DIGITAL DIASPORA

THE **SUNY** SERIES

CULTURAL STUDIES IN CINEMA/VIDEO

WHEELER WINSTON DIXON | EDITOR

DIGITAL DIASPORA

A Race for Cyberspace

ANNA EVERETT

Published by
State University of New York Press, Albany

© 2009 State University of New York

For information, contact State University of New York Press, Albany, NY
www.sunypress.edu

Production by Marilyn P. Semerad
Marketing by Anne M. Valentine

Library of Congress Cataloging-in-Publication Data

Everett, Anna (date)
   Digital diaspora : a race for cyberspace / Anna Everett.
      p. cm. — (Suny series, cultural studies in cinema/video)
   Includes bibliographical references and index.
   ISBN 978-0-7914-7673-4 (hardcover : alk. paper)
   ISBN 978-0-7914-7674-1 (pbk. : alk. paper)
1. Computers—Social aspects—United States. 2. African Americans and
mass media—United States. 3. Digital media—Social aspects—United States.
4. African diaspora. I. Title.
   QA76.9.C66E95 2009
   303.48'34—dc22

                                                            2008017373

                    10 9 8 7 6 5 4 3 2 1

To Wheeler and James,
for never losing faith in this project.

CONTENTS

ILLUSTRATIONS

ACKNOWLEDGMENTS

I am grateful to many people who helped me during the course of completing this volume. First and foremost, I gladly acknowledge the fact that this book would not be possible without the efforts of Wheeler Winston Dixon and James Peltz. I have to thank Wheeler Winston Dixon for his enthusiastic and unwavering support of this project over the years that it took to reach completion. His belief in this project has sustained me through many difficult episodes and life-changing events that intervened during the various stages of this work. I also owe a great deal of thanks to James Peltz for his amazing editorial guidance and commitment to this project over the long haul. I thank especially Aldon L. Nielsen and George Lipsitz for reading the manuscript and offering their much appreciated suggestions and ideas. I am eternally grateful to Rosi Braidotti at the University of Utrecht for encouraging me in this work by inviting me to share early stages of this research as the 2001 Belle Van Zuylen Chair in Women's Studies. I thank my other colleagues at the University of Utrecht whose insights and intellectual generosity helped enormously in the development of this work, namely, Anneke Smelik, Berteke Waaldik, Mischa Peters, Joost Raessens, and Gloria Wekker. I also thank Nina Lykke at the University of Linkoeping. I am very grateful to Jim Palmer, the late Stan Brakhage, Melinda Barlow, Phil Soloman, Suranjan Ganguly, Staci Steers, Patti Bruck, and Bruce Kawin, my faculty colleagues at the University of Colorado at Boulder, who created a very supportive and nurturing environment when I began this project. I also am indebted to my wonderful colleagues at the University of California at Santa Barbara. Thank you

Charles Wolfe, Janet Walker, Connie Penley, Lisa Parks, Edward Branigan, Bhaskar Sarkar, Cristina Venegas, Peter Bloom, Jung-Bong Choi, Anna Brusutti, Dana Driskel, Cynthia Felando, Paul Portuges, Dick Hebdige, Claudine Michel, Jude Akudinobe, Joe Palladino, and Kathy Carnahan.

Some portions of this work have appeared elsewhere and in a different form, including excerpts, in chapter 2, from "Double Click: The Million Woman March on Television and the Internet," in *Television After TV: Essays on a Medium in Transition*, edited by Lynn Spigel (Durham, NC: Duke UP, 2004). Chapter 2 also contains excerpts from an article of mine in a special *Social Text* journal issue on afuturism, entitled "The Revolution Will Be Digitized: Afrocentricity in the Digital Public Sphere," *Social Text* 71, vol. 20, no. 2 (Summer 2002): 125–46. I am grateful to Thomas A. Robinson at Duke University Press for permission to reprint materials from both these texts. Some research from chapter 3 was first published as "The Black Press in the Age of Digital Reproduction: Two Exemplars," in *The Black Press: New Literary and Historical Essays*, edited by Todd Vogel, copyright © 2011 by Rutgers, the State University, and reprinted here by permission of Rutgers University Press; my thanks to Michele Gisbert for her attention to my request. A portion of my research on computer games in chapter 4 was published as "Serious Play: Playing with Race in Computer Games," in *Handbook of Computer Game Studies*, edited by Joost Raessens and Jeffrey H. Goldstein (Cambridge: MIT, 2005); I thank Pamela Quick at MIT Press for permission to reprint this work. All these texts have been useful introductory or preface materials leading up to the fullness of this volume that has changed and expanded over the years. Finally, I must give special thanks to Susan Walanski, my student researcher at the University of Colorado, Boulder, who was tireless in helping track down all those websites at the start of this research project. Anita Brown, Anne Walker, Ruth Ojimbo Ochieng, Rita Mijumbi-Epodoi, Ken Anderson, Kalamu Ya Salaam, and Mukasa E. Ssemakula, thank you so much for your assistance with the production of this manuscript. Last, but certainly not least, I thank the manuscript readers for SUNY Press and the editorial staff for their diligence and careful attention to many details in this work. I am especially grateful to Marilyn Semerad for her eagle eyes, her pleasant disposition, and her amazing focus on quality control. I also gladly thank Barbara Stroup. Their contributions have enhanced this book beyond measure. It has been thoroughly rewarding working on this book, with so many talented friends and associates. I look forward with great anticipation as other new work in this area emerges. Once again, thank you Aldon L. Nielsen for all your care and assistance.

INTRODUCTION

Introductions sketch the discursive framework for what follows, and what follows immediately are prefatory remarks that speak to my profound ambivalence about the evolution of digital culture as it intersects with issues of race. The focus of this project is on early instances of African diasporic engagements with cyberspace. I begin by acknowledging my ambivalence about the rhetorical terms of the emerging technocratic order, an ambivalence that during the earliest phases of this project seemed particularly justified each time I booted up my personal computer to compile my years of research into this topic.[1] In powering up my PC, I was confronted with DOS-based text that gave me pause. Before access to the then state-of-the-art MMX technology powering my system was granted, I was alerted to this opening textual encoding: "Pri. Master Disk, Pri. Slave Disk, Sec. Master, Sec. Slave." Programmed here is a virtual hierarchy organizing my computer's software operations. Given the nature of my subject matter, it might not be surprising that I remain perpetually taken aback by such programmed boot-up language informing me that my access to the cyber frontier indeed is predicated upon a digitally configured "master/slave" relationship. As the on-screen text of my first high-end computer ran through its string of required boot-up language and codes, I often wondered why the programmers chose such signifiers that hark back to our nation's ignominious past. I doubt that the Hegelian slave/master dialectic was the referent to which those earlier programmers alluded. And even though I resisted the presumption of a racial affront or intentionality in such a peculiar deployment of the slave and

1

master coupling, its choice as a signifier of the computer's operations nonetheless struck me. Still, my lingering discomfiture over that master-slave rhetorical enigma seems a fitting segue to this volume, *Digital Diaspora: A Race for Cyberspace.*

THE HISTORICAL SITUATEDNESS OF
AFRICAN DIASPORIC CONSCIOUSNESS

There can be little doubt that African diasporic consciousness originated in the darkened abyss below the decks of European ships during the infamous Middle Passage of the trans-Atlantic slave trade. Severed from the familiar terrain of their homelands and dispatched to the overcrowded bowels of slave vessels, the abducted Africans forged out of necessity a virtual community of intercultural kinship structures and new languages in which to express them. During the first half of the twentieth century African diasporic scholar-activists W. E. B. Du Bois and C. L. R. James argued that these historical events created the preconditions for Africans in the New World to be among the first people to experience modernity. In 1969 James asserted:

> The vast change in human society came from the slave trade and slavery. All the historians tell you that. . . . It was slavery that built up the bourgeois society and enabled it to make what Lévi Strauss thinks is the only fundamental change in ten thousand years of human history. The blacks not only provided the wealth in the struggle, which began between the old [aristocratic] society and the new bourgeois society; the black people were foremost in the struggle itself. (James 396)

Commenting on James's position, Aldon L. Nielsen states that despite subsequent historians' questioning of "the exact amounts of capital generated by slavery and made available for industrialization . . . there is little question that slavery was central to the evolution of modern capitalism and industry" (*C. L. R. James* 56).

Other contemporary theorists such as Paul Gilroy, in *The Black Atlantic: Modernity and Double Consciousness*, echo James and Du Bois's positions to elaborate further that the trans-Atlantic African diasporic consciousness of African Americans, African Caribbeans, Black Britons, and others is directly attributable to the post-Enlightenment demands of a modernity that followed the invasion of the European body snatchers into Africa seeking black bodies to power the impending Industrial Revolution. Despite the well-documented dehumanizing imperatives of the colonial encounter, the ethnically and nationally diverse Africans in the New World developed self-sustaining virtual communities through paralinguistic and transnational communicative systems and networks of song, dance, talking drums, and other musical instrumentations that enabled this heterogenous mass of people somehow to overcome their profound dislocation, fragmentation, alienation, relocation, and ultimate commodification in the Western slavocracies of the modern world. Poet Amiri Baraka recounted a poignant memory related to this legacy. Referencing the unvanquished yearning of African Americans to reconnect with the African homeland, Baraka tells a story about the drummer Tony Williams's virtuoso drum performance in Africa spoken in the metalanguage of the talking drums. The Africans' response, according to Baraka, was that they greatly enjoyed Williams's drumming but that they did not understand a word he was saying. Apparently, the centuries of cultural distance had profoundly mainfested an alienation effect. Whether or nor this is an apocryphal tale, the point about the difficulty of exile and return holds. Yet history is rife with African diasporic peoples' "hopes that the days of Cyprian and Augustine shall again return to Africa; when the giant sins and the deadly evils which have ruined her, shall be effectively stayed" (Crummell 340).

It was particularly in the nineteenth century that transnational movements designed to advance an African diasporic consciousness in opposition to the European negation of black culture and humanity began to emerge. During the 1850s, for example, a free African American, English-educated Alexander Crummell began advocating a "repossession of Africa, in trade, commerce, and moral power, by her now scattered children in distant lands" (Liggins Hill, et al. 337). Likewise in the following decade, Martin Robinson Delany espoused the necessity for post–Reconstruction-era African Americans to emigrate to Africa. For Delany, the first black to serve as an American commissioned officer of high rank (he was a major in the Union Army), legal emancipation of the African body in America after the Civil War was a hollow victory indeed (Liggins Hill 475). What Delany understood was that the state had legal recourse to de facto slavery: witness the later *Plessy v. Ferguson* Supreme Court decision, which held that even freed African Americans were not entitled to full citizenship protections. Through the African Colonization

Society, Crummell, Delany, and others sought to establish "the day of Africa's redemption" (Walker 339) and, by extension, redemption for the continent's newly manumitted sons and daughters of modernity's enslaved African expatriates.

By the turn of the twentieth century, W. E. B. Du Bois became another prominent African American scholar and writer assiduously promoting the idea of African diasporic consciousness, though not in these exact terms. He organized a series of pan-Africanist conferences with the expressed goal of recuperating African culture and civilization and repositioning them to a rightful place alongside other world cultures. In fact, Du Bois became a naturalized African citizen of Ghana, where he spent the last days of his very long life. In the nineteen-teens, the Jamaican Marcus Garvey founded one of the most successful organizations in modern history devoted to African diasporic self-empowerment and determination, the Universal Negro Improvement Association (UNIA). Based in New York and noted for the potent slogan "Africa for Africans at home and abroad," the self-educated Garvey and his more populist Back to Africa movement did much to advance African disaporic consciousness historically even though his own UNIA ultimately collapsed or imploded under the tragic weight of its own success. Filling the void left by the UNIA's demise were other black individuals and loose confederations dedicated to fostering panAfricanism in the Americas and throughout the colonial world.

Another mode of twentieth-century pan-Africanism was articulated by Aimé Césaire and Léopold Senghor, two Francophone African scholars living in voluntary exile as college students in France. In the late 1930s and throughout the 1940s they became exponents of a panAfrican movement specific to the unique needs of Francophone Africans. Theirs was the Negritude movement. In answer to charges that negritude was paradoxically "racialism" and "an inferiority complex" at once, Senghor explains:

> Negritude is nothing more or less than what some English-speaking Africans have called the *African personality* (emphasis in original). It is no different from the "black personality" discovered and proclaimed by the American New Negro movement. . . . Perhaps our only originality, since it was the West Indian poet Aimé Césaire who coined the word negritude, is to have attempted to define the concept a little more closely; to have developed it as a weapon, as an instrument of liberation and as a contribution to the humanism of the twentieth century. (27)

Here Senghor also is careful to stress a key element in the ontology of negritude, what he calls its "philosophy of being" (30), and that is negritude's necessary role as a humanism of the twentieth century. As Senghor puts it, "negritude, by its ontology . . . its moral law and its aesthetic, is a response to the modern humanism that European philosophers and scientists have been preparing" (30). Among the types of European modern humanism that negritude sought to negate was the racist ideology expressed by Hegel: "[W]e may conclude slavery to have been the occasion of the increase in human feeling among the Negroes" (Hegel, quoted in Gilroy 41).

Back in America, Melvin B. Tolson (whose formidable work as an educator was captured in the 2007 film *The Great Debaters*) was carrying the panAfrican banner as the first and only American citizen to be named poet laureate of a foreign country. The fact that the foreign country was in Africa underscores the powerful responsiveness to African diasporic consciousness exhibited by such black scholars, activists, and poets as Tolson. To commemorate his 1947 appointment as poet laureate of the African nation of Liberia, Tolson penned a well-known epic poem entitled *Libretto for the Republic of Liberia*, published in 1953. Tolson's nomination to this diplomatic honor was due largeley to his successful 1944 book *Rendezvous with America*, wherein Tolson articulates well the dual predicament of the black American during the interwar years. On the one hand, according to Tolson biographer Robert M. Farnsworth, *Rendezvous* makes a strong assertion that African Americans were "a part of the national American identity from its beginning." And on the other hand was Tolson's belief that the events of World Ward II obliged America to assist in the decolonizing efforts of "Africa chafing under colonial rule" (Farnsworth 108).

As the 1960s dawned, panAfricanism was joined by black nationalism as a new manifestation of African diasporic consciousness. Fully a century after the Civil War and the Emancipation Proclamation, African Americans were weary of the consistent failures of the Booker T. Washington-style accommodationist logic governing race relations in America. Despite black Americans' heroic efforts to demonstrate their patriotism by making the ultimate sacrifice in the Revolutionary War, the Great War, World War II, the Korean War, and the Vietnam War, it was apparent that the nation was unwilling to recognize and fairly grant its black citizenry full citizenship protections and benefits. After the ironies of engaging in all manner of white assimilationist strategies such as trying skin-bleaching creams, hair straighteners, and every other deracination product or identity altering commodity available, at the height of the civil rights movement in the 1960s large numbers of African Americans effected a symbolic return to their African roots. This return was signified most forcefully by several visible phenomena: the widespread participation of black students in college activism for increased black curricula and black professors on historically white campuses, a rethinking of European standards of beauty, and a formulation of Afrocentric sociopolitico-cultural rituals, such as Kwanza and the founding of alternative black K–12 schools and camps. Among this newly awakened racial pride and consciousness Huey Newton and Eldridge Cleaver founded the Black Panther Party for Self Defense in Oakland, James Brown sang "Say It Loud, I'm Black and I'm Proud," black cultural workers such as Leroi Jones (aka Amiri Baraka) and Hoyt Fuller and charismatic political freedom fighters including Malcolm X erected the foundations on which a new black nationalist political and aesthetic movement would be built. This new African diasporic consciousness presented itself on the level of everyday people's participatory expressions. Black Americans began wearing natural hairstyles (called "Afros") and dashikis (African-inspired patterned mini robes), and they began peppering their speech with words in Swahili, the transethnic African-European hybrid language.

This brief overview is necessary to contextualize the ideological primacy and the historical development of an African diasporic consciousness in oppressed New World Africans who fomented the decolonizing movements that herald what is termed the "postcolonial era." Many, including this writer, are not convinced that colonization is over. For us the economic institution has morphed into the new global oligopolies thriving in the post–Cold-War, postmodern era (which arguably can be equated with globalization). The point here is that without such an overview and context, it becomes a near impossibility to understand and fully account for the historical and epochal shifts as well as mutabilities in the ideology of African diasporic consciousness motivating the black nationalist ethos spanning the nineteenth-century African Colonization Societies on through the twentieth-century black nationalist or Afrocentric movements of the 1960s to the present day. This book, then, explores the discursive richness of African diasporic consciousness in terms of its migratory trek through the evolving technospheres of cyberspace during the early years.

Since 1994, there has been a proliferation of electronic bulletin boards, chat rooms, home pages, list serves, electronic directories, and black web rings (precursors to blogs and social networks) on the Internet and the World Wide Web that are specifically targeted at African and African diasporic net users. This volume considers the persistence of the African diasporic consciousness in cyberspace and the digital age. Among the areas of concern here are the often overlooked or unacknowledged fact of historical and contemporary black technolust; early technology adoption and mastery, representations of race and the new digital technologies in film, TV, video games and the Internet, and the theorizing of African diasporic issues vis-à-vis the super information highway and other digital media technologies in education, culture, and politics.

CHAPTER ONE

Toward a Theory of the Egalitarian Technosphere: How Wide Is the Digital Divide?

In the eary 1970s, a new communications network began to take off in America. . . . Visionaries saw it unleashing creativity and opening the door to an egalitarian future. It was CB Radio. By 1980 it was almost dead; it had collapsed under the weight of its own popularity, its channels drowned under a sea of noise and chaos. Could the Internet go the same way?

—Christopher Anderson, "The Internet"

Historically. . . . Nothing might seem less realistic, attractive or believable to black Americans than the notion of a black public sphere . . . [Blacks] are drawn to the possibilities of structurally and effectively transforming the founding notion of the bourgeois public into an expressive and empowering self-fashioning.

—Houston A. Baker Jr., "Critical Memory and the Black Public Sphere"

[T]he contemporary black public sphere is partly the creature of the political economy of a global, advanced capitalist order, but in the past it has offered—and may yet again offer—a space for critique and transformation of that order. If not, then all this is only idle talk.

—Thomas C. Holt, "Afterword: Mapping the Black Public Sphere"

My years of research into the African diasporic presence online suggests that 1995 was a watershed moment in the transformation of the Internet from a predominately elite, white masculinist domain. Although a number of African American early adopters infiltrated this would-be gated cybercommunity prior to this benchmark, black connectivity online seems to have achieved a critical mass in 1995 when the Yahoo search engine initiated a separate category for Afrocentric content on the World Wide Web. In his 1995 study of the Internet for the *Economist* magazine, Christopher Anderson gives an indication of the magnitude of its unprecedented growth. His estimation of the World Wide Web's massive expansion is significant and particularly revealing for our discussion. Anderson noted that the Internet doubled in size since 1988. "At the same time," he observed, "the Web grew almost 20-fold; in just 18 months users created more than 3 million multimedia pages of information, entertainment and advertising" (3). Although he concedes that exact numbers were difficult to ascertain, he calculates that at least 20 million "users" were online as early as October 1994. If we accept his evocation of "Moore's Law," a phenomenon named after Gordon Moore, founder of the Intel Corporation, "which says that computing power and capacity double every 18 months" (4), then the unwieldy nature of any attempt to survey the contents of the Internet after 1995 is apparent.

The difficulty of delimiting the cybertext for analytical purposes in many ways replicates problems encountered by early analysts in their formulation of a critical hermeneutics of television. Like television, the dynamic and fluid nature of the Internet makes it "too big and too baggy to be easily or quickly explained. No single approach is sufficient to deal with it adequately" (Newcomb ix). With this in mind, I have opted to frame my own findings on the African diasporic niche within the Internet in terms of a snapshot or moment-in-time approach so that some useful perspective on this difficult, moving target of analysis might emerge.

Also, in all the years since I began this targeted history of a new media technology in a state of becoming, I have discovered some important and quite intriguing methodological and theoretical problems. My previous research on early twentieth-century black print publications did not prepare me for what I want to call the "hyper-ephemerality of the cybertext." What this means is that conducting Internet content analysis presents a unique set of problematics involving access to and availability of the material under scrutiny. The fleeting nature or short shelf life of most individual, grassroots and private, nonprofit and nongovernment organization (NGO) websites and social networking sites necessitates the immediate downloading and printing of those sites that might be considered worthy of study because, as I have learned the hard way, a second page or site view may not be possible. Too many of these sites disappear without a trace, or they are upgraded to the point of unrecognizability. This fact of textual instability, mutability, and morphing does not even address the push to out-perform TV in terms of immediacy, instantaneity, and freshness, whereby independent websites, social networks, YouTube, and especially blogs, unburdened by apparatuses and functions of official media's ideological gatekeeping, freely disseminate information globally and instantly. These are among the challenges of historicizing contemporary or present day events.

FORGING A DIGITAL BLACK PUBLIC SPHERE

As I watched in amazement the incalculable stream of orderly black female bodies (and their supportive male counterparts) that swelled the streets of Philadelphia on 25 October 1997, my overwhelming feelings of jubilation, incredulity, pride, and optimism soon gave way to thoughts of fear, concern, and pessimism. Driving my ambivalence about even the scant network and cable TV news broadcasts of the phenomenally successful Million Woman March was my understanding of how televised coverage of the civil rights movement and its aftermath in the late 1950s and early 1960s contributed to a national backlash against African American aspirations for social, political, economic, and educational equity. Gil Scott Heron did not get it quite right when he famously said that "the revolution will not be televised." I contend that it is precisely because the revolution *was* televised that the conservative forces of counterrevolution were able to mobilize a traumatized nation to effectuate a civil rights backlash and retrenchment from the revolutionary social change movements of

Lyndon B. Johnson's idealized "Great Society." California voters' late twentieth-century passages of several anti-affirmative action propositions—including #209, the anti-affirmative action measure, #187, the anti-immigration ruling, and the 1999 passage of a juvenile justice initiative that sentences minor offenders as adults—are legatees of this revolutionary history captured on TV. Moreover, today's precipitous and steady decline in African American and other racial minority students' enrollments at prestigious universities nationwide clearly attests to the regressive consequences of the 1960s' counterrevolution and its subsequent legal deinstitutionalization of these underrepresented groups' access to elite higher education in the nation since the 1978 University of California *Regents v. Bakke* decision.[1]

Despite this recent history's profound influence on today's racial and political economies, the role of the Internet in the undeniable success of the 1997 Million Woman March may have allayed, temporarily, fears that the nascent technocratic order would automatically exclude the marginalized black masses from the still-evolving information infrastructure. In fact, my project of tracking and analyzing black "homesteading on the electronic frontier," to borrow an apt phrase from Howard Reingold, remains guardedly optimistic about the Internet's democratizing potential, especially given its demonstrably pivotal role in mobilizing a throng of grassroots activists in the 1997 Million Woman March on Philadelphia. (More about the march later.) This is also true for later hip-hop music culture that began organizing global summits and mounting a strong web presence around the year 2000 (figure 1.1).

In his seminal 1993 book *The Virtual Community: Homesteading on the Electronic Frontier*, Rheingold observed that "computer-mediated communications" technologies owe their phenomenal growth and development to networking capabilities that enable people "to build social relationships across barriers of space and time" (7). It is specifically to this point of spatial and temporal ruptures produced by recent technological advances that the present study of the Internet as a promising site for the establishment of an egalitarian technosphere is initially directed. First, it is useful to emphasize an important lesson embedded in Rheingold's ethnographic informant account of the "computer-mediated social groups" he has dubbed "virtual communities" (1). Of the myriad ways that grassroots groups adapted the inchoate Internet technology "designed for one purpose to suit their own, very different communication needs" (7), none was more symptomatic of technology's overall elasticity and unpredictability than the rapid and unanticipated growth of the "Internet Relay Chat

FIGURE 1.1. Old School Hip Hop site. One example of the Hip Hop Culture's early presence online.

(IRC)" phenomenon among noncomputer experts. Reingold sees the lure of the IRC (and more recently "blogs" and social networking sites) as being inextricably bound up with its recombinant nature[2] as an interactive medium that conjoins "the features of conversation and writing" (3). Second, this technological hybridization of speech or orality (conversation) and literacy (writing) that privileges neither, not only furthers the Derridian project of negating epistemological exaltations of logocentrism (privileging speech) over techne (writing),[3] but it also suggests a parallel or affinity to various traditions of black technocultural syncretisms. For example, much has been written about black appropriations and mastery of Western musical technologies and instruments to craft and express such uniquely black musical idioms as jazz and the blues.[4] As Bruce R. Powers puts it in *The Global Village*, "Unlikely combinations produce discovery" (McLuhan and Powers ix). Thus the seamless combination of conversational strategies and writing on the proliferating IRC channels has produced for black *early adopters* of and latecomers to the Internet and other digital media technologies a discovery of the latest inchoate mass medium to be appropriated for unfettered social and cultural expressions. This is possible, of course, because their complete domination by the interests of corporate capital remains somewhat elusive, for the time being at least. Meanwhile, it appears that computer mediated communication (CMC) is refashioning the concept and utility of a viable black public sphere in the new millennium.

HISTORICIZING DEMOCRATIC TURF WARS AND THE PRIVATIZATION OF THE PUBLIC SPHERE

The problematics of space and place in American culture have been thoroughly addressed by legions of African American and feminist cultural workers in and outside the academy. Literature produced by blacks and women across decades has served to denude past and present attempts to yoke social relationships based on race and gender to highly repressive structures of public and private spheres of influence. While an extensive survey of this vast data does not bear reduplication here, a sketch of certain historical struggles over access to the public sphere is necessary to our appreciation of black people's harnessing of the democratizing possibilities of postindustrial society's rapidly congealing information technocracy.

For starters, it is instructive to recall how the historical subjugation of racial minorities and women by means of the politicization of space and place in American civil society spurred frequent mass mobilizations by these groups to take their long-standing grievances to the streets. As the measured social gains of the 1950s civil rights movement begat the second wave of the women's movement in the 1970s,[5] the goals of social and political equity that eluded the post–Civil War Reconstruction and suffragists' voting rights efforts a century earlier became increasingly difficult for the white male-dominated power structures to withhold. Indeed, a century of violent protests against American racism and patriarchy had borne out Frederick Douglass's truism that power concedes nothing without a demand. Acknowledging this reality, there can be little doubt that blacks and women adroitly seized temporary and limited access to the public sphere to voice dissent over their relegation to places of powerlessness in domesticated private spaces. Although the once ever-present dangers of lynchings and rape posed a real threat for transgressing this rigid public-private divide, blacks and women refused to be deterred from their "demands" for unrestricted access to the public portals to power.

If such epoch-making, nineteenth-century demands as Reconstruction, the suffrage movement, and passages of the Fourteenth and the Nineteenth Amendments to the U.S. Constitution proved insufficient to the task of opening up the public sphere to genuine attempts at resolving the Negro and women "questions," how, then, do we account for those grudging concessions to similar demands brought by the generation of the 1960s? While the uncomplicated view might suggest answers attributable to a natural or historical evolution of public attitudes, a more probing analysis uncovers the central role of less passive determinants at work. The advent and persuasiveness of new telecommunications technologies such as the telephone, radio, film, and television inaugurated new technological methods of social arbitration that factored greatly in this historical contest of wills. But, as Paul Arthur points out in his essay "Jargons of Authenticity," there was a double-edged sword attenuating this mechanical intervention in public debates about space and place. Arthur's disclosure of the limitations of documentary films to provide "the highest quotient of immediacy, responsiveness, clarity, and verisimilitude" (110) during fierce public debates around Franklin Delano Roosevelt's radical New Deal reforms has obvious relevance to later concerns about television's pervasive and sensational coverage of 1960s-era social changes. Arthur reminds us that the "truth claims" of 1930s film documentaries such as *The City* (1939) relied on the genre's "chimera of objectivity" (118) to obfuscate "a tangled reciprocity" existing between documentary realism and Hollywood fiction (108). He suggests that Depression-era spectators' inability to disaggregate these seemingly representational antinomies structuring *The City's* political thrust rendered them impervious to the film's propagandistic narrative intent. For him, *The City's* aural and visual verisimilitudes helped assure widespread acquiescence to the film's favorable portrayal of FDR's controversial vision of the welfare state. Arthur astutely demonstrates how documentary films of this sort functioned to legitimate the investment of scarce funds into untried reorganization schemes because they proffered the idyllic, ordered suburban community as a simple remedy to the complex ills gripping the nation's disordered cities. Arthur writes:

> The polemical thrust . . . is readily apparent. Depersonalization in the metropolis is figured as a disorienting clash of graphic elements, whereas the humanizing appeal of the planned community is reified in familiar Hollywood conventions of spatio-temporal harmony and continuity. The

alleviation of urban disorder by social engineering is argued verbally and demonstrated visually. . . . As Grierson himself was quick to note, emphasis on the "creative treatment" of reality works to blunt the charge of propaganda. (112)

This model of pressing film technology into service for the preservation of established power regimes is replicated when television supplants its film and radio predecessors as the preferred method for disseminating official discourses on place and space in the last half of the twentieth century.

TELEVISION AND THE ELECTRONIC
PARTICIPATORY DEMOCRACY MODEL

The centrality of television in building public consensus around the urgent need for social reform during the "turbulent sixties" has been well considered.[6] Coincidentally, the new television industry was experiencing its own growing pains. As African Americans heightened their public campaign for full citizenship in the late 1950s and early 1960s, the fledgling television medium was embarking upon its own period of redefinition. In an attempt to regain audience trust, to dig itself out of the quagmire of its infamous, self-induced quiz show scandals of the late 1950s, and to thwart threatened federal regulatory action from the Newton Minow Federal Communication Commission, the television industry enacted a series of self-regulating reforms that included "high-quality documentaries" and "the expansion of news coverage from 15 to 30 minutes" (Kellner 50). These measured reforms culminated in an unprecedented stream of uncensored, real-life, and even real-time or "live" violent imagery so unsettling that American television viewers are still reeling from the impact. In his book *Television and the Crisis of Democracy*, Douglas Kellner explains the significance of television's programming shift in this way:

> Audiences thus began to see dramatic images of the civil rights struggle:
> Filling their TV screen were pictures of demonstrations, bombed churches,
> and blacks beaten and hosed by Southern police, chased by dogs, and bru-
> tally arrested. The 1960s also witnessed such high-quality documentaries
> as "Harvest of Shame," "Hunger in America," and "The Tenement," which
> dramatized the plight of the poor. . . . Television's ideological functions and

conservative reluctance to embrace controversy as a consequence of its total commercialization rendered TV entertainment increasingly irrelevant to the vast process of social and cultural change that was occurring. (50)

Not only did television bring the violence occurring in the disorderly public sphere into the genteel domestic sphere of American living rooms, but it also redeployed the concept of an electronic participatory democracy instituted by FDR's well-received Depression-era "Fireside Chats" via radio. By resurrecting the representational strategies of 1930s documentary films, television's coverage of the chaotic 1960s likewise conveyed potent imagistic reductions of urban chaos versus suburban order that served to reassure if disinform the nation about complex issues during both generations' periods of national crisis. Additionally, the televising of Richard Nixon's declaration of innocence to charges of political influence peddling in the now-infamous "Checkers" speech during the late 1950s and the Kennedy and Nixon presidential debate in the early 1960s set the stage for a new order of American political life. This transformation of political life was now predicated on television's hegemonic adjudication of the nation's electoral victories. And though it is the case that America's televisual confrontation with the harsh realities of itself as a race-, class-, and gender-conflicted society unraveling from within lead to such social reform measures during the 1960s as voting rights, school busing programs, and affirmative action legislation, Kellner rightfully points out that this incessant flood of violent images over time also served to undermine sustained mass support for these reforms over the long haul (53). Again, the idea that the revolution *was* indeed televised seems clear.

Because television routinely covered the civil rights, free speech, antiwar, environmental, and women's liberation movements and the brutal police methods used to contain them, in one seamless stream, reactionary conservative forces had little difficulty conflating these leftist groups' access to the public sphere with national chaos and social disintegration. "Conservatives," Kellner notes, "began complaining of a liberal bias in television following Spiro Agnew's attack on the medium in 1969." Kellner further states that "following the turmoil of the 1968 Democratic Convention, the news networks reconsidered their policies of covering demonstrations and social upheaval, and moved to a more conservative terrain, backing off from controversy" (54). Thus, this early experiment in unrestricted access to the public sphere, now policed by a conservative televisual panopticon, was deemed a resounding failure.

Now that television had "shown" how forbidding the public sphere (read the urban streets) had become for the orderly advancement of democratic ideals, it (TV) was uniquely situated to privatize the public business of deciding the progression of American democracy at this critical juncture. Rather than hazard the perceived dangers of mingling with radical members of an unruly society, viewers could instead base their "informed" judgments about crucial events of the day on televised summaries of important issues from the safety of their suburban tract homes. Following these developments, the Supreme Court's response to the civil rights movement that mandated forced racial integration of American uncivil society has been accompanied by a steady erosion of public confidence in the safety of the nations' public spaces.

Clearly, then, the persistent fear most Americans harbor about both real and imagined dangers lurking in the public sphere (irrespective of exculpating crime statistics or personal experiences) can be traced particularly to television's penchant for privileging the sensational over the substantive, rant over reason, fear over fact, and profit above all else.[7] Given this set of reportorial imperatives, how could the public's situated knowledge based on decontextualized overcoverage of the economically destitute urban centers, and its undercoverage of white flight and its concommitant redistribution of wealth to support suburban sprawl yield anything but racial polarization and social conflagration. Even though the law officially struck down most "separate but equal" statutes underpinning America's apartheidlike segregation of our public spaces, one tactic of resistance or noncompliance with the nation's new racial order was and continues to be massive white flight from racially integrated cites and schools. In effect, white flight becomes a most effective escape clause in the law ensuring what Derrick Bell describes as "the permanence of racism" in America.[8] Failing that, gentrification (or "urban renewal") of once-blighted areas achieves another form of racial and economic segregation of communities. In fact, once the suburban fortress of de facto racial separation was firmly erected in the late 1940s and early 1950s, with the assistance of racially restrictive FHA loan policies, the mass media's captains of consciousness did not hesitate to enlist the culture industries in naturalizing this particular construction of a class- and race-stratified American social reality. The widespread installation of television sets into suburban homes was essential in selling a new and improved, highly constructed "antiseptic" image of social space in postwar America.

Lynn Spigel demonstrates how 1940s and '50s television borrowed its "antiseptic model of space" from earlier electrical communications technologies "like the telephone and the telegraph" (110) to distill its own normalizing discourse on social divisions of space, place, and race for its middle-class suburban family audience.[9] For Spigel, nineteenth-century utopian beliefs in "the magical powers" of electrical telegraphy to purify the environment of "the grime and noise of industrialization" (110) have their corollaries in much of the early promotional hypes extolling the benefits of radio and television. Not surprisingly, this "antiseptic model" of mechanically and electronically driven participatory democracy has morphed into present-day utopian discourses promulgating the new digital democracy as society's panacea for the dawning millennium.

BLACK TECHNOPHILES ARE IN THE VIRTUAL HOUSE: THE PHENOMENAL RISE OF BLACK PARTICIPATION ONLINE

In the cacophonous rush to judgment by new media technology gurus, academics, politicians, entrepreneurs, and cyberpunk novelists, all striving to divine the eventual contours of the surging information society, concern over issues of racial equity or the impact of the growing black presence in cyberspace has been conspicuously muted, until recently. This deafening silence in evolving discourses on new information technologies during the mid-1980s and late 1990s, what Theodore Roszak terms "the cult of information," might be owing to a general presumption of black nonparticipation in the incipient technosphere or perhaps to a belief in something akin to what I am calling "black technophobia." After all, the recursiveness of theories claiming "scientific" evidence of black intellectual inferiority means that such theories will always manage to find new means of attaining cultural currency, as Charles Murray and Richard Hernstein's 1994 book *The Bell Curve*'s long-term standing on national bestseller lists illustrates. Consequently, the overwhelming characterizations of the brave new world of cyberspace as primarily a racialized sphere of whiteness inhere in popular constructions of high-tech and low-to-no-tech spheres that too often consign black bodies to the latter, with the latter being insignificant if not absent altogether. Any close scrutiny of early editions of specialized computer magazines, such as *Wired* and *Mondo 2000*, mass market advertisements for computer products in both print and electronic media, cyberpunk novels, and even scholarly treatises on the intersections of technology and culture bears out this troubling future vision. Although blacks have recently become increasingly prominent as consumer users of computer products in both television commercials and print advertisements, nonetheless, many mainstream cybercritics and cyberpunk subcultural elites have produced imaginative figurations of a cybernetic future untroubled by the complication of blackness. Still, black people have forged a more expansive view of technological progress.

From 1995 to the present, the swelled ranks of black people throughout the African diaspora connecting to the Internet, particularly to the World Wide Web, have forced a new reckoning with the rapidly changing configuration of the new electronic frontier. For a time, the structured absences of black bodies that have marked most popular imaginings of the brave new world order were in danger of reifying an updated myth of black intellectual lag or black technophobia. Instead, I want to suggest an alternative scenario—a fact of black technophilia. In fact, the unanticipated dramatic upsurge in black participation on the Internet from 1995 onward captured the imaginations of print headline writers across the country. The headlines are suggestive of a black-technofuturist enthusiasm that harkens back to the celebratory discourses of Filippo Tommaso Marinetti, the Italian poet, novelist, and critic of the Industrial Age, widely regarded as the founder of a protechnology sentiment termed "futurism."[10] Consider this sampling of sensational headlines from the not too distant past: *The Washington Post,* "Revving Up Their Computer Power: Now Black Americans Are Outpacing Whites on Online Services" (19 September 1997); the *Boston Globe,* "Suddenly, a Boom in sites Geared toward African Americans" (2 January 1996); *Metro Paper* [San Jose, CA], "Laptop Over Hip-Hop: The African American Pocket-protector Crowd Upgrades to the Next Generation" (6–12 November 1997); *Los Angeles Times,* "The Virtual Pie Shop and Other Cyber Dreams: The Inner City Computer Society Promotes the Practical Applications of Technology and the Wonders of the Internet (21 November 1995); The *Los Angeles Sentinel,* "For the Kids' Sake: Turn off TV, Turn on PC" (8 August 1996) and "Getting Plugged into the Computer Age" (21 September 1995); the *Denver Post's Connectime* Magazine, "At Netnoir, History Is Now" (January 1997); *USA Today,* "Seeing a Future with More Blacks Exploring the Internet" (20 February 1997); and in the *American Visions* Magazine, "New Black Cyberhood on the Web" (February/March 1997); and the *New York Times,* "Virtual Community for African-Americans" (8 October 1998).

As the race for cyberspace began revving up for what may well be its determining lap, the forceful entrance of a black Marinettian contingent at last century's end and the dawning new millennium signaled African diasporic peoples' refusal to be excluded from this all-important running. And while the mainstream press did take notice of this emergent black cyberfever, the sporadic nature and incredulous tone of much of the coverage betrays a sense of condescension, ghettoization, trivialization, and a general air of dismissiveness. For example, Dana Canedy's 8 October 1998 *New York Times* full-page feature article highlighting "black oriented sites," entitled "Virtual Community for African-Americans," exemplifies many of these tendencies. In one discussion, subheaded "A Contemporary Bookstore," Canedy describes the site of a black retail partner of Amazon.com in this way: "The problem is that it could be so much more. Mosaicbooks.com bills itself as a showcase for 'the latest in black and Hispanic literature,' so beyond the Book of the Month picks, you won't find much of the classic work of authors like James Baldwin and Langston Hughes." Now, given the wide availability of the works of Baldwin and Hughes, it is not clear why Canedy is so distressed by a showcase being provided for "the "latest" in literature. Where is the problem here? Similarly, in his critique "For Buppies With a Capital 'B,'" Canedy takes Buppie.Com to task for being not quite good enough:

> Even some of the more current information seemed forced into categories that don't quite fit. This past summer, for example, under Issues Affecting Us, there was an article in [sic] about President Clinton's top Secret Service agent for being forced to testify before the grand jury in the Monica Lewinsky matter. First of all, the account never clearly stated whether the agent is black, which is relevant only because the article was included on a black-oriented Website. More to the point, the site never addressed the issue of how this article would affect African-Americans.

Again, where is the problem here? Many of the issues and circumstances that affect African Americans are not determined or influenced by black agents or black participation no matter how organized and valiant efforts are to the contrary. Nonetheless, their impact on black lives is no less significant or deterministic as far as the fate of this community is concerned. (Consider, for example, the remarkably high black voter turnout in Florida for Democratic candidate Al Gore in the Y2K [year 2000] U.S. presidential election—the real Y2K Bug event!) The assumption that

African Americans should only care about so-called black issues has its corollary in the racist presumption that nonblack people would or should *not* be interested in "black" issues. Despite a generally dismissive tone, Candy singles out one black website on which to heap measured praise. The feature's lead article, entitled "Library/Black Oriented Sites," provides capsule descriptions of nine specified sites ranging from the highly specialized, such as the National Association of Black Scuba Divers, to the more familiar, namely *Essence* and *Black Enterprise* magazines' online editions. Candy finds: "Overall, black-oriented sites have a lot of the same information, although *Net Noir*, for one has worked hard to be more comprehensive and is designed so well that it stands apart from the pack." I offer these observations even though Candy's equivocating feature story does what few popular press journalists had by 1998, and that is to acknowledge, promote, and qualitatively consider the fact and diversity of black online engagement. Still, the diminution of these black-oriented sites betrays an arbitrary evaluative criteria. More typically, however, black homesteading on the electronic frontier gets discussed with a focus on individual websites and net users in isolation and figured as anomalous.

Consider two other examples of rhetorical incredulity over black Internet use during these early years. One centers on a valiant struggle for computer literacy in a Harlem housing project, and the other spotlights one woman's discovery of the joys of e-commerce for her small pie shop in Compton, California. The problem with the first article, a 29 July 1997 *Village Voice* article, entitled "Tech Tyke: A Six-Year Old Brings Computer Education to the Projects," is, yet again, one of narrative emphasis. Athima Chansanchai's laudatory report on six-year-old Jerra Bost's prodigious feat of teaching in her father's after-school computer program that "attracts anywhere from 40 to 60 kids" is undermined by the stress on the program's only two working computers that were salvaged, "four primitive software programs, which have been eclipsed by a decade's worth of progress," the center's sweltering heat, Jerome Bost's (Jerra's dad) fifteen unsuccessful grant proposals for funding support, and a familiar disparagement of the Harlem neighborhood.[11] Plucky survivalist narrative frame aside, the prospect of future success as conveyed here is negligible at best and impossible at worst. A similar discursive thrust problematizes the 12 November 1995 *Los Angeles Times* feature story "The Virtual Pie Shop and Other Cyber Dreams." Confounding the four-column-width photo of four capable-looking black members of the Inner-City Computer Society, posed in front of a computer screen displaying a member website, is Randal C. Archibold's color commentary. From his story introduction and throughout, Archibold positions Rutherford, her Mid-City storefront pie shop, and the Compton neighborhood far behind and even outside the technological norm and its concomitant adoption curve. He writes,

> Just a year ago, the only bytes Rutherford understood were the ones taken from her blackbird pie or oatmeal cake. . . . Members like Rutherford show what the society is all about . . . sparking awareness of computer technology and the Internet among those who never thought it could do anything for them.[12]

Highlighting the effectiveness of the Computer Society need not hinge on negating African American small business owners' familiarity with and routine usage of computers in business.

The article quotes one group member as saying, "Our biggest obstacle is fear of the technology." A professor at Florida Atlantic University claimed in the article, "It's extra difficult to write something for the inner city. . . . The inner-city people I have dealt with really want to know where the business loans and jobs are. . . . People have asked me, how does my page on the Internet show how to get a bank loan? The Internet doesn't answer immediate needs" (Archibold E1–2). If we accept this professor's characterization of what black people wanted and expected from online services and given that these desires were expressed in 1995, then it appears that writing for the inner city was "extra difficult" because these black people were ahead of the curve. We can make this assertion because these "immediate needs" and more indeed are answered on the Internet as traditional businesses such as banks and loan services have rushed to embrace e-commerce. As with the *Village Voice* article, this story concludes somewhat pessimistically, "But few novices seem to have Rutherford's zeal. Sure, she has found frustration: Her modem doesn't always work, and the other day she was trying to figure out how to type commands into her machine without the aid of a mouse. Nevertheless she speaks effusively about the possibilities of a virtual pie shop" (Archibold E1–2).

No wonder the rhetoric of "the digital divide" functions to obfuscate a parallel "digital bridge"[13] reality as descriptive of blacks' relationship to the digital revolution. The situation of mainstream coverage of this virtual community's online activity parallels the issue discussed earlier about mainstream press coverage of violence and crime, wherein an overemphasis on sensational and unusual criminal acts occurs simultaneously with a deemphasis on the declining rates of crime. In both cases, the impact of the information disseminated is often heightened or blunted by the proportion and tone of the issue's presentation. It is for these reasons that Canedy's and other popular press accounts of black technolust serve to contain and marginalize the impressive fact of black early adopters in the once superelite culture of the embryonic information age.

AFROFUTURISM, MARINETTI REDUX, AND THE DIGITAL AGORA

Perhaps our nation's ongoing ignorance of African American early adoption of and involvement with prior innovative media technologies, such as the printing press, cinema, radio, and, to a lesser extent, video authorizes much of today's myopic consideration of black technological sophistication. Symptomatic in this regard is the fact that most popular science fiction discourses address little, if anything, of African Americans' longstanding fascination with science fiction, including the science fiction literature of African American journalist George S. Schuyler that was serialized in the black press during the 1930s. Even best-selling contemporary science fiction authors Samuel Delaney and the late, recently deceased Octavia Butler do not enjoy the celebrity of their white counterparts. Lately, however, the emergence of an academic rediscovery of an African diasporic niche element of science fiction and technoculture has resulted in what Mark Dery terms "Afrofuturism." In *Flame Wars: The Discourse of Cyberculture*, Dery poses the question, "Why do so few African Americans write science fiction?" to members of the black digerati, Samuel R. Delany, Greg Tate, and Tricia Rose (179). A master of the genre since his early twenties, Delany provides an important rationale for and insight into the relative dearth of black participation in an expressive mode thought by many to be a particularly well-suited expressive conduit for the peculiarities of the black experience in Western culture. That many of the future visions of science fiction literature are thinly veiled mythological reworkings of actual historical and contemporaneous scientific developments and phenomena surprises no one. However, Delany's cogent observation that black people's disproportionate participation in a literary tradition premised on an imaginary future is attributable to the systematic erasure of their actual past, might. Citing the infamous practices of the slave trade dedicated to the complete annihilation of "all vestiges of what might endure as African social consciousness," Delany makes clear the historical and deep structural impediments that explain "the historical reason that we've been so impoverished in terms of future images."[14] Despite the formidable "efforts of the white, slave importing machinery" to destroy all African cultural remnants, Delany reminds us that "some musical rhythms endured" as did "certain religious attitudes and structures" (191). From the outset of this discussion, Dery sets forth his working concept of 'Afrofuturism,' an umbrella term that aims to elucidate some of the specificites of what might be regarded as black-inflected or Afrocentric science fiction. It bears quoting at length. According to Dery, Afrofuturism is:

> Speculative fiction that treats African-American themes and addresses African-American concerns in the context of twentieth-century technoculture—and more generally, African-signification that appropriates images of technology and a prosthetically enhanced future—might, for want of a better term, be called "Afrofuturism." The notion of Afrofuturism gives rise to a troubling antinomy: Can a community whose past has been deliberately rubbed out, and whose energies have subsequently been consumed by the search for legible traces of its history, imagine possible futures? Furthermore, isn't the unreal estate of the future already owned by the technocrats, futurologists, streamliners, and set designers—white to a man—who have engineered our collective fantasies? . . . But, African-American voices have other stories to tell. . . . [I]f there is an Afrofuturism, it must be sought in unlikely places. (180–82)

Clearly, unofficial histories, both distant and recent, remain among the unlikely places that any serious attempt to uncover black participation in the often progressive vision of science fiction and fact-based technological social transformation will be found. Fleshing out some of the enduring spiritual and musical African remnants that Delany mentions by tracing some of the historical contours of black technomastery are Greg Tate and Tricia Rose. In tandem, they construct a useful mapping of the foundations of black scientism and technolust. Through the expertise and insights of these black digerati, the impetus driving the present Afrofuturism phenomenon more easily comes into view. For Greg Tate it is important to recall Africans' ancient technological and scientific primacy in any discussion of Afrofuturism and other myriad manifestations of black participation in science fiction:

> I see science fiction as continuing a vein of philosophical inquiry and tech-
> nological speculation that begins with the Egyptians and their incredibly
> detailed meditations on life after death. SF represents a kind of rationalist,
> positivist, scientific codification of that impulse, but it's still coming from
> a basic human desire to know the unknowable. (210)

More contemporarily, Tate finds it equally important to recognize the
science fiction impulse that suffuses the writing of twentieth-century
black writers Clarence Major, Ishmael Reed, and "the Nigerian writer
Amos Tutuola [among others], whose work uses Yoruban mythology in
a SF rather than a folkloric manner" (208). But it is in sequences of
Ralph Ellison's *Invisible Man* that Tate finds one of the earliest and
unmistakable instances of black literature breaking into what is traditionally thought a white genre's canon formation (207). Another
unlikely place where black science fiction resides in full view and yet
somehow remains invisible to the mainstream is urban and underground
black youth culture, including graffiti art and music. As Tate reveals,
even hip-hop is informed by a science fiction sensibility, "And then
there's Public Enemy's *Fear of a Black Planet*—I don't know if it gets any-
more sci-fi than that! . . . Black people live the estrangement that science
fiction writers imagine" (210–11).

Tricia Rose continues the exploration and extends it to considera-
tions of black technological mastery in the realm of mechanized and technocultural aesthetics. Again, stressing the profound intersection of mech-
anization and funk, and black musicians' virtuoso mastery of new musical
instruments within old musical traditions, Rose asserts:

> Digital music technology—samplers, sequencers, drum machines—are
> themselves cultural objects, and as such they carry cultural ideas. These
> machines force black musicians into certain ways of producing sound
> inside certain parameters, in this case nineteenth-century European musical
> constructions. . . . I resist the reading that by definition suggests that being
> black and funky means that one can't occupy certain spaces. (213)

Rose also rejects the Frankfurt School assumption that machine culture is
inherently fascist and devoid of creativity. Thriving as a result of a funky
and mechanical music mesh is precisely "what hip-hop is," in Rose's estimation. Commenting on Afrika Bambaataa and Arthur Baker's appropri-

ation of the black music inflected white German electro-pop band Kraftwerk's "*Trans-Europe" Express*,[15] for their "electro-boogie classic '*Planet Rock*,'" Rose is careful to contextualize this particular mode of reverse-cultural poaching historically.

> Electro-boogie took place in a historical moment—"Planet Rock" was released in 1982—when factory production and solid blue-collar work were coming to a screeching halt in urban America. Urban blacks were increasingly unemployed, and their best options were to become hidden workers for service industries or computer repair people. People said, "Look, technology is here; we can choose to be left behind or we can try to take control of the beast." What Africa Bambaataa and hip-hoppers like him saw in Kraftwerk's use of the robot was an understanding of themselves as *already* having been robots. (213)

What Rose illuminates here is Bambaataa's and subsequent hip-hop artists' apparent understanding of how the regimentation of their everyday lives benefits the ever-increasing demands of late capitalism that too often position black people as mindless, robotlike alien Others. But Rose sees the creative break-in as instantiating a meaningful act of white-face musical ventriloquism, with black musicians "taking on the robotic stance" *to play* with the robot imagery, and not *be played* by its profound alienation effect. "Kraftwerk gets taken up in a way that may or may not" fit with cultural studies' models of resistance, according to Rose. Yet she gets to the heart of black fascination with Euro-technopop: "Kraftwerk's own position may or may not be understood as resistive. I'm interested in reading effects in context, which is why technology can be emancipatory for hip-hop—because of its effects, not because it is naturally emancipatory" (214). Rejecting the idea of an inherent value neutrality or positivism in technology, Rose is clear about the specific ends to which black musicians adapted Kraftwerk's electro-pop symbols of regimentation to further their own needs to control the beast.

A part of controlling the technological beast and its elitist scientific applications is black artists' skill at recoding science and technology for black life in situ. This activity of demystifying and rearticulating science in terms of black popular cultural relevance is called "droppin' science" in the hip-hop vernacular. Rose explains the hip-hop catchphrase "droppin' science," as sharing knowledge, knowledge that is generally inaccessible to people, together with a fearlessness about stating what you believe to be the truth. There is also the implication that the information that you're imparting is going to revolutionize things because this is the truth that has been deliberately and systematically denied. Science, here, stands for incontrovertible evidence. Science is understood as that space where the future takes place. (214–15)

Hip-hop is not the only musical means by which African Americans succeeded in controlling the beast of technology. Rose also points to iconoclastic musician Sun-Ra and his unique fusion of African musical cosmology and Western musical traditions as emblematic. Sun-Ra's famous "flying saucer imagery," for Rose, "is about accepting the mystical powers that one knows, culturally," and it is about mystical processes and deductive reasoning that together produce new visions of society (215). One value of Sun-Ra's brand of "droppin' science" is his fusion of ancient Egyptian cosmology and a unique black science fiction futurist imaginary. For Rose it is important to see within Sun-Ra's creativity an astute reconciliation of black peoples' two histories or double consciousness. She writes, "If you're going to imagine yourself in the future, you have to imagine where you've come from; ancestor worship in black culture is a way of countering a historical erasure" (215). Rose, along with Delany and Tate, adroitly uses Dery's Afrofuturism heuristic to make it impossible to ignore the ways in which black folks historically have been and remain today on the cutting edge of transforming technology and their relationship to it (215).

DROPPIN' SCIENCE: AN-OTHER
FUTURIST MANIFESTO GOES ONLINE

Clearly, no discussion of Afrofuturism or black technoculture is complete without evoking the historical primacy of Filippo Tommaso Marinetti's influential Futurist Manifesto. It could be argued on theoretical grounds, coupled with the major task of putting aside Marinetti's fascism, that the progressive futurist zeitgeist of Marinetti informs many African diasporic peoples breaking in and hacking in to the fortresses of today's sites of technological experimentation. This is especially evident in the community-based efforts of technology-savvy groups who endeavor to bring cutting-edge technologies to the 'hood.

Whether the pioneering "black geeks online" (as one African American virtual community once dubbed itself) or others were familiar with Marinetti's futurist manifesto,[16] his modernist poetics on twentieth-century revolutionary technologies seem particularly resonant with this new energetic spirit of black technomastery. Typical of the sort of passionate futurist rhetoric contained in Marinetti's Manifesto are such passages as: "We shall sing the great crowds tossed about by work, by pleasure, or revolt; the many-colored and polyphonic surf of revolutions in modern capitals the nocturnal vibration of the arsenals and the yards under violent electrical moons." Decrying what he considers the "gangrene" influences of the past, Marinetti continues, "Do you mean to waste the best of you in useless admiration of the past that must necessarily leave you exhausted, lessened, trampled?" ("Joy of Mechanical Force").[17] Echoes of a Marinettian sensibility can be found in the computer-mediated frustrations of one contributor to an African American CMC or listserv on 26 February 1995. Sharing his outrage at a *Newsweek* special edition dedicated to the "information revolution" that excluded any mention of blacks, the contributor, whom I will call "Max," posted the following call to digital arms under the subject heading "Digital Racism Is Already Here":

> Personally, I am appalled that in the middle of Black History Month, *Newsweek* Magazine dedicated the February 27, 1995 issue to the information revolution and completely omitted any mention of the thousands of African Americans and people of color that are very active in shaping the information highway. It is evident to me that racism transfers very smoothly to a digital format. The number of you on my mailing list alone who will receive this message is large enough to nip this trend in the bud, but only if you act NOW! . . . They will not be able to ignore a flood of email, faxes, and phone calls from ALL of you. . . . Now is the time to let *Newsweek* and the world know exactly what it means that the revolution has begun. ("Digital Racism," AFROAM-L)

For Max, it is clear that *Newsweek*'s erasure of blacks and other peoples of color from its future vision projects a view from the past necessarily inferior to the real future rapidly taking shape in the digital domain. It is equally clear that Max is enlisting the new technology to foment widespread rejection of older media practices. *Newsweek* becomes Max's equivalent of what Marinetti describes as a "useless admiration of the past that must necessarily leave you exhausted, lessened, trampled."

As I stated, I initiated this study in late 1994 and early 1995, which happened to coincide with the birth of the Internet browser, navigator, or search engine phenomenon designed to make the revolutionary technology more user friendly to net novices.[18] At that time, when I entered the key word string *black* and *African American*, singly and together, the response from Yahoo (then the only Internet search engine) returned a count of twenty-one "matches," accompanied by the term "new" in brackets. It is partly from this universe that my particularized use of the "early adopters" category derives. Rounding out my "early adopters" universe are two archival databases maintained by participants of the online discussion groups or listservs that either preceded the advent of the Internet search engine or were omitted by them. Those black sites or individual participants referenced in this study that do not appear on either the 1995 Yahoo listing or the above-mentioned private discussion group/listserv constitute the "later arrivals" segment of this study.

STAKING CLAIMS ON THE CYBERFRONTIER: BLACK EARLY ADOPTERS AND LATER ARRIVALS— SOME GENERAL CONTOURS

The hyperbolic rhetoric designating the Internet and the World Wide Web as "super information highway" and as the gateway or on-ramp to the information age did not go unnoticed by the African diasporic community. While some remained skeptical of the discursive onslaught of utopic claims for the revolutionary digital democracy, many were affected by the gold-rush mentality that seems to have triggered a bout of global cyberfever. To outline the progressive possibilities of an egalitarian technosphere in the information age, I consider a few separate but related instances of the African diasporic engagement with the plenitudes of cyberspace. These examples posit another prism through which we might begin to reconsider the powerfully charged rhetorics of "the digital divide" and promises of "universal access."

The first is a virtual community called "Naijanet," which centers on an elite group of "early adopters" whose activities and concerns revolving around African connectivity to the Internet present us with a new set of issues vis-à-vis postcolonialism and geopolitical change at the intersection of globalization and the information age. Another representative group affords an opportunity to examine more popular uses of the Internet to arbitrate popular culture issues and debates given the competing demands of old and new school approaches to digital media technologies. And finally, the Million Woman March (and my study of a few black geeks) round out this core group of early IT adopters featured in this work. With its more grassroots centered approach especially to harnessing the Internet's growing influence, the Internet's role in the Million Woman March became the most promising for interrogating the powerful emancipatory power of this new medium for actually realizing the promise of technological social change, at least at this juncture. While it is important to acknowledge this study's construction of a high-tech/early adopters and low-tech/latecomers schism as a result of selecting these specific four cases, it is equally necessary to point out the fluidity and permeability of these heuristic boundaries on important levels. Operating on one level is the class and educational level of the black elite groups that mirror mainstream divisions. But the precarious nature of black social, economic, and educational mobility militates against such rigid categorizations. On another level is the prevalence of the "bootstrap" ethos suffusing much of the black diaspora's "self-help" politics that render demarcations of an essential division into high and low untenable.

One example of this bootstrapping praxis is seen in the Black Geeks Online organization's "Taking IT to the Streets" campaign of summer 1997. On Saturday, 5 July 1997, the Black Geeks took their online computer literacy activism off-line to the streets of Washington, D.C. In what they describe as "Taking IT (information technologies) to the Streets," the group organizers enlisted corporate sponsorship to host a one-day information technology expo to, "bring the 'Net to the un-connected."[19] As they put it, "Though we are a virtual organization based on the web, it is our goal to connect people of color from around the world—both on and offline. Our purpose is to share our talents and time to promote computer literacy and educate others about the power and potential of Internet technology" ("Taking IT to the Streets).

Besides confounding entrenched notions of black technophobia, considered together these four cases offer interesting materialist critiques of the Frankfurt School's alarmist views of "one-dimensional" cultural or technological determinism, and they suggest a revivification of the more optimistic Gramscian organic intellectual model in postmodern society. Although it would be difficult to equate this emergent black technophilia with some certain triumph of black critical consciousness (advocated by bell hooks) over the mental shackles of consumerist false consciousness (warned against by Horkheimer and Adorno), it is clear that the proliferation of black Internet sites signals a new era in black diasporic cultural production, dissemination, and consumption.

ESTABLISHING CYBERGATEWAYS TO THE
AFRICAN DIASPORA: GEOPOLITICS IN THE DIGITAL AGE

It is important to understand that the current scramble for domination and domestication of the Internet and the World Wide Web recalls that unleashed on the African continent by the West in the nineteenth century. This "Scramble for Africa" analogy as a narrative frame for contextualizing the stakes involved in the Internet revolution was dually inspired. One inspiration was the spate of newspaper articles covering the apparently surprising alacrity of African Americans' entry onto the fast lanes of the global infobahn discussed earlier. Another suggested itself as news surfaced of the global media corporations' scramble to colonize the Internet through their highly publicized strategies of merger mania and media convergence tactics. And while print reports detailing an unanticipated surge in black online connectivity only hint at what any netizen (virtual citizen of the Internet) or netnovice today who types in the key words *black* and *African* as any portion of a keyword search quickly discovers, these search commands yield up to more than a million "results," "hits," or "category matches" (in the argot of Internet search engines Lycos, Hotbot, Alta Vista, Ask Jeeves, Yahoo, Google, and many others).[20] This study reveals that in fact as early as 1991, some technosavvy black people throughout the African diaspora had mounted their own scramble for a secure share of the Internet spoils in the intensifying global grab for Internet dominance.

As one of history's most profound and far-reaching cycles of corporate expansion and domination since the Industrial Age's robber barons and corporate trusts,[21] today's megamedia mergers threaten to obliterate any remaining optimism about preserving the last vestiges of a viable and unsponsored public sphere. Indeed, the political engine of deregulation responsible for powering the economic force of the ascendant global media behemoths has the capacity and intent now to rock our worlds. No sooner had the centripetal forces of technological innovation produced newer, democratizing models of mass media diversity such as cable, satellite, Internet, wireless, and other wide-ranging digital communications systems, than the older media concerns set in motion a centrifugal counter-model of mass media monopolizing and reconsolidation, better known as convergence. Because these newer media were poised to undermine what Ben Bagdikian calls "the media monopoly" (Sklar), many believed the decentralized nature and transnational reach of these new media industries signaled a new age of participatory democracy and by extension progressive social equity and creative cultural rejuvenation. It seemed that finally new multimedia forms might function to serve and promote the diverse communicative needs of a changing, multicultural world. The arrival and rapid diffusion of the Internet and the World Wide Web were central to this vision of inevitable global transformation, as the Internet's role in prodemocracy movements in several developing nations attests. One contemporary critic, who underscores the connection between the Internet and geopolitical change, is Ingrid Volkmer. In Volkmer's estimation:

> the Internet can be regarded as an icon of a globalized media world that has shifted global communication to a new level. Whereas television was a harbinger of this new era of global communication by reaching a worldwide audience with worldwide distribution and innovative global programming (such as that of CNN and MTV), the Internet reveals the full vision of a global community. . . . [T]he implications are obvious: national borders are increasingly disappearing within cyberspace. (48)

Not only do national borders increasingly disappear in cyberspace; they are replaced by new kinship structures now predicated on the fluidity of cybernetic virtual communities and homelands.

In his important work *Imagined Communities: Reflections on the Origin and Spread of Nationalism*, Benedict Anderson reminds us that "nationality, or . . . [the] world's mutiple significations, nation-ness, as well as nationalism, are cultural artefacts of a particular kind" (4). It is essential to Anderson that we understand how nationness is often historically determined and its meanings subject to change over time (4). And yet for Anderson it is crucial to recognize the profound emotional legitimacy of nationalisms despite the challenge of subnationalisms within many tenuous nationalist borders, as the dissolution of the Soviet Union, the fall of the Berlin Wall, and the bloody coups responsible for reconfiguring many Third-World nations clearly attest. "Nation, nationality, nationalism," as Anderson points out, "all have proved notoriously difficult to define, let alone analyse" (3). Clearly then, the historical changes and technological innovations responsible for the Internet threaten to exacerbate the slippery and increasing fragility of traditional nationalisms while simultaneously strengthening the affective dimensions of a newer, virtual, or cybernationalism now unbound by traditional ideological, political, economic, geographical, and even temporal boundaries and limitations. Moreover, it is the aim of this work to proffer new definitions and analyses of that new brand of cybernationalisms and virtual communities that comprised an emergent African digital diaspora as it existed in the early years of the Internet's global formation.

IMAGINED AFRICAN COMMUNITIES IN CYBERSPACE OR DIGITIZING DOUBLE CONSCIOUSNESS

In the late 1980s, Marshall McLuhan and Bruce R. Powers studied "the structural impact of technologies on society" (x). In their book *The Global Village: Transformations in World Life and Media in the 21st Century*, the authors remarked that "electronic technologies have begun to shake the distinction between inner and outer space, by blurring the difference between being here or there" (148). Additionally, they observed that "man's nature was being rapidly translated into information systems which would produce enormous global sensitivity and no secrets" (viii). Although it was the phenomenal communications revolution wrought by video-related technologies to which McLuhan and Powers addressed themselves, their observations have obvious and profound implications for digital technologies such as the Internet. Without a doubt McLuhan's conceptualization of the global village has been a useful heuristic for grasping the incredible lure of the Internet's global reach. However, his later ideas about the technological breakdown of boundaries between inner and outer spaces and information technologies' production of "enormous global sensitivities and no secrets" are equally, if not more, generative. For these ideas provide important frameworks for thinking about how digital media erect new possibilities for concretizing my rhetoric of an African digital diaspora capable of enacting a new millennial manifestation of W. E. B Du Bois's powerful trope of black "double consciousness."

As early as 1992 the African diaspora was willfully and optimistically dispersed into the transnational ether of the Internet by many tech-savvy African nationals and expatriates living and working abroad. For these Afrogeeks (as I have dubbed them) the lure of cyberspace represents "the possibility of vast, unexplored territory" (Balsamo 116) capable of sustaining new modes of postcolonial African unity, of sorts, often untenable on the continent given the political and military economies of "real" space. Among African early adopters of the Internet and the World Wide Web were those visionary techevangelists or cyber-witchdoctors, if you will, who conjured such new Africanities online as Naijanet, the Association of Nigerians Abroad, the Buganda Home Page, the African National Congress Home Page, and others. By 1997, more black diasporic websites began appearing, including ones for the Republic of Ghana, the Afro-Caribbean Chamber of Commerce, Camden (UK) Black Parents and Teachers Association, Canadian Artists' Network: Black Artists in Action, Egypt's Information Highway Project, and Africa Online, among others too numerous to list here. Although the named sites are exemplary of most that I actually visited and analyzed during the early phases of my long-standing study, I want to stress again the importance of acknowledging the existence of many more websites that I noticed, many of which are long defunct. This fact of the vanishing cybertext is a significant research problem, and apparently it is particularly acute for experimental, avant-garde and outré—the most marginal, and unusual—nonmainstream online ventures. So one of my burdens of history, to borrow a phrase from Hayden White, is producing and preserving a critical archeology of these first Afrocentric websites. My historical burden has not been lessened by the reduction of this rich, early constellation to a smaller orbit of extant stars (at least at this writing) and those now defunct, that I have preserved serendipitously through my habitual downloading since the 1994 heyday of Internet homesteading on through the present moment. While it is impossible to elaborate on most of these sites' specific identities, impact, and developmental trajectories, it nonetheless is important to acknowledge the historical fact of their online existence.

NEW AFRICANITIES AND THE REVERSE AFRICAN BRAIN DRAIN OR A DIGITAL AFRICAN BRAIN REATTACHMENT

The first steps "toward developing a Nigerian online network took place in 1991" when a Nigerian at Dartmouth College began forwarding to select friends email news about the home country.[24] From this inauspicious beginning sprang Naijanet, one of the Net's most robust and enduring Afrocentric virtual communities. In a 1999 article for the online journal

West Africa Review, Misty L. Bastian reports that since 1992 "Naijanet has spun off at least six related online networks" and that at its height of influence and popularity in 1995 "Naijanetters" numbered approximately 750 strong (Bastian, "Immigrant Nigerians"). One difficulty that I encountered having to do with locating more specifically African virtual communities to research was this (CMC's) penchant for insularity, which Bastian conveys well as a result of her own participant observation of the group:

> Basically, an interested party needed to know a Naijanetter in order to learn the address to subscribe. The subsidiary nets were (and remain) even more difficult to access. People who have heard of the subsidiary nets would, during the later 1990s, post to Naijanet and request their subscription addresses from Naijanetters "in the know."

My own contact with a Naijanetter "in the know" did not occur until 1997, when several of my early investigations were nearing completion. My researches led me to one of Naijanet's subscribers, a Nigerian technology scientist who agreed to share his personal database of Naijanet communications with me to benefit my research. It is this personal database that informs much of my interaction with Bastian's published Naijanet historiography.

Now, we begin first by considering what a digital retransplantation of the African brain or reversing the brain drain phenomenon portends for rethinking issues of postcoloniality. One of the more recognizably transformative aspects of postcoloniality being wrought by the digital age is a new discursive Africanity obtaining in chat rooms and listservs of several Nigeria-centered subnets engendered by Naijanet. According to Bastian the six Naijanet subnets are

> Oduduwa (the Yoruba net), ANA-net (a net for the Association of Nigerians Abroad, an activist group), Naijawoman-net, soc.culture.nigeria on Usenet, Igbo—net, and Rivnet (a net for indigenes of southeastern Nigeria's Rivers State). A number of people who were once important "netizens" of Naijanet have also begun to construct Africa or Nigeria pages on the World Wide Web; these pages act as clearinghouses of information about African and Nigerian issues on the internet at large.

This fracturing of Naijanet's success into these "fission nets," in Bastian's terms, suggests the possibilities for a virtual tolerance and acceptance of

ideological and political dissent and democratic practices that remain elusive in Nigeria's militarized postcolonial (although I prefer the term
"recolonized")[23] reality. Bastian's participant informers at Naijanet
revealed that the not-too-surprising issues that provoked the splintering
of Naijanet generally concerned the politics of indigenous language pluralism, expatriate political activism, gender oppression, nettiquette, ethnic cleansing, and tribalism. To be sure this is familiar terrain for post-
colonial conflicts, and expectations of passionate expressions of conflicts
by now typify the communicative exchange in user groups and listservs,
particularly in this age of "globalization and its discontents."[24] However,
the fact that Naijanet and its "fission-nets" formed and sustained a voluntary web ring of mutual support and nationalist solidarity is remarkable indeed.

This postindependence conceptualization of a virtual Nigerian con-
sanguinity is remarkable because, as Emeka J. Okoli reminds us, "the
British arrogantly realigned Nigerian political structures to serve their
own interest at devastating consequences on relations between Nigerian
ethnic populations, which include between 178 and 300 languages and
more than 250 cultures, each having its own customs, traditions"
(32–33). And notwithstanding the fact that Nigeria's putative independence in 1960 has been ineffectual in bridging the bitter divisions
between such major ethnic groups as Housas, Igbos, and Yorubas, neither
has it alleviated their mutual suspicions (33). However, as Sandy Stone
points out, use nets and email networks are new spaces that instantiate
"the collapse of the boundaries between the social and technological, biology and machine, natural and artificial" (85). Thus, Naijanetters used the
new spaces of the Internet to refuse crucial elements of Nigeria's
intractably debilitating colonialist legacy and through CMC reimage a
new Africanity in cyberspace.

Obviously, it would be naïve to expect a miraculous vaulting over
decades of deep-seated ethnic and tribal hostilities, even given the phe-
nomenological and experiential accelerator that is Internet time. Yet outside the state panopticon diverse expatriate Nigerians in virtual communication found common ground for airing divergent and convergent
views. In cyberspace, they were not governed by the volatile "press/gov-
ernment relationship that makes it a no-win battle between the pen and
the sword" that defines Nigeria's state-controlled press and media institutions (Okoli 39). Still, as Bastian's recent ethnography conveys, Naijanetters were not immune to intense ethnic and gender rivalries of the sort

that plague Nigerians on the continent. By contrast however, these new online social spaces and democratic media forums facilitated face-to-face meetings, "but under new definitions of both 'meet' and 'face'" (Stone 85) and, for Naijanetters, under less-threatening conditions more conducive to nonlethal expressions of opposing views, philosophies, and perspectives. This is not to imply that Naijanet's tolerant, digital public sphere was a flame-free zone. Far from it, as the network's eventual splintering amply demonstrates. In that regard, Bastian has noted:

> Even though some netizens suggested censuring the people who "flamed" in the past, most participants during this period insisted that "Naija" was a community where all opinions were valued and where discourse consequently had to be freeflowing. Some of the most radically egalitarian on Naijanet actually decried the formation of alternative nets, saying that those who split off Naijanet wished to fractionalize the true spirit of the net—and therefore the true spirit of "Naija," the virtual nationalist space they were struggling to create. ("Nationalism")

Because the digitized postcolonial condition forestalls the necessity of putting real flesh and blood bodies dangerously on the line in service to the nation-state, taking primacy over ethnic group allegiance, Naijanetters used their virtual bodies regularly to challenge and contest one another, as well as amplify problems in the homeland. One challenge that simultaneously embodied and threatened the "true spirit of Naija" was the insistent articulation of African women's long-standing discontent vis-a-vis gender oppression. Just as "Naija's" free speech ethos helped foster painfully honest dialogues and vigorous debates about the politics of language-chauvinism and ethnic "tribalism" (Bastian, "Nationalism"), so too were grievances and recriminations about the persistence of women's "double colonization" given voice—at least for a time.

This concept of "double colonization" is discussed in postcolonial feminism as a particularly acute system of gender oppression whereby "women in formerly colonized societies were doubly colonized by both imperial and patriarchal ideologies" (Ashcroft, Griffiths, and Tiffin 250). In decolonizing struggles for African cultural restoration, the matter of women's double colonization too often was sublimated under a "first things first" offensive promulgated by men who saw it as ancillary to the larger fight against Western racism and imperialism (Petersen 254). Naijanet's cell divisions along gender lines indicate how these postcolonial issues get refracted signifcantly in the African digital diaspora. Because name-based gender marking is not always evident in Nigerian languages, Bastian reports that women Naijanetters "were tired of being addressed as 'Mr.' or 'Brother' in every post." Other gender-specific frictions ensued, and when some men uttered sexist remarks and commentary romanticizing abusive traditional practices against women such as female circumcision, Naijawomen-net was formed. It is telling that despite the fact of most women's continued participation in both nets after the split, with some even forwarding information to Naijanet, the majority of men ignored Naijawomen-net (Bastian, "Nationalism"). It is important to underscore, however, that African men in the digital diaspora were confronted with, and some took notice of, the women's insistent liberation agenda within many black nationalist decolonizing strategies.

Among the more fractious and irresistible matters to afflict Naijanet's digital village upstarts were members' intense reactions to homeland news of recurring military coups, human rights abuses, and the frustrations of their mediation through Nigeria's powerful state-controlled mass media hegemony. One of Naijanet's more politically minded fission nets willing to engage these hot-button issues directly and vociferously was the Association of Nigerians Abroad (ANA-net).[27] Because of its political outspokeness, ANA's CMC approach presents fertile ground for reccontextualizing aspects of the postcolonial condition in the digital era.

Resisting the lure of a presumed white mask of émigré (white-skin) privilege that often hides Africans' black skin experiential reality in global politics, ANA members were committed "to the concept of Nigerian nationalism, even during the dark days of the Abacha military regime" (Bastian, "Immigrant Nigerians"). Moreover, ANA members were determined to broadcast—or cybercast—their vehement political dissent against "power hungry despots bent on taking [Nigeria] back into the Stone Age,"[28] to progressive-minded netizens willing to enlist the medium in an array of postimperialist moves. In a scathing indictment of Nigerian military rule in 1995, in the form of a press release, ANA articulated its outrage at the "Stalinist-style terror" being visited upon "the Nigerian people." Using the occasion of Nigerian poet-writer Ken Saro-Wiwa's and other political prisoners' unconscionable murders to demonstrate that indeed, the subaltern could and would speak, ANA's press release made these charges and appeals:

A year ago the Association of Nigerians Abroad (ANA) predicted that the Nigerian military cabal will unleash the most brutal and lawless acts of irresponsibility on Nigeria. Since then, the evil and satanic regime has gradually and systematically chosen to re-enact Stalinist-style terror on the Nigerian people. . . . The latest act in these series of atrocities is the deliberate judicial murder of Mr. Ken Saro-Wiwa and 8 other Ogoni political activists. At the same time, the military regime holds more than 80 political detainees in prisons scattered all over the country. . . . We therefore urge the international community to enact urgent measures to bring an end to the tyrannical regime in Nigeria. If this is not done as a matter of urgency, the consequences for Nigeria and the entire world community will be enormous. (ANA online, "Association")

To underscore the urgent need of rethinking Nigeria's place in the world community of nations, outside her often-shadow status as the major oil supplier to the West, second only to OPEC, ANA reminds the international community of its recent moral victory against another despotic African regime—apartheid South Africa. Recalling the immense pressure brought to bear by an outraged global citizenry on South Africa for its scandalous human rights abuses, ANA sought to reawaken that activism against Nigeria's then-current military government with the added irony that "Nigeria was an active proponent for economic sanctions and total isolation of [South Africa's] racist regime" (ANA online, "Association"). Anticipating some recalcitrance on the part of some Western leaders, ANA's subalterns spoke truth to power on the matter and in this way:

With all due respect to the British Prime Minister, Mr. Major on the hardship that economic sanctions may cause, our generation accepts and prefers the hardships of economic sanctions to the wanton killing of our citizens by a brutal regime. Besides, the oil-wealth has only gone to benefit the ruling cabal not the average Nigerian. Indeed, sanctions represent the best available tool that could lead to a speedy emancipation of Nigerians from military colonisation and oppression. (ANA online, "Association")

While it might be tempting to view ANA's confrontational speech through jaundiced eyes owing to its members' presumed free speech privileges and protections here in America, we must not overlook the significant political risks always attendant upon exiles. For despite their liminal positioning astride Africa and America, and functioning under what Gayatri Spivak suggests for such subalterns is a fixed sign of otherness (269–71), ANA members were resolute in their efforts to "move with the world into the 21st century" with the Internet put in service toward Nigeria's political freedom. To that end, in 1999 ANA initiated a scholarship program for Nigerian university students, and the Internet was used as a fundraising tool in this endeavor. The website announced that "by the end of 2003," the organization had awarded twenty-two scholarships to Nigerian students at Nigerian universities.[27] The names of all the students and their respective universities are published and made available for view on their website in 2004.

In one of the foundational texts of postcolonial discourse, "The Occasion for Speaking," from his book *The Pleasures of Exile*, West Indian novelist and critic George Lamming observed in 1960 that the act of writing is linked with the expectation, however modest, of being read (16). He also said, "The pleasure and paradox of my own exile is that I belong wherever I am. My role, it seems, has rather to do with time and change than with the geography of circumstances; and yet there is always an acre of ground in the New World which keeps growing echoes in my head. I can only hope that these echoes do not die before my work comes to an end" (17). It seems that Lamming's utterances not only prefigure new modes and codes of struggle and transformation beyond himself, but his occasion for speaking to ask "what the West Indian novelist has brought to the West Indies" represents an African diasporic echo to which ANA members' online work responds.

Apparently, among the pleasures and paradoxes of exile for ANA members is that the Internet makes it possible to belong to and be in both Africa and America or some other diasporic locales at once. What this condition of digitized exile permits is an ideological boundary crossing with material force in digital space wherein expatriates can act oppositionally to those neo-imperialist interests that willingly or inadvertently benefit their host nation. As mentioned earlier, later developments resulted in ANA's ability to use their website to solicit and evidently secure funds from Africans living abroad and others sympathetic to the cause to support their scholarship program for Nigerian students on the African continent. In 1995, though, ANA seized upon the frontierist, Wild West ethos, embodied in a *Wired* Magazine press release titled "Cyberspace Cannot Be Censored" (quoted in Barwell and Bowles 708). At that moment, ANA challenged the neo-imperialist practices of powerful Western oil corporations in their host countries. Indeed, in 1995 ANA used its website to hold the Anglo-American Shell Oil Company accountable for human rights violations, repressions, political abuses, and environmental devastation in Nigeria. In its 13 November 1995 press release, ANA specified ten demands of the international community on behalf of the "People of Nigeria," including

> freezing of all new loans, extension or rescheduling of old loans; we particularly applaud the decision of the IFC to freeze a $180 million loan and equity package that would have been used by the Nigerian regime, Shell, Elf, and Agip Oil Companies to build a gas plant and oil pipelines in the ravaged Niger Delta; A world-wide boycott of all Shell Products. We hold Shell equally responsible for the death of all nine activists and for the decimation of the oil producing areas of the Niger Delta. (ANA online, "Association")

If Lamming's midtwentieth-century contemplations of the peculiar pleasures of exile revolved around the cultural dissonance West Indian writers experienced negotiating the "idea of England" and living its exile reality (Lamming 13), ANA members more than thirty years later clearly invite new rules of exilic engagement with their American and other "Others." Unlike Lamming's writer in exile, who "has not only to prove his worth to the other, he has to win the approval of Headquarters, meaning . . . England" (13), ANA's global exiles living "in the USA, Canada, Australia, Japan, the UK, South Africa, Botswana, Russia, Saudi Arabia, Finland, and so on,"[28] wanted proof of *their* "other's" own worth. To a large extent, this "proof" entailed unequivocal international support for the struggle against Shell Oil. As ANA's 1995 online press release put it:

> There is a moral responsibility which must be borne by certain governments and multi-national companies whose desire for profit and the proverbial black gold has blinded them into unholy alliances with the evil regimes. In particular, we note the roles being played by Shell Petroleum in Nigeria. Shell's operation in Nigeria is one of the worst nightmares visited upon Nigerians and the Ogoni people in particular.

Shell was named as a litigant in the "special Tribunal which tried and convicted Ken Saro-Wiwa and the other Ogoni activists, and is therefore morally implicated in their deaths. . . . Shell must be stopped." ANA insists, "Every litre of petroleum product from Nigeria marketed by Shell is being extracted at the expense of the blood and the lives of our patriots whose families and land are being destroyed mainly for the benefits of a tyrannical elite and of Shell and its shareholders." These are strong words,

words of the order likely responsible for Saro-Wiwa and the others' political assassinations. Again, Lamming's words about the occasion for the
exile's speaking are instructive, "The exile is a universal figure. The prox-
imity of our two lives to the major issues of our time has demanded of us
all some kind of involvement. Some may remain neutral" (12), as many
Naijanetters attempted,

> but all have, at least, to pay attention to what is going on. On the political
> level, we are often without the right kind of information to make argument
> effective [sic]; on the moral level we have to feel our way through problems
> for which we have no adequate reference of traditional conduct as a
> guide. . . . Sooner or later, in silence or with rhetoric, we sign a contract
> whose epitaph reads: To be an exile is to be alive. (12)

Alas, it was ANA's very alive exiles who paid attention to what was going
on and issued a digital call-to-arms against Shell to help secure Nigeria's
salvation and Saro-Wiwa's redemption.

What makes ANA such an interesting study during its earlier
period, besides its contrast to many chat groups' functional self-centered-
ness, MUDs, and other online groups' hedonistic role-playing digital
playgrounds, is its historical self-consciousness about engendering a new
activist political agency in its formation of a digital disapora. In a welcome letter to its site visitors in the mid-1990s, the group's president,
Usman G. Akano, had this to say about the organization:

> The ANA is an association of Nigerian professionals, academics and stu-
> dents who are resident abroad, and friends of Nigeria with genuine inter-
> ests in issues Nigeriana. . . . The Association of Nigerians Abroad is unique
> among Nigerian organizations for the breadth of its developmental goals,
> the diversity of its membership, and its commitment to see Nigeria take
> her rightful place among the comity of nations. The ANA's business is also
> conducted almost entirely via the internet, perhaps the only full-fleged
> organization born of the information super-highway. This web page,
> designed, created and implemented through volunteer effort by a group of
> dedicated ANA members on our WWW sub-committee, is a small exam-
> ple of what ANA is all about. As you move around from page to page and
> from one link to another, you will come to learn more about ANA. . . .
> [J]oin us in the task of making the Nigerian corner of the world a better
> place for all. I thank you for your visit.[29]

Comfortable in the i-speak (Internet speech) of the net's argot (replete with such direct interactive appeals as "join us," "your visit," "as you move around," and new technology verbiage, "information super-highway," for example), Akano emphasizes his commitment to the organization's goal of supporting "the development of Internet communication in Nigeria." By 19 November 2000, the ANA website deployed more graphics and intra-site links (links internal to ANA's own pages, as opposed to extrasite links or what are more commonly called "web rings"). Sound files, animated gifs and icons, and an expanded array of features, topics, issues and visitor surveys were other structural changes and interactive elements indicating the site's technical sophistication, growth, and development over the years. For example, the site boasts a "Free Fax Service to ANYWHERE in the world. . . . [C]lick here to JUST DO IT!" Offers to "Set Up Your Home Page" are made to visitors of ANA.

During the website's late 1990s iteration there were regular departments that included "About ANA," "Join A.N.A.," ANA Executives," "ANA Committees," "ANA Publications," " Nigeria News," "Guardian," "Post Express," "Nigerian Universities," "Business in Nigeria," "FALLEN HEROES," "Nigerian Gallery," "NIGERIA HISTORY," and "Enter ANA Chatroom."[30] This became a full-service site following the rhizomatic structuring principles of many large-scale, nonprofit group-run, information-rich websites with pages and pages of data and discourses. Added to the obligatory copyright page, ANA's tag line is "All images ©www.ana.org® 1999 This Site is Designed by NIGERIANS." Finally, and lest anyone is left with the impression that the ANA of 2000 and beyond is not as politically active and confrontational as in 1993–9, let me briefly mention the letter posted on the site from 3 March 2000. In a letter to Nigerian President Olusegun Obasanjo, ANA expressed "its profound sadness at the recent colossal loss of lives and destruction of properties in Kaduna and Abia States as a result of the Sharia controversy." As expected, ANA brooked no compromise in its rhetoric of outrage,

> While the Association condems the brains behind these attrocities against innocent citizens of Nigeria, it expresses its disappointment at President Olesegun Obasanjo's lukewarm approach of a mere pronouncement that the Sharia law is "unconstitutional" and will "die a natural death" to this serious constitutional problem. . . . As a result of the national controversey and the danger it posed to the country's nascent democracy, the world

awaited President Obansanjo's executive initiative by utilizing all the judicial means available to resolve the issue. The President's inaction until the
outbreak of violence clearly sent the wrong message."[31]

The letter concludes with declarations of several resolutions. As with the
Shell censure, ANA is once again using the Internet to keep a vigilant eye
on Nigerian affairs, which all but ensures that Africa's digerati in exile will
not lack "the occasion for speaking." ANA's occasion for speaking continues up to the present. Indeed, at this writing the site has been redesigned
and updated to meet the organization's changing needs and functions. Its
more streamlined look is consistent with the more easily navigated site
designs employed by most professional news and information organizations on the web today. At present, the site's menu buttons consist of these
categories: About ANA, Executives, Committees, Publications, Join ANA,
Press Releases, Contact, Scholarship, Information, Chat Forum, What's
New, Nigerian Newspapers, and Search.[32] Unfortunately, the revamped
ANA website does not feature an archive of the site's earlier iterations used
in the compilation of this important case history. Once again, we are confronted with the hyperephemerality of digital texts.

SPEAKING IN DIGITAL TONGUES: DISEMBODIED
AFRICANS POUNDING DIGITAL TALKING DRUMS

Accompanying those expatriate Nigerians of Naijanet and ANA to the
online ether were other Africans on the continent and in the diaspora who
were most instrumental in constructing and beating the digital talking
drums of Internet connectivity for new cyber homelands. Most prominent were African diasporans producing such websites as the African
National Congress (ANC), the Buganda Homepage, Egypt's Information
Highway, and those affiliated with Africa Online, among others. When
Duncan Harford and others affiliated with the ANC launched the African
National Congress' website in early 1995, they were responsible for what
was then called the organization's "Electronic Communications Unit." In
1997 the ANC "underwent a process of restructuring" that resulted in the
formation of the Unwembi Communications Company responsible for
all aspects of the ANC website and its general IT agenda and goals.[33] As
of September 2004, the Unwembi Communications website describes its
origins in the following manner:

Established in 1997, Unwembi has its roots firmly planted in the *African National Congress* and the founding members of Unwembi were all actively involved in this movement long before the creation of the company. Having initially developed the ANC's website, it soon became apparent that in the new South Africa, the dissemination of information would play a crucial role in helping to strengthen democracy in South Africa. With this as a cornerstone, Unwembi quickly developed a website to disseminate information produced by the Government of National Unity (GNU) in 1996, later it became the www.polity.org.za website, subsequently sold to Creamer Media. . . . Subsequently Unwembi has expanded to take advantage of the outgoing convergence of electronic and print media.[34]

Under the site's more current listing of its selected clients, the ANC does not appear either as a government or NGO clientele of the organization. However, the ANC's own website does specify in these words "site by

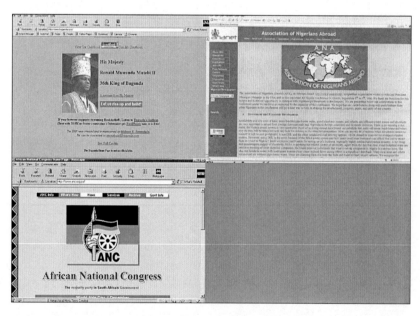

FIGURE 1.2. Array of screen shots from African and African diasporic web sites including Buganda Pages, featuring King Ronald Muwenda Mutebi II, circa 1999. Courtesy and © of Dr. Mukasa E. Ssemakula, ANA (Association of Nigerians Abroad) hompage, and ANC (The African National Congress). These groups and individuals recognized early on the need for an online presence.

Unwembi," which contains a hot-link button to the Unwembi website. As with the Association of Nigerians Abroad (ANA), the African National Congress' website has been updated along similar streamlined design aesthetics, with an added feature of streaming banner text that asks "what is the ANC" in various languages, including English and Afrikaans, among other dialects[35] (figure 1.2).

AFRICAN AMERICANS SPEAKING IN DIGITAL TONGUES

It is common knowledge among academics that Western or Eurocentric cultures traditionally use the term *lingua franca* to represent a generic translinguistic communications code. *Webster's Collegiate Dictionary* describes lingua franca as "any language that is widely used as a means of communication among speakers of other languages."[36] For me, a new

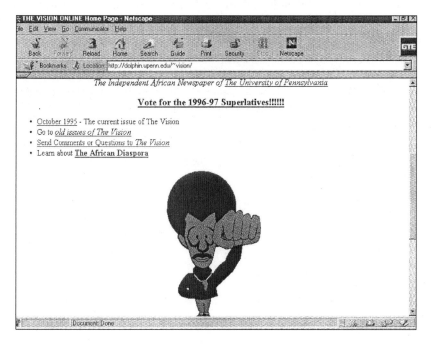

FIGURE 1.3. Screen shot of *Visions* splash page. A very early example of black iconography on the Web. Posted in 1997, *Visions* was a student-produced African newspaper and web site at the University of Pennsylvania.

transnational universal language is rapidly displacing the more familiar lingua franca trope. As globalization secures its position as the newest New World Order, the Internet, with its computerized zeroes and ones and digital communications infrastructure, seems to be the new lingua franca due to its more "universal" or translinguistic capacities. With this in mind, I have combined a familiar form of the Protestant religious practice known as "speaking in tongues" (a practice which dominates in many African American churches, and signifies a believer's privileged claim to and status of spiritual salvation) with the form of black speech known as Ebonics. I merge these black cultural modalities to inflect the global rise of digital and Internet culture with a specifically African American sensibility.

Among the first African American early adopters of the Internet speaking in what I am calling the "digital tongues" of zeroes and ones are black-oriented listservs located within HWCUs (historically white colleges and universities), HBCUs (historically black colleges and universities), black presses, black businesses, black grassroots activist centers, black nonprofit and nongovernmental organizations, and the personal websites of individual black citizens (figure 1.3). In conclusion, let me propose a particularly apt analogy. While watching a single candle flame's persistent burning against the opposing strong blasts of wind from an open window of a loft apartment during my visiting professorship in the Netherlands, I was struck by the fact that the candle flame was bent every which way but not extinguished. Accordingly, I became hopeful that digital grassroots activism and its flames of emancipation and liberation could and would persist despite the countervailing winds of increasing corporate media dominance of the ascendant Internet and other digital media technologies.

CHAPTER TWO

Digital Women:
The Case of the Million Woman
March Online and on Television

The Internet was definitely a factor in helping to get the word out to Sisters about the [Million Woman] March. From August 10th, 1997 to 12:01 AM, October 25, 1997, the official Web Site took 1,010,000 hits from around the world. . . . This doesn't take into account the number of hits or e-mail at the regional MWM Web Sites across the country.

> —Ken Anderson, email communication
> with author (30 October 1997)

I speak today because I'm fearless, and I even speak because of my fear. . . . I speak today because I really have no choice.

> —Congresswoman Maxine Waters, speech, *Million
> Woman March*, TV, C-SPAN (25 October 1997)

It was a beautiful day wasn't it? I've rarely been as proud as I was on Oct. 25th, and I think most of us felt the same. We also found that we don't need the mainstream media to publicize or endorse our events/ourselves.

> —Sis. Mickey, "Congratulations Sistahs," email
> communication with author (29 October 1997)

> There was now more of a risk that the women and their skills
> would become entangled with each other and wander off on
> their own. . . . They weren't only processing data for the boss.
> If they were pooled with their colleagues, their working envi-
> ronment was a hive of activity . . . a multiplicity of informal
> networks, grapevine gossip riding on the back of formal work-
> ing life.
>
> —Sadie Plant, *Zeroes + Ones: Digital*
> *Women + the New Technoculture*

The failure of television networks to recognize the existence and significance of black women's technolust was evident in the anemic coverage of
the phenomenally successful 25 October 1997 Million Woman March on
Philadelphia. Due to an apparent disinterest in the year-long planning
efforts of march organizers and supporters,[1] the mainstream broadcast
media were ill-prepared for the magnitude of the event transpiring before
their own collective televisual gaze. The spectacle of a massive stream of
orderly black female (and supportive male) bodies, detached from the
familiar frame of a newsworthy urban riot or rap music concert run
amok, clearly left mainstream journalists scrambling for explanations in
that revealing manifestation of black-white cultural disconnect, while
betraying traditional practices of dominant media myopia. Could the *Los
Angeles Sentinel* be right in its critique of television media and the Million
Man March two years earlier, when it asserted: "One may rest assured
[that] coverage would have been extensive and comprehensive if the
march had erupted in violence"?[2]

   That the Million Woman March drew its inspiration from the Million Man March is apparent and widely acknowledged. Not so apparent,
however, are the Million Woman March founders' motivations and ratio-
nales for such an undertaking. Besides adhering to what Elsa Barkley
Brown describes as a tradition of "negotiating and transforming the public sphere" in ways that advance "African American political life in the
transition from slavery to freedom" (111), march organizers specify key
elements of their contemporary approaches and methods. To begin, we
note that the march was conceived and orchestrated by two Philadelphia
locals. Phile Chionesu, a small business entrepreneur, was its visionary
and founder. Aiding in the realization of that vision was march cochair
Asia Coney, a longtime public-housing activist (Quinones Miller 2).[3] Ten

days prior to the march, both women were interviewed by the *Final Call,* the weekly publication of the Nation of Islam. Among the most telling and insightful pieces of information about the march that emerged was why Philadelphia became the march site.[4] The obvious response that it was where march organizers Chionesu and Coney resided clearly is a factor. However, Asia Coney's thoughtful answer to the question of locale overturns such easy assumptions. To the *Final Call*'s question of "Why have the March in Philadelphia?" Coney's reply is significant:

> We recognized initially that Philadelphia was the first capital (of America). We understand that many historical events and programs were started here. The Benjamin Franklin Parkway was designed by a Black man. We watched as a bomb was dropped on Osage Avenue and acted like it happened in another country. One of the major primes of this march is to go back to the root. In a sense, this being the first capital, we had to bring it home. We had to bring it to Philadelphia. As you well know, the brothers went to Washington. The following year they went to New York. There was no need to continue to highlight those particular locations. But, to make folks understand that there is a clear connection, we didn't just pick it out of the sky. Philadelphia is where it started. So, it is clear there was no place else to go.

These resolute women not only were attuned to the historic symbolism of staging this black womanist act of sassy self-articulation at a site of previous repression and liberation, but they also recognized their present role in swaying the winds of social change as the new millennium dawned. To the question of why even pursue this march, Chionesu responded:

> Black women have made achievements for many years and now is the time that we must take another step forward. Now, we must put it all together and prepare something we can give to our daughters and to our entire race as a people. This is a timely situation because we see all the changes that are occurring in the world, and we must make the preparation to be a vital part of what is getting ready to occur. (*Final Call*)

One of the changes to speak of was in the way these black women imagined their differentiation from their male counterparts. Distinguishing their agenda from that of the Million Man March, while still acknowledging its profound influence, Chionesu states:

> The Million Man March, for many of us, showed in a very magnificent way that the coming together of a body of men brought about some very positive aspects. We saw brothers come back and immediately become responsible for family and community. . . . We were going to be in step with our brothers. We say, once again, that the brothers atoned; we are now stating clearly that we will assist in setting the tone. (*Final Call*)

The tone that these women were intent on setting was that of motivated women committed to the idea of reinventing black families and communities as full-fledged partners with their male counterparts in the post–civil rights liberation struggle for societal transformation, including efforts to reassert the ongoing need for black political and economic justice and fundamental social change.

Another change occurring in the world that the women insisted on confronting was computer literacy. By all accounts, the march's phenomenal success owed much to the Internet. Both the traditional mainstream media and the march organizers foreground the Internet in mobilizing the massive sea of black bodies that turned out for the march, but in varying degrees and effect. Where the television and print media betray their rivalry with the new digital media by insinuating a culpability of sorts in facilitating this unauthorized takeover of Philadelphia's streets, march organizers, by comparison, betray their technolust by harnessing the new agenda-setting momentum of the Internet for the cause of African diasporic unity.

Still, what is so remarkable here is black women's strategic deployment of the Internet to orchestrate a massive, grassroots movement,[8] and the fact that these low-tech, low-profile, urban women had compelled the racially biased mainstream media to cover in fact (the event's success) what they ignored in theory (its very possibility).[6] And given the historical disinclination of patriarchal structures, including media institutions, to accord women their rightful places in the annals of technological advancement,[7] this deliberate avoidance of the newsworthiness of the Million Woman March, until it was well underway, is hardly surprising. As Laura Miller observed in considering the problematic rhetorics of "cyberbabe harassment," no matter how revolutionary the "technologized interactions of on-line communities may seem . . . gender roles still provide a foundation for the intensification of social controls that proscribe the freedoms of men as well as women" (50). Since, as Miller asserts, the media accept "the idea that women, like children, constitute a peculiarly vulnerable class of people who require special protection from the elements of society [that] men are expected to confront alone" (52–53), the fact of black women's sophisticated engagement with cyberactivism was likely unfathomable.

Nonetheless, the significance of the Internet's role in the success of the Million Woman March testifies to the marginalized black masses' refusal to be reduced to what Paolo Carpignano and colleagues term television news' "edited public"[8] or to what I call "inevitable road-kill" on the fast-moving information superhighway. In the main, this chapter tackles "the persistence of television" (to borrow Lynn Spigel's terms) in the age of digital reproduction along two discursive tracts. The first concern is the issue of television's differing responses to the civil rights revolution of the 1960s and black people's later revolutionary assemblies at the Million Man March and Million Woman Marches in 1995 and 1997, respectively. The other is a consideration of black women's particular engagement with the Internet, in the glaring absence of television, to foreground black people's unabated and unabashed liberation struggles for self-determination and autonomy by any means necessary (figure 2.1).

FIGURE 2.1. MWM logo and crowd scene rendering on poster. Artistic rendering of MWM crowd and official March logo, courtesy and © copyright of Ken Anderson.

MEDIATING BLACK WOMEN'S HISTORIC
INTERVENTIONS IN THE PUBLIC SPHERE

Historically, African disaporic peoples in the New World and in Africa have been excluded from and victimized by the contradictory logic of the Habermassian ideal bourgeois public sphere. Houston Baker's idea of "black critical memory" to explain disaporic people's long-standing attraction to "the possibilities of structurally and affectively transforming the founding notion of the bourgeois public into an expressive and empowering self-fashioning"[9] contributes another nodal point of entry for considering the implications and impact of the Million Woman March's unanticipated achievement, especially outside the televisual panopticon.

What was so striking about the near absence of network television cameras in the history-making Million Woman (and Million Man) March was the remarkable contrast it makes to the ubiquitous television presence during the epochal events of the 1950s–60s civil rights movement. During that era, the spectacle of such black women as Fannie Lou Hamer and Rosa Parks transgressing the "accepted bounds"[10] of domestic spaces to make their voices heard in the public sphere clearly made for riveting television. At the same time, Lynn Spigel reminds us of the failure of fifties TV to reconcile its idealized depictions of rigidly masculinized public and feminized domestic spaces with the reality of women's increased roles in the workplace. "[T]he housewife image," Spigel argues, "might have had the unplanned paradoxical effect of sending married women into the labor force in order to obtain the money necessary to live the ideal [pictured in fifties-era sit-coms]." For, as she points out, "both the advertising and the homes themselves were built on the shaky foundations of social upheaval and cultural conflict which never were completely resolved" (78). Indeed, Fannie Lou Hamer's televised "Is This America?" speech at the 1964 Democratic National Convention in Atlantic City signaled a pivotal moment in the history of television's relationship to the civil rights campaign. Despite President Johnson's directive that the networks kill the live feed of her speech, the networks aired Hamer's powerful speech in its entirety later that night.[11] Perhaps the anomaly of seeing these resolute black women foregrounded in this confrontation with authority was compelling because, as Kay Mills observed, "black women were able to play such an active role in areas where leadership was foreclosed for men because the black women were invisible to white eyes."[12]

The march recalls even earlier instances in the mediation of black women's efforts at social and political liberation and bears recounting here. In the nineteenth century, black women freedom fighters such as Harriet Tubman and Sojourner Truth established a formidable tradition of breaking through the idealized public sphere's ossified gender divide. And though the scope of this work precludes a full engagement with this impressive black herstory and its obvious lessons for our own time, Congresswoman Waters's "I Speak Today" address at the Million Woman March so evokes historical accounts of Sojourner Truth's 1851 "Ain't I a Woman?" speech, that a revisitation of Truth's speech—in brief—is warranted.

One of the earliest mediated instances of a black woman "speaking truth to power," to borrow a phrase popularly invoked by Anita Hill (of the infamous 1990s Clearance Thomas—Anita Hill Congressional Hearings), was Sojourner Truth's famed 'Ain't I a Woman?' speech at the 1851 Women's Rights Convention in Akron Ohio.[13] Due to conflicting accounts of Truth's extemporaneous talk, it is impossible to extricate the legend that springs from Frances Gage's 1863 "Classic Report" and contemporaneous newspaper claims to carry her exact words. Regardless of the enduring debates and our inability to know the speech's textual specifics ever, at issue here are indices of significant continuities and ruptures that characterize nineteenth-century mediations of black women's public speech acts and those of our own time. In the former, print media's representation of black women's entry into modernity is muted. And in the latter, black women's self-presentation through digital media herald their postmodern arrival. Whereas the limits of nineteenth-century race and gender identity politics dictated that Truth, a former slave, could only address the all-white assembly (gathered to discuss women's suffrage) on the sufferance and authority of white abolitionists, the simultaneously public and clandestine communicative possibilities of late twentieth-century Internet technology enabled Million Woman March organizers to authorize their own addresses to a global assembly, on their own terms through computer-mediated communications (CMC). For these women, (in McLuhanesque terms) *the medium was the message* to a large extent.

Clearly, the decentralizing communicative force of the Internet marks a significant rupture in television's historic containment and cooptation of black women's "sass." In her excellent book *Black Women Writing Autobiography: A Tradition within a Tradition,* Joanne Braxton historicizes "sass" as a survivalist speech act utilized by black women during and after slavery. Sass, for slave women, Braxton notes, employs verbal warfare and defensive verbal posturing as tools of liberation (30). This impertinent speech also denotes self-esteem and self-defense. Braxton additionally alerts us to this potent term's African etymology:

> Sass is a word of West African derivation that is associated with the female aspect of the trickster. The *Oxford English Dictionary* attributes the word's origin to the poisonous "sassy tree." A decoction of the bark of this tree was used in West Africa as an ordeal poison in the trial of accused witches, women spoken of as being wives of Exu, the trickster god. (30)

To be sure, it is the sass contained in both Sojourner Truth's "Ain't I a Woman" and Maxine Waters's "I Speak Today" utterances that reflects notable continuities in black women's ongoing and relentless public and personal strategies for negotiating political and sociocultural autonomy. Compare these two sassy utterances, for example. Frances Gage's excerpted eyewitness account of Truth's speech reads:

> That man over there says that women need to be helped into carriages, and lifted over ditches, and to have the best place everywhere. Nobody helps *me* any best place. *And ain't I a woman?* . . . I could work as much, and eat as much as a man—when I could get it—and bear the lash as well! *And ain't I a woman?* I have borne children and seen most of them sold into slavery, and when I cried out with a mother's grief, none but Jesus heard me. *And ain't I a woman?*[14]

Now, hear the rhetorical resonance in this excerpt from Maxine Waters's address to the march's throng:[15]

> I speak today because I'm so very happy. . . . I speak today because I'm vulnerable. I speak today because I'm strong, I speak today because I'm fearless . . . I speak today because I am a woman, a black woman bonded with other black women, determined to love, to be loved, to grow, to create, to live. I speak today because I really have no choice. I speak because my very soul is stirred, inspired and excited. We the women hailing from this nation, [in] all shapes, sizes and views have something to say today. I speak today because I am determined that we will all be free, we must be free. As a black woman, a mother, a wife, a grandmother, a sister, I am you, and you are me.

Besides the masterful rhetorical refrains ("Ain't I a Woman" and "I Speak Today") punctuating their historically situated societal reprimands, these speeches are also yoked by their skillful deployment of sass as a means of resistance to the double repression of race and gender most identified with the black woman's experience in the West. It is true that the sassy, unruly black woman image is a familiar and romanticized media archetype, particularly in her signifying economy as the mammy. Think of Hattie McDaniel's 1939 Academy Award–winning portrayal of a sassy slave mammy in *Gone with the Wind* and her television progeny (i.e., *Beulah* and Florence in *The Jeffersons*). As a means of countering mainstream culture's cooptation and commodification through Hollywood's fictional black sass put in the service of privileging whiteness, Truth's and Waters's real sass foregrounds their enduring emancipatory allure.

UPLOADING SASS TO THE ONLINE AGORA AND DOWNLOADING IT TO THE STREETS

Webmaster Ken Anderson's 1997 revelation that the official MWM website, not counting the regional ones, tallied more than 1 million hits (visitors to the site) in a two-month period[16] does much to collapse the bipolar base on which our racialized technological superstructures frequently rest, both comfortably and too predictably. Of late there has been much discussion in the popular media about bridging the digital divide.[17] These belated mainstream calls for universal access to new media are certainly necessary. However, it is equally necessary to acknowledge the sass of black women who have already begun to bridge the divide. Rather than decry the disproportionate rate of computer technology diffusion within the black diasporic community, everyday African American women found an ingenious remedy, or tactic of cultural intervention, via the Internet.

In *The Practice of Everyday Life*, which he terms an homage to "a common hero, an ubiquitous character, walking in countless thousands on the streets,"[18] Michel de Certeau's unpacking of certain postmodern practices of bricolage or "making-do" is instructive. For example, when we learn that black women office workers downloaded march organizers' directives from the official website and made Xerox copies for their computerless counterparts, we are reminded of de Certeau's discussion of French workers' "diversionary practice of '*la perruque*.'" *La perruque*, according to de Certeau, is the worker's own work disguised as work for his employer. . . . Accused of stealing or turning material to his own ends and using the machines for his own profit, the worker who indulges in *la perruque* actually diverts time (not goods, since he uses only scraps) from the factory. . . . In the very place where the machine he must serve reigns supreme, he cunningly takes pleasure in finding a way to create gratuitous products whose sole purpose is . . . solidarity with other workers. (24–25)

MWM Webmaster Anderson reports how black women laborers' use of this worker unity tactic galvanized hundreds of thousands:

While I was at the march, Sisters walked up to me . . . and told me that they would not have heard about the march without the Website. I have heard from at least 30 Sisters who printed out the entire Web Site and shared it with friends, neighbors, and co-workers who weren't online yet. This is very flattering, and I appreciate every Sister's attention to and use of the Web Site.[19]

There is a significant issue underlying Anderson's informant account. In addition to his optimism regarding black women's guerrilla tactics and instances of *la perruque* in their embrace of the Internet, Anderson makes us privy to something truly amazing in black women's tactics of "making do." By making virtual computers available to black women who "weren't online yet," march supporters with access to actual Internet technology, either through their jobs or in-home Internet service providers (ISPs) effectively transformed low-tech, sixties-era mimeograph activism into high-tech, new-millennial digital news and information flows. We should not be surprised by these women's keystroke activism because, as Ellen Seiter reminds us, "huge numbers of female employees occupy clerical jobs that use computers for processing payroll, word-processing, conducting inventory, sales, and airline reservations—more than 16 million held such positions in the United States in 1993" (237). Given this level of feminized computer mastery in the nation's workforce, black women's recourse to this technological precondition for successful grassroots organizing seems less unimaginable and much more consistent with poor people's strategies of resistance. So, out of necessity and through the economy of computer-mediated communication (CMC), these black women subverted their marginal status as technology consumers and laborers into that of technology innovators and producers. Through their clandestine cultural production of sassy online discourses, these women, in effect, downloaded the digital agora and took it (information technologies) to their offline sisters, to the streets of Philadelphia, and to cable and local television airwaves.

SELF-AUTHENTICATING NARRATIVES AND "TEMPORARY AUTONOMOUS ZONES"

Once it became apparent that network television would not assist in march organizers' efforts to get widespread media coverage of their historic undertaking, organizers set about the task of formulating alternative modes of producing and disseminating their self-authenticating narratives. In their refusal of a racialized invisibility, march organizers utilized a number of alternative media options. Using consumer-grade camcorder technology to document their mass mobilization, organizers created a composite video-ethnography combining available footage from local and national broadcasts with heavily edited cable television coverage of the unfolding march. In this way, they temporarily made cable and local TV realize their potential as "citizen technologies" (Loudon 36). At the same time, documentary footage of the event captured by march supporters' ubiquitous camcorder usage paired with mainstream TV's limited coverage ensured the marchers' authentic imprimatur on and claim to any mechanical/digital reproduction and retelling of the day's historic events.

Indeed, it is the case that the march's camcorder videotape recodes the logic of technological determinism to make it serve the arsenal of resistance available to these contemporary freedom fighters. This tape reads as a replay of late 1960s counterculture video practices "founded on a belief in liberation via the democratic pluralism of television—[wherein] anyone could control the means of production, [and] anyone could and should be an artist" (Mellencamp 200). The production values of this compilation tape testify to the audiovisual proficiency of this "colonized class'" to not only represent but present these black women's "oppositional cyborg politics,"[20] a grassroots politics facilitated by march organizers' emergent technomastery. The video is framed at its beginning and end with an artistically rendered, computer-generated title page announcing the Million Woman March and its historic date, 25 October 1997. The ensuing documentary footage is contextualized within an audio-visual representational field composed of a voice-over excerpt from

FIGURE 2.2. Screen shots from MWM video documentary with Representative Maxir Waters and Winnie Mandela. These screen shots are from the Million Woman March pr duced videotape of the 1997 march, with excerpted video footage from C-SPAN. Courte and © of Ken Anderson.

Maxine Waters' "I Speak Today" speech that enlivens a sepia-tone snap-shot image taken from the march's crowd. This is followed by a transition wipe into slow-motion video footage of a teenage girls' marching band leading the march's throngs. Stark is the conspicuous absence of national television coverage save one segment from NBC's *Today* show combined with that network's local affiliate coverage in Philadelphia (Channel 10), and C-SPAN's full—if delayed—cablecast. It is the small, iconic text-box image that alternated between identifying the day, "Sat.," and its show schedule that suggests C-SPAN's coverage was not "live."

My own channel surfing on the day of the march failed to locate any-thing but cursory mentions of the march in network and cable news pro-grams. Although the story did make the front page of the *New York Times* newspaper the next day (26 October 1997) replete with a three-column-width color photo of marchers, it remains perplexing that event-driven TV news bureaus would ignore the rousing speeches of such iconic figures as Maxine Waters, Winnie Mandela, Dick Gregory, Malcolm X and Betty Shabazz's daughters, and others, not to mention the phenomenal pictures of the unprecedented crowds in Philadelphia captured by the "mass-cam" and sky cams of local Philadelphia news organization helicopters (figure 2.2). Marking the convergence of new and traditional media, the video ethnography produced by march organizers concludes with credits high-lighting their Internet address, which loops back to diegetic footage of several marchers stressing their excitement about returning to their communities and sharing their wonderful experiences in online chat sessions, and through their own video diaries.

Apparently the repressed zeitgeist of sixties-era counterculture video art and activism, promulgated by the activist groups TVTV, Ant Farm, the Video Theater, Videofreex, Global Village, and others (Mellencamp 200), has returned with a new media vengeance. Video vans have been displaced by the digitized mobility of the Internet's streaming video functionality. In fact, march organizers posted to their website calls "to gather copies of video and photos taken at the Million Woman March. "We would also like," they requested further, "to have you record your experiences coming to, being at, and returning home from the march. . . . We are compiling an international record of the Million Woman March. We really need your help."[21] In some ways, this cyberactivism approach marks a new media redux of the agit prop trains used by the "Soviet constructivist filmmakers," who, to paraphrase Patricia Mellencamp, would have loved the speed of the Internet (201) and its amazing ideological use value.

In an attempt to rectify or circumvent the commodified logic of network newsgathering, the march organizers' use of the camcorder and the Internet embodies the spirit of what Hakim Bey refers to as "The Temporary Autonomous Zone." Echoing de Certeau and Sadie Plant's sentiments about the efficacious "data piracy" (Bey's terms) strategies of women and working-class groups to use the master's tools in subversive maneuvers, Bey describes temporary autonomous zones as enclaves of "intentional communities, whole mini-societies living consciously outside the law and determined to keep it [so], even if only for a short but merry life."[22] Though Bey acknowledges that the temporary autonomous zone is a failed romantic notion from another time that "remains precisely science fiction—pure speculation" ("Temporary"), he nonetheless recommends it conceptually today "because it can provide the quality of enhancement associated with the uprising without necessarily leading to violence and martyrdom" ("Temporary"). The fact that black women and their supporters used the march to construct their own very real and apparently necessary temporary autonomous zone cannot be minimized or dismissed. For this reason, it is useful to consider the march as a documented enactment of what Chela Sadoval terms "cyborg feminism and the methodology of the oppressed," a cyborg consciousness "developed out of a set of technologies that together comprise . . . a methodology that can provide the guides for survival and resistance under First World transnational cultural conditions" (375).

As these examples of black women's technolust clearly illustrate, any fair assessment of black computer literacy confounds dominant culture's technorhetoric that reifies black people unproblematically as poster children for the disabling digital divide discourse. Underscoring the incongruence between the image of black technophobia and a black technophilic reality is Ken Anderson's account of the revolutionary usage of the Internet. As Anderson, the self-proclaimed "humble servant to the cause," aptly puts it:

> There is a complete strategy around the issue of using this medium to spread the word, increase activism, increase the number of Sisters on the Net, increase networking opportunities for Sisters worldwide, and to provide real-time communications utilizing chat sessions and email. . . . [T]hese are indeed exciting times. Just when no one thought women of African descent were paying attention, along come[s] the MWM and its Internet presence.[23]

Anderson's remarks, then, seem to confirm Sadie Plant's and others' beliefs that subordinate classes of women and blacks *could* use the master's tools to dismantle his house of racial domination and masculinist privilege, to rephrase Audre Lorde's famous saying. In her discussion of Alan Turing's ideas about the subversive potential of machines' detournment on the slave-master relationship, Plant provides us with a particularly useful analogy for considering the march organizers' tactical use of the Internet for their own unedited global publicity and promotion. In *Zeroes + Ones*, Plant gives us a sense of Turing's prescience regarding man's inability to restrict machine power or subordinated groups' use of that power. For Turing, man's presumed dominion over the "rest of creation" does not necessarily translate into an assured superiority over his own machine creations. Quoting Turing, Plant writes:

> We like to believe that Man is in some subtle way superior to the rest of creation. . . . It is best if he can be shown to be *necessarily* superior, for then there is no danger of him losing his commanding position." But Turing's words were laced with irony. He relished the possibility that machines would undo this necessity. . . . Turing knew that this attempt to produce highly programmed slave machines would backfire. It is the "masters who are liable to get replaced" by the new generation of machines. (88)

Through their masterful use of the new generation of computer machinery, march organizers effectively bore out Turing's late 1940s prophecy. Indeed, as a result of their unanticipated usage and mastery of the Internet, black women, in this instance, succeeded in upsetting "the old distinctions between the user and the used" (89), the master and the slave.

Utilizing the Internet the march's digerati were able, albeit temporarily, to undo their representational enslavement in the racialized agenda-setting economy of broadcast television's master class. Moreover, they mobilized their virtual community online to effect an "intrusion of the real"[24] into broadcast television's denial (at that time) of the Internet as a viable, real world broadcast alternative. Viewed in this way, the political, social, and economic achievement of the Million Woman March cannot help but reaffirm one's cautious optimism about the much-hyped democratizing potential of the Internet despite its increasing Wall Street corporatization and post–September 11 governmental surveillance. While most mainstream media remained indifferent to the march's sociopolitical agenda, its economic impact was not ignored by online reportage. AFAMnet and the *Philadelphia Inquirer*'s online venue (via philly.com) both reported that an astounding $21.7 million windfall was generated by the march for the local Philadelphia economy. According to Tom Muldoon, president of the Philadelphia Convention and Visitors Bureau, "The impact [of the march] was felt as far away as Dover, Del. (88 miles from Philadelphia) where the Sheraton was sold out."[25] Tanya Hall, executive director of the Multicultural Affairs division stated, "We were delighted that this historic event was held in Philadelphia." "The incredible economic impact of the march emphasizes the tremendous economic strength of African-American women in this country" ("Successful").

In the afterglow of the Million Woman March's success, event organizers posted a note of thanks to their ground-breaking global constituency. "What is important," organizers proclaimed, "is that Sistahs from around the nation and the world came together. . . . A great deal was done with very little. The power of Sisterhood is amazing. This was a day for Sisters to come together for repentance, resurrection, and restoration. Thank you for being involved and connected."[26] When we consider that popular perceptions of technological mastery tend to position blacks outside of what Theodore Roszak terms "the cult of information," this particularized instance of black women's technolust demands a rethinking.

While march organizers' emphasis on Internet connectivity brought African diasporic women "together for unity, the uplift of [black] families and communities, love, common ground, understanding and respect" (MWM, "Platform Issues"), their tactical seizure of the World Wide Web, in the absence of television coverage, makes the march a significant research project for assessing black women's untouted participation in the new electronic agora.

First of all, as early as 1997, the forward-thinking online participation symbolized by the march enacts black women's reclamation of their historic space and place in the construction and maintenance of a viable, newly configured, "subaltern counterpublic," to use Nancy Fraser's terminology. The march also gives lie to the twinned mythologies of black and female technophobia. Not only did these women astonish the nation by replicating the remarkable mass-mobilization feat of the Million Man March two years earlier[27] but, unlike their male counterparts, the women amassed their impressive number of local and global enthusiasts through the grassroots organizing of "people who were little-known outside Philadelphia's urban neighborhoods" (Janofsky). Even though the Million Woman March featured high-profile keynote speakers, including California Congresswoman Maxine Waters, political activist Winnie Madikizela-Mandela (exwife and political partner of former South Africa President Nelson Mandela), Michigan Congressman John Conyers Jr. (one of the few men invited to speak), and popular film and TV actress Jada Pinkett (among other celebrities), it is important to note that the march organizers were what musician Sylvester (Sly) Stone terms "everyday people."

The Million Man March, in contrast, was the brainchild of former prominent NAACP leader Reverend Benjamin Chavis and controversial Nation of Islam leader Minister Louis Farrakhan. And despite the fact that "neither the NAACP nor the Urban League endorsed the Million Man March . . . both civil rights organizations benefited from its success and have increased membership," according to the *Chicago Defender*.[28] Consequently, both events actualize Nancy Fraser's concept of "subaltern counterpublics" that clearly demonstrate how members of "subordinated groups" today find new ways to "invent and circulate counter discourses, which in turn permit them to formulate oppositional interpretations of their identities, interests, and needs" (67)[29] outside the limitations of mainstream discursive agendas.

MODEM MAMAS: MIDWIVES TO THE
BIRTH OF A DIGITAL NATION

As early as July 1997, regional march organizers in Philadelphia instructed visitors to visit their websites: "Feel free to make copies of this webpage and share it with other Afrikan women." Among the agenda items for march organizers in the Midwestern states was the solicitation of computer needs and expertise.[30] In fact, from the outset these women were demonstrably adept at enlisting the web to promote their premarch conference, organizing and fundraising activities that became pivotal to the success of the main event. The three themes of "Repentance, Resurrection, and Restoration" for the march came about as Chionesu and other coordinators met to define their platform issues. As ideas circulated, Chionesu noticed, "A lot of words with 'R's kept coming up—respect, resolution, etc. But, when we heard repentance we knew that was one. . . . Once you do repentance then you can do resurrection, then you can begin to stand up. . . . Then you can bring about restoration, which is about taking back those things that were stolen from us."

For cochair Coney, the march's themes enabled supporters and detractors alike to grasp the event's purpose and objectives, which were most notably the cessation of institutional violence against black people, reparations for slavery, and black self-help and self-determination, among others. Coney was further motivated by a sense of historical agency and intervention: "I would like to be able to look back and say that I was one of the individuals responsible for bringing about a major change" (Chionesu). What the *Final Call* interview with march cochairs Chionesu and Coney conveys, particularly in retrospect, is these women's profound optimism against incredible odds. Indeed, by their comments we understand their self-perceptions as midwives to a new movement. Undergirding their faith in the power of sisterhood were the efforts and tremendous sacrifices of regional organizers and lay march supporters. Expressing their thoughts in the *Call* just two weeks prior to the big day, the women were striking in their confidence and self-possession. To the question, "You are two weeks now from the event, how do you feel?" Chionesu replied:

> Mixed emotions. Excited, obviously elated because we are really beginning to see the manifestation of our works. . . . It's a feeling that is almost

indescribable. But the flip side is that we also know that the work is really just beginning. Now the birthing process is about to come to its point of fruition. The child, in a sense, is about to be brought forth. Now we have to raise this child. Raising a nation is a lot of work. Raising a people is a lot of work. So, although we see how wonderful October 25th is going to be, we know that on October 26th the work will have just begun.

What Chionesu could not know at this point was how difficult the work of maintaining their success after the march would in fact be. For accompanying the postmarch accolades were a number of detractions, ironically from several vociferous sources in digital spaces online and a host of other problems. Shortly after the march event, organizers posted an "International Scam Alert" on their website advising supporters of the flood of counterfeit march memorabilia: "[A] number of individuals and groups are . . . using familiar sounding names and images to make money for themselves only." They continue, "A poster being circulated by Michael Brown is not the official poster sanctioned by the National Organizers and Founders of the Million Woman March."[31] In an effort to foreclose disinformation circulation, organizers also posted requests that supporters check the website for updates "before interviews are given in order to reduce the misuse or misinterpretation of information" ("Million Woman March: International Scam Alert"). In addition to policing the boundaries of their new proprietary information and commodity rights, organizers encountered a plethora of postmarch criticisms and diatribes, congealing coincidentally in the online ether that had nurtured their grand vision.

FLAME WARS: BATTLING FOR AND AGAINST THE MARCH

One of the most vitriolic condemnations of the march was an editorial produced by Gary Hull for the Ayn Rand Institute's MediaLink department. Hull's online article, entitled "The Pied Pipers of Tribalism: The 'Million Woman March' Should Have Promoted Individualism Not Tribalism," seeks to discredit at once the march and progressive educational practices in higher education. Hull writes:

> Lurking behind the rally's love of all things African was the insidious message to every listener: Ditch your brain; subordinate your will; accept the notion that your life has no reality except as an appendage of the tribal

organism. These ideas are not originated by the leaders of the march. They come from the humanities departments at our colleges and universities. The organizers merely spread in the culture of what college professors now teach in class. . . . Travelers on the Million Woman March will find that this tribalist road leads only to poverty, dictatorship and slavery.[32]

It is highly improbable that march organizers were wounded by this particular online pillory, especially considering organizers' strength and resolve to achieve their formidable feat against tremendous odds leading up to and including the march itself. At the same time, philly.com tallied a host of mixed reviews of the march from several online editorial forums including "Letters to the Editor" pages at both the *Philadelphia Inquirer* and the *Daily News*. From the *Daily News*, Ken Wyllie of Philadelphia wrote, "In a time [when] we preach equality, the news media showed gross disrespect for our women. It is sexist, disgusting and dead wrong. . . . The American media owe our sisters an apology." A less affirming response was posted by Della Rucker of Philadelphia, who wrote, "Women who feel it is just an African-American problem should have referred to it as just that. Instead, they are being racist, trying to justify themselves."[33] On 2 November 1997, Donna White of Claymont, Delaware, wrote into the *Inquirer* stating, "The essence of the cluster was that of strength unknown. . . . Some of us can even testify to the rewards of the march and will extend the knowledge to others. . . . My sisters, remember not only who you are, but all that is yours." J. Collison, from King of Prussia, wrote, "Do we get a turn now to have a march for whites only? No, of course not. That would be racist."[34] Despite a diversity of views from the public, the majority of commentary posted to philly.com was supportive of the march. However, as time passed, the difficulty of sustaining the march's tenuous international coalition became evident as the organization apparently imploded under the weight of its phenomenal success.

From a series of candid conversations posted to several of the regional Million Woman March websites we gain a clearer sense of the philosophical and organizational fissures that threatened the longevity and institutional aspirations of the organization. Among the indications of the rifts emerging within the organizational ranks of the Million Woman March are posted comments contained in march participant Ifama's online article "The Buttnaked Truth about the Million Woman March." Following the organizers' directives to supporters to share their views of the march, Ifama's essay included both compliments and complaints about the march. Ifama begins her discussion of the march with a section she calls "I think Most of Us Missed the Point!!" Because her remarks are telling in an ethnographic vein, they merit extensive quoting, especially as they highlight the role of the Internet in connecting herself and others to the event. Early on in her essay, Ifama confesses her interest in "just about any gathering" that would give her strength to persevere as an oppressed African American:

> Then one day, I was surfing the Internet, looking for nothing in particular and BAMN!!, there it was, a web site for a Million Woman March. My heart skipped. I clicked on it and pulled the site up, read the small bit of information that was there and my spirit said, "Ifama, this just what you need to be rejuvenated," so being one who listens when my spirit talks to me, I got busy. . . . I kept revisiting until I got more information . . . and it was on.[35]

Although her initial euphoria was tempered by the apparent disappointing realities of organizational politics, Ifama remained loyal to the cause's larger vision. Still, Ifama decided to air the full spectrum of her ambivalent thoughts as a participant thoroughly involved before, during, and after the march. For Ifama, one major complaint centered around a perceived conflict between orchestrating a grassroots movement and the organizers' recourse to conduct the meetings according to Robert's Rules of Order. Her posted comments were thus:

> I personally got involved because this was a "grassroots" movement. Because after reading the platform issues, I knew that this was an effort to bring us together to address them. The personalities of the people who called the march were not a concern because the platform issues were VALID. Now, I have always considered all African folks "grassroots" but I guess there is some sort of separation because the coordinators kept referring to [themselves] as the "grassroots" folks as opposed to them being only God knows what else. NEway [sic], we, the "grassroots" folks were ready to get busy and do whatever needed to be done to make this success. (Ifama)

In Ifama's use of the transitional "NEway" (an Ebonics-style reinscription of the word *anyway*), we detect her intuitive participation in and modification of the web's developing cyberlexicon comprised of "emoticons" (with expressive or emotional icons) and acronyms.[36] But primary for Ifama, the idea of erecting a hierarchical structure for achieving the march's stated platform was problematic. She continues:

> Well you know, here comes the thing I hate most: STRUCTURE!! Now I ain't one for structure, cause if you know what you got to do, you just commit and do it. I mean, forming committees to me is set up for failure cause it always got to have a head and that's where the trouble starts. . . . They even started at first with that euro-Robert Rules of Order mess. Well, that did not last too long cause, on the real we can't keep the European [sic] structure up too long amongst ourselves. (Ifama)

Other frustrations for Ifama included the level of disinterest in the black consciousness-raising videos brought along for the bus rides and failure of the bus riders to "sit in the assigned seats" *en route* to the main event. As she puts it: "Our bus was equipped with a video and small television sets and I tried to show movies like *Sankofa*, etc. But NOOOOO, they wanted to sleep on that but stayed awake long enough to watch some other brainwashing movies that another Sista brought." It is interesting that Ifama, who professes "the thing I hate most: STRUCTURE," was vexed because people refused the structure of assigned seating. Ultimately, she capitulated to those on the bus ride that she organized instructing them to "sit where you want, just get on the damn bus." Notwithstanding these and other vexations, basking in the afterglow of the march's unmitigated success, she writes:

> Once I was amongst all of those Beautiful Sistahs, I knew that it was all worth it. It seemed that all of the negative energy that had covered me earlier just disappeared. . . . Being amongst African women who came on a hope and little information was enough for me. No, it did not get no press. I met a lot of Sistahs, made some business contacts, gathered some ideas for me to do when I got back home and it was all good!!! . . . All in all, my spirit is rejuvenated and I definitely have some new ideas. (Ifama)

Ifama's observation that the march "did not get no press" is essential for understanding the importance of the Internet in facilitating the march's iteration of Chela Sandoval's ideas about cyborg feminism and resistance to oppression. Again, the mainstream press' willful avoidance of this important newsworthy story underscores the apparent racial biases at work in the nation's news media industry, and this fact was not lost on march participants, including Ifama. In her remarks about resisting "the negative talk about the organization of the march or the lack of being able to hear folks talk" (a reference to the technical difficulties of the sound equipment in reaching the march's throngs), Ifama makes explicit an important sore point in African Americans' ongoing frustration with the mainstream media. When Ifama stated, "We can always read it or see it on CNN (or so I thought)," she clearly articulated what many march supporters reasonably expected but ultimately were denied.

MEDIATING THE MEDIATION: A MARCH SUPPORTER ANALYZES MAINSTREAM MEDIA'S ANEMIC COVERAGE

One march supporter from the Ohio region, who attended that area's march "Take Off Rally" but not the march itself, expected nonetheless to experience the history-making event televisually. Identifying herself online as Mama Khandi, this march supporter heeded organizers' call for "Online Commentary" and posted an essay to one of the regional march websites. Her essay is entitled "Million Woman March Online Commentary before—during—the Aftermath."[37] Here Mama Khandi documents her frustrated efforts to transcend her bodily absence at the march itself by experiencing what she anticipated would be extensive television coverage. To her surprise, Mama Khandi did not turn up any significant national media coverage of the Million Woman March, despite her diligent television surfing. The lack of mainstream media coverage unfortunately reaffirms black people's skepticism and distrust of the agenda-setting prerogative of American news media. And Mama Kandi's poignant expressions of disappointment and disdain give voice to African Americans' long-standing weariness in battling against traditional media manipulations of blackness in the nation's racial imaginary. Moreover, they help us to appreciate these black women's tactical use of the Internet as an effective temporary autonomous zone capable of circumventing mainstream media's erasure of legitimate black concerns via the digital dissemination of their messages to a receptive mass audience constituting itself in cyberspace.

Khandi, functioning here as a newly empowered "cyborg citizen or citizen journalist,"[38] initiates her critique of television's near whiteout of the march by describing the up-beat tenor of the Columbus, Ohio, region's press conference and send-off event, which she notes "was well

attended by many members of the press of all the major local networks."
And given the apparent media interest in and unimpeded flow of march
information to the attending journalists, Khandi's expectation of widespread or national television coverage is reasonable if misplaced. However,
once again, it is Khandi's emphasis on the march's and other black entities' "entrance onto the internet!" that underscores the major role that this
newer technology represents for evolving digital media's notions of citizenship (Grey 24), and a "decentering of the television mainstream."[42]
This is especially the case for grassroots groups' heightened participation
in America's evolving digital public sphere. After specifying some important content of week-long premarch seminars sponsored by the Million
Woman March Organization, Khandi casts her ethnographic gaze on the
unexpected glaring absence of all network television coverage of the event.
She chronicles her frustration as follows: "This writer has been watching
and scanning cable stations since 5am, October 25 and coverage of the
MWM was/is scarce at best." Khandi begins by specifying CNN's (Cable
News Network's) "diss" (disrespect) of the historic event. She writes:

> CNN has continued to provide the minimum coverage that has occurred,
> approximately 1–3 minutes of coverage every half hour. CNN's white cor-
> respondent Cynthia Tornquist and white male correspondent Skip
> Loescher were the reporters for the Million Woman March. Skip kept stat-
> ing that the objects of the march included investigation of the CIA's
> involvement in drugs in the Afrikan community and independent Afrikan
> schools. They kept playing the same clip from Phile Chionesu's speech as
> if she never said anything else.

What Khandi found so unconscionable about CNN's truncated coverage
was not the network's seeming indifference and cadre of only white cor-
respondents, after all she chastised the lack of coverage by BET (Black
Entertainment Television). For Khandi the most unfortunate element in
the minimal coverage was that it was devoid of any Afrikan perspective.
She continues:

> The unfortunate part of such commentary is the perspective. There are/were
> no Afrikan reporters with CNN (nor coverage by BET) to give an Afrikan
> centered perspective to their reporting. Tornquist never mentioned the sem-
> inars that took place all week, nor the Official Program of Speakers that does
> not include various [celebrities]. She stated that there was not publicity and

that the MWM was organized by "flyers, word of mouth and the internet." CNN stated that MWM methods of publicizing the march [were] "unconventional promotions." As an Afrikan, in reflection, when has Afrikan promotion ever been "conventional." When have We ever controlled media/seized the means of production? Rather [a]bsurd comment actually.

After witnessing march organizers' unavailing efforts to play by the rules of "conventional" promotional protocols, as the press conference episode discussed above indicates, Khandi's too-through attitude here is better understood. And despite the cyberrant tone of her sassy outrage, underlying Khandi's criticism of television's perfunctory coverage of the march are some important and enduring concerns that black people have about traditional media's hegemonic gate-keeping function. For example, Khandi raises a key point of frustration regarding the way mainstream media and other ideological state apparatuses play the numbers game in representing the popular appeal of underground movements often distilled via the disputed crowd estimates.

It is the case that crowd estimates are routinely controversial as the numbers tend to be manipulated upward or downward depending on the political imperatives of the reporting source and their desired influence on public opinion. Where march organizers estimated the crowd turnout at upwards of a million supporters, Khandi points out CNN's preference for citing Philadelphia officials' count insisting "that only 300,000–500,000 Afrikan women attended the march." And given that CNN's reporter "Cynthia Tornquist, stated that . . . she sees a sea of Black faces 'as far as the eye can see,'" Khandi implies a suspect agenda at work in what she suggests is a willful official undercount. Other points of contestation for her are CNN's representational economy in effect especially as a rationale for Tornquist's emphasis on the march's lack of jumbotrons or adequate speaker systems and the network's decision to run textual excerpts from the march against what Khandi describes as "the amerikkan flag." The semiotics of CNN's mise-en-scene is particularly troubling for Khandi because the official logo of the Million Woman March was not used until later in the broadcast. In addition to challenging the crowd numbers rhetorically, Cyborg Khandi posits her own semiotic counteroffensive by posting a wide-shot photograph of the march's crowds alongside her revisionist online critique of CNN's representation of the disputed numbers.

Feminist scholar Jacqueline Bobo's insights regarding black women's unrelenting efforts to disrupt mainstream media's "standard depictions of black women" help us appreciate Khandi's audacious counterdiscursive strategy for her online community, and the intentional semiotic collision with CNN's reportage. In *Black Women as Cultural Readers*, Bobo discusses what it means for black women to function as an interpretive community for its members and for the larger body politic. For Bobo it is important to understand black women's commitment to undermine mainstream culture's reification of negative images of black women through what Stuart Hall terms "lines of tendency" (39) in historical cultural production and representational practices that systematically demean black women. Bobo writes:

> Black women are also knowledgeable recorders of their history and experiences and have a stake in faithfully telling their own stories. . . . Black women have thus underscored their existence as "collective subjects" who reaffirmed that they would take whatever measures were necessary to protect their rights and defend their cultural image. (36–43)[40]

Clearly, the Internet became one measure Khandi found necessary to protect black women's dissenting voices and cultural image, which thereby disrupts CNN's and other mainstream media's lines of tendency to dissimulate black women's difficult realities. Just as Tornquist is cited expressing skepticism "about what exactly would be accomplished by this march," Khandi returns the skepticism: "It has been quite interesting watching this white woman reporting and trying to answer the questions of her interpretation of the march, when asked by the in-studio reporter at the Atlanta CNN studio."[41] In this instance, Khandi's oppositional use of cyberspace repositions CNN's Tornquist and her discourse filtration as the objects of suspicion in what theorist Jacquie Jones names the "accusatory space" of hegemonic media discourse, a privileged imaginary space reserved for the accusation of black female bodies.[42] Khandi also coopts CNN's Headline News flow structure to organize her own critical updates on the cable giant's "tidbit" coverage of the march's highlights. Khandi reports:

> At approximately 9:30pm Maxine Waters' comments were finally broadcasted [sic] on CNN Headline News. . . . This writer can only assume that this "tidbit" reporting will continue for the rest of the evening with bits and pieces of the march not previously broadcasted. Stay tuned as this commentary will be updated with each new piece of news. And of course, as sistas begin to file their reports w/me, the information will be passed on.

For Khandi, it is not enough merely to point out the inadequacy of CNN's oscillating sound bytes. By uploading passages she deemed important from CNN's stingy coverage of the march's speakers and adding her own commentary, Khandi activates the web's metadiscursive function to amplify and annotate CNN's meager updates with key political messages so crucial to the march constituency and their public information campaign. Specific points in CNN's coverage that Khandi posts to her website are Congresswoman Maxine Waters's insistence that black women will "fight against racism and marginalization" and for their homeless and incarcerated sistas, despite a national "atmosphere of mean-spirited politics" and Winnie Mandela's report that African women's powerful solidarity and self-empowerment are proof of their successful resistance to the "spiral of oppression" (Khandi).

However, Khandi's cyberwomanist intervention does not inhere so much in her amplification and "remediation" of CNN's coverage of Congresswoman Maxine Waters's and Winnie Mandela's political sentiments, as in her defiant reception and no-holds-barred digital deconstruction of that coverage. For instance, Khandi makes it quite apparent that CNN's delayed airing of its mere "sound bites" containing Waters's indictment of "the CIA [for] bringing drugs into the Afrikan community" and Winnie Mandela's political woes in Azanie until the early morning hours the day after the march was neither benign nor inconsequential. She is particularly alert to the fact that CNN's revised crowd estimates that put the numbers of attendees at approximately 300,000 to 1 million were not broadcast until 3:00 a.m. on the morning of October 26. Khandi's intense rhetorical posturing expresses her derogation of both CNN's and Philadelphia officials' numbers game. Khandi reports: "9:14am . . . CNN reports that the Richard Allen City (filthydelphia) poLICE have stated that there were approximately 1.5 million people in attendance at the Million Woman March." "10:00am . . . CNN reports its final comments showing the same footage that they had been showing. No further reporting after that, that this writer saw. And I watched for another 3 hours before finally cutting off the tv."

For those following her directive to "stay tuned" for reports filed by other sistahs, Khandi delivered on the promise. By 5:30 p.m., the day after, Khandi posted this media-surveillance communiqué from Sistah Marpessa, hailing from the Delaware MWM region:

> Right now (about 5:30 EST) just flicked onto CSPAN and Julia Wright with Pam Africa beside her are indicting the U.S. Government and the

Philadelphia city and PA state government for attempted murder of Mumia Abu-Jamal and the MOVE organization and demanding freedom for PP/POWs [political prisoners/prisoners of war] on behalf of revolutionary women around the world. This is from the MWM yesterday, don't know if they are showing the whole thing or not.

In a deft deployment of strategic cyberheteroglossia (multiplicity of disparate voices online) that typifies web culture and computer-mediated communication, Khandi supplements her womanist rant with the following hyperlinks: (1) "Commentary attachment #1: MWM, the question of 'why only Afrikan women?'"; (2) "MWM Commentary Journal entries of MWM attendees and other Afrikan's commentary statements"; "Delaware Co-coordinator Sista Marpessa's MWM Survey Questionnaire"; "MWM National Call for Video, Photos, Journal entries for an International Record"; "CNN MWM newscast links w/Quicktime.mov video clips"; "Final Call articles about the Million Woman March"; and "Other Commentaries by Other Journalists." What is striking in Khandi's technologically engendered analysis is how its urban-edged rhetoric manifests Donna Haraway's point about cyborg irreverence toward patriarchal structures of domination.[43] Haraway has remarked that "[t]he cyborg is resolutely committed to partiality, irony, intimacy and perversity. It is oppositional, utopian, and completely without innocence" (151). If we focus on Khandi's word play, vis-à-vis the "filthydelpia," and "poLICE," as a measure of the black community's opposition to Philadelphia's well-known, divisive racial politics, we easily recognize a manifestation of Haraway's compelling idea of cyborg irreverence and perversity in confronting these persistent struggles.

In terms of her cyberdiscourse and media analysis, Khandi resists replicating mainstream media's reduction of highly complex sociopolitical phenomena to such familiar binary oppositions as left/right, good/bad, trustworthy/suspect, and significant/insignificant. Instead, she capitalizes on the Internet's information-rich message relay structures and its dialogic or two-way communications function by posting an array of critical views and positions both sympathetic and contrary to her own, and she invites commentary and participation by visitors to her site.

Central to this investigation of Mama Khandi's hyperbolic remediation of mainstream media institutions' Million Woman March coverage is its evidentiary status as proof of black women's insurgent cyberfeminism and specific hacktivist impulse. What Khandi's sassy online discourse suggests is the new media agenda of black people in general and black women in particular to hack into dominant culture's lock on representing blackness for mass society in the information age. It seems quite clear that the real life lessons of political activism that Khandi learned as a regional march organizer were easily transposed to the virtual realm of cyberspace, especially given its potential to extend the cause of the Million Woman March beyond the willful blind spots of mainstream media.

DISAPPEARING AND REAPPEARING
TEMPORARY AUTONOMOUS ZONES (TAZ)

Because the march was a local event with international underpinnings, it should not be surprising that Philadelphia's mainstream media eventually capitulated to extensive coverage of it (figure 2.3). From a retrospective vantage point after the march's unmitigated success, stories about its fractious beginnings became fodder for these press' online march postmortems. Discussions of march organizers' working-class independence and grassroots origins were emphasized in postmarch coverage. Given the local press' disinterest in and incredulity about the march, and as if these dominant media required a certain failure of any long-term success from this unsanctioned underground effort, the Philadelphia press apparently seized upon the fact

FIGURE 2.3. Screen shot from MWM video documentary featuring footage from local TV news.

that the march organizers failed to maintain their fragile coalition. In her series of updates on the march, Karen E. Quinones Miller, *Inquirer* staff writer, reported the fracturing of the organization in articles titled "One Year Later, Marching Apart" (25 October 1998) and "Million Woman March Organizers Split Group" (12 October 1998). At the heart of the split, Quinones Miller found, was the co-chairs' revelation, "We both decided that we had to move forward, but we did not necessarily agree on the direction." In fact, Chionesu and Coney announced at a town meeting that "one organization is now two,"[44] the Million Woman Universal Movement and Sisters of the Million Woman March. Cognizant of how the split could countermand the march's unifying effect, Coney insisted, "You will not see Phile and I attacking each other, and you can be clear that if she needs me, I will be there, and vice-versa" (Quinones Miller).

At the arrival of the new millennium, Coney and Chionesu reaffirmed their mutual commitment to the cause when they both participated in the April 2001 Race in Digital Space inaugural conference held at the Massachusetts Institute of Technology.[45] Notwithstanding their remarkable ability to "astonish the country by attracting hundreds of thousands of women" (Quinones Miller) to Philadelphia in 1997, the organization's implosion may be most exemplary of Hakim Bey's observation that the temporary autonomous zone's (TAZ) "greatest strength lies in its invisibility." He goes on to say, "As soon as the TAZ is named (represented, mediated), it must vanish, it *will* vanish, leaving behind it an empty husk, only to spring up again somewhere else, once again invisible because undefinable in terms of the Spectacle."[46] As if confirming Bey's thesis, the spirit of the Million Woman March influenced another iteration of the TAZ when it was put in effect in 2000 as the predominately white women-led Million Mom March was called to push forward a revived gun control campaign after the 1999 Columbine High School massacres.

Despite their inability to translate the formidable organization feat of the march into an equally powerful societal force imagined as the "Million Woman Movement," black women who made the march happen, nevertheless, can be assured of their fin-de-siecle historical impact.

CONCLUSION

Although the commercial imperatives of network television's teleological ratings' illogics (Meehan 126) invariably position black women at television's demographic margins, black women used the Internet's counterlogic of decentralization to reposition themselves at the center of public life in America, if only for a day. Surely, the role of the Internet—as well as camcorders—in constructing a TAZ enabled march organizers to disabuse the nation momentarily of the view that women required special protection both *from* and *in* the public sphere. Having said that, one point must be made. We are well advised to adopt Herman Gray's suspicions of "uncritical celebrations of the practices of collective and individual subjects (the working class, women, people of color) as resistance" (3). Thus, to remain vigilant in our efforts to scrutinize both the hyperbole of new media deification and demonization we must strain to situate our knowledges of new and traditional media production and consumption in actual cases of peoples' often unanticipated media use. In that vein, I demonstrated that television's persistence is equally matched by the persistence of black women not to be ignored as they take their historic grievances to the streets, with or without the televisual panopticon. In the 1980s the short-lived maverick television news and information program *South Africa Now* began each show emphasizing television's then unparalleled influence with the adage, "If it's not on TV, it doesn't exist." At century's end, the arrival of the Internet modifies this once widely held truism. Perhaps the new media adage should be: "If it's not on TV, it most likely *does* exist on the Internet."

CHAPTER THREE

New Black Public Spheres: The Case of the Black Press in the Age of Digital Reproduction

We wish to plead our own cause. Too long have others spoken for us.

—Samuel Cornish and John
Russwurm, "To Our Patrons"

A significant development for African Americans and new technology has been the establishment of both local and national "Drum" lists. These Drum lists, which are essentially e-mail mailing lists, allow one African American to communicate with many others. . . . The result is a digital cascade of information which is not unlike the sounds of call and response delivered by the drums our forefathers used in Africa.

—R. Cadet, "Net Emerges as Delivery
Tool for Black News and Views"

Since Samuel Cornish and John Russwurm's 1827 founding of *Freedom's Journal,* the first African American–owned and -controlled newspaper,[1] the black press has functioned as a reliable register of African American struggle and progress in the United States. At the same time, it has served as a potent political and ideological force in galvanizing mass support for a wide array of black protest and cultural movements. Conceived from the outset as both a political and an ideological weapon for the eradication of slavery and other antebellum atrocities, the earliest black political pamphlets, newspapers, magazines, and other forms of black writing established a tradition of protest literature that has been a prominent feature throughout the history of the press' "uplift" mission or journalistic freedom fighting. Equally important as its struggles for racial justice, particularly during heightened moments of political and economic crises, was the press' role as cultural arbiter and promoter.[2] While extensive research exists on the black press' intervention in such historic events from the abolitionist crusades to contemporary struggles against antiaffirmative action and other civil rights backlash politics, work remains to be done regarding the present and future of the black press in the information age. At the dawn of this much-anticipated new millennium with a nascent postindustrial, new information order in tow, it is time to consider the black press' strong presence in cyberspace.

The advent of the digital revolution—specifically the Internet—has ushered in a new developmental phase of black journalistic purpose and praxis. However, before any meaningful consideration of the black press' online migration and digital metamorphosis can proceed, it seems necessary to address, with some level of specificity, what we mean by the phrase *black press*, given the radically transformed publishing realities engendered by the digital media environment responsible for what I call "digitextuality." There are two ontological questions driving this need to rethink the "black press" appellation as a fixed and familiar referent. First, there must be an effort to grasp the fundamental incommensurabilities one confronts when comparing the disparate natures of the communicative processes governing digital informatics on one hand and its print counterpart on the other. Second, the brave new world of cyberspace forces a reckoning with the complexities of race and identity that our familiar categories from the past too often disavow. What this means is that our possessive investments in racial communities (to paraphrase George Lipsitz) are less secure than ever because the fact of virtual bodies and their troubling manipulations in cyberspace destabilizes our presumptive knowledge of people and institutions in new and manifold ways. The point is that print journalism issuing from brick and mortar publishing organizations is less likely to be racially misidentified than are digital texts emanating exclusively from the ether of online publishers who can operate under a virtual cloak of identity anonymity. As it stands now, not only are we confronted with the question of how many "black presses" are online but we also need to be concerned with how to authenticate black presses in cyberspace from masquerading opportunists and bigots. Although it is understood that contemporary theories justly instruct us to bracket such essentializing terms as *real* and *authentic*, it is clear that our efforts beg another weighty question that we may not be able to answer here about racial passing online: does it matter? In fact, there is a website devoted to identity concealment online. The site, Anonymizer.com, began in 1995 to offer what it terms "anonymous shell accounts" for seven dollars per month. And though it claimed to offer a "cyberpass" for anonymous surfing, and to insure privacy, the site's frequently asked questions page boasts, "Our server will retrieve the document from xxx.com, without revealing your identity and then send the document back to you" ("Anonymizer FAQ").

Regarding the differing communicative modes that characterize print and digital texts, George Landow and others have proffered convincing arguments for the existence of significant structural differences separating the communicative modes of print and digital media. For Landow, one key point of departure here is that autonomous or standalone print texts normally are identified by their unified and centralized natures (*Hypertext/Theory*, "What's a Critic to Do?" 23), whereas the hypertext structure of digital texts, particularly those found on the web, are defined conversely by a "dispersed, multiply centered network of data organized by a key feature known as electronic linking" (23).

As crucial a distinction as this useful opposition between traditional print and still-evolving digital texts propounds, more at issue for our investigation of black presses online are the practical consequences of Landow's cogent observation that "networked electronic communication changes our experiences of publication" (13). What he means by "networked electronic communication" is that once text and other data are transformed into digital form they can be endlessly duplicated, up or downloaded on several computers via a network and "manipulated simultaneously by many users" (9). Further, Landow notes that electronic communication "produces new forms of textuality" (13) and "new habits of reading and writing" for which, he asserts, the newspaper offers a precedent with its agglomeration of discrete subjects and categories (24) in one stand-alone edition or issue. And while this comment seemingly reassures us that familiar information regimes and practices do ultimately domesticate scary new ones (websites, after all, the logic implies, are simply new and improved newspapers/newsletters, right?), Landow's point about the "ease with which hypertext permits manipulation, searching, and (to use the new jargon) re-purposing" (27) rescinds this comforting notion.

It is not so much that the digital revolution and hypertext drive the final nail in the coffin of the author,[3] as the author's proprietary rights seemingly have been held in abeyance given the highly debated antitrust ruling against Bill Gates's Microsoft Corporation and pending decisions on other intellectual property rights. Only time will reveal the full impact of the Microsoft decision on the final configuration of this shape-shifting new information order on minority groups and other information have-nots. What is certain, however, is the advent of hypertext and other digital forms of textual plasticity, what I term "digitextuality"[4] (a concept that marries digital form to intertextual content). As Landow points out, among the pivotal features of this new communication revolution separating it from traditional print systems are linking and new modes of electronic interactivity or multimedia convergence.

Linking, which is essentially a computerized system enabling instantaneous textual navigation and retrieval that permits readers of digital data to jump from text to text instantaneously with the click of a computer mouse, does not simply redefine digital information systems structurally against the manual linearity of older print information regimes. It is this digital collision with intertextuality (again, "digitextuality") that compels Landow to go so far as to assert that hypertexts cause a mode of perceptual and cognitive blurring that "has a marked effect on the conception and experience of boundaries and limits" (Landow, "What's a Critic to Do?" 27).

It is specifically this idea of seamless digital boundary crossings of generic, disciplinary, temporal, and spatial lines (that also engender class, national, generational, gender, and the always problematic racial blurring of established norms and hierarchies) that vexes any discursive engagement with would-be immutable identity categories in cyberspace. This is not to suggest that the notion of fixed identity categories has been uncontested before now. I raise this because the present project clearly is imbricated in these newly evolving nuances and distinctions. How then to define the

particularities of the black press in cyberspace now that the drastically rev-
olutionized nature of "the text," of publication, of authorship, of information dissemination and retrieval, and of the reader all signify so significant
a shift in the basic terms and concepts of our topic? The pertinence of this
need to rethink what constitutes the black press in the digital age becomes
evident to anyone confronted with the sheer volume of sites claiming black
affiliation. In fact, this problem did not manifest itself to me until I was
well into my own research that required consultation with such popular
search engines as Yahoo! Google, Lycos, Alta Vista, and Hotbot, among
others. (These searches supplemented my investigation of such black site
directories as the Universal Black Pages, Melanet, Everything Black.Com,
the Afrocentric Mall, etc.) Relying on such specified key words and phrases
as *black, black press, African American, African American press, black diaspora, African diaspora,* and so on, which yielded a number of "hits" and
"site" and "category matches" in the hundreds of thousands (figure 3.1), I
was thrust into the sort of panning for gold mentality that surely must

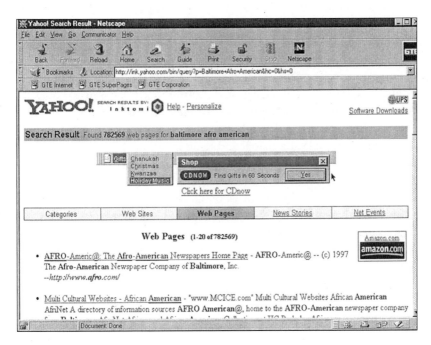

FIGURE 3.1. Yahoo screen grab. Even in 1999 the number of hits on African
American black press key words on Yahoo had exploded to approximately 782,569.

have defined the prospecting life at the height of California's nineteenth-century Gold Rush, except that I was prospecting for the rare black gold of "legitimate" black press websites hidden somewhere amid what I soon discovered were inflated numbers for these mainstream search engines' "category matches."

Complicating the search was the plethora of listings for those black press sites that only exist as online publications. This further confirmed my need to reconceive what I meant by the "black press" now that my print signifier has become entangled in the digitextual blurring of a new black press signified in cyberspace. The plethora of "category/site matches" presented me with numerous informational "black" sites that mimic the information function of dedicated print newspapers and magazines even though these digitexts more accurately might be described as data banks or directories featuring black or Afrocentric content. Moreover, the fact that many of these online black sites that bear no stylistic or ideological resemblance to traditional print newspapers, magazines, or journals feature journalistic and news departments or sections served to compound the problem of specifying and delimiting the object of study. Nonetheless, a number of sites were selected as exemplars of the black press migration to cyberspace and their imbrication in the developing discourse of digital culture.

Quoting Jean-Francois Lyotard, Landow cites this very instructive idea: "Any piece of data becomes useful (exploitable, operational) once it can be translated into information. . . . After they have been put into digital form, these data can be synthesized anywhere and anytime. . . . They are thereby rendered independent of the place and time of their 'initial' reception, realizable at a spatial and temporal distance: let's say telegraphable" (Landow, "What's a Critic to Do?" 27). This observation makes clear the fact that the new modes of digital reproducibility have radically altered the nature and conditions of black publication. Whereas the conditions of possibility that engendered the historic print black press (i.e., startup capital, expensive linotype machinery, a national and global distribution system, and sales agents) no longer represent the formidable impediments that once plagued chronically undercapitalized black press ventures.[5] Today almost anyone with access to a computer and an Internet service provider can establish a virtual black press operation to plead his or her own cause. Additionally, there now exists a whole new industry devoted to creating and maintaining websites specifically targeted at the lucrative black consumer market. A 1997 *New York Times* article quotes one Chicago research firm as estimating African Americans' annual spending for magazines alone at $175 million (Pogrebin B3). New e-commerce industries now put ownership of a virtual press within reach of any group or organization interested in exploiting this lucrative market segment.

In the face of these monumental shifts and formidable transformations, it should be clear why traditional frameworks and assumptions for discussing what we think of as the black press are fast becoming untenable. Obviously, we must reconsider what constitutes the black press now that the age of cyberspace all but removes brick and mortar obstacles to mass publishing operations. Even more crucial, in my view, is the pressing need to grapple with a new kind and increasing level of ontological uncertainty one confronts when interacting with putative black press entities in the digital sphere. It is this problematic of verifying racial authenticity or the ease of enacting racial masquerades in cyberspace—the equivalent of virtual blackface—that leads to the second ontological quandry, one brought about by "the vanishing divides between nature and technology," to use Allucquere Rosanne Stone's terms (82). If we accept cyberspace's much theorized decoupling of minds and bodies how, then, can we know that we are interacting with "real" black bodies behind the plurality of black presses in the virtual public sphere? While this ontological uncertainty is ultimately a hard-to-answer question bound up in an epistemological enigma, I think the urgency of this matter will be underscored as we move on to that part of our discussion centering specifically on selected black press websites.

To confront and acknowledge the newly expansive conceptualization of the "black press," given the increasing difficulty of sorting out actual black press entities from their online iterations and simulacra, I will deploy scare quotes judiciously around the term "black press" to indicate my suspicions of the latter. With this effort to delimit an otherwise endless and unreliable slide of racial signification in this quest for black presses in cyberspace, it seems logical, as a point of emphasis, to focus our sampling on a number of websites established by several legitimate and prominent black press organizations. Among these will be the *Philadelphia Tribune*, the *Indianapolis Recorder*, the *Baltimore Afro American*, and the *Charlotte Post*; *Ebony* and *Jet* Magazines; and *Callaloo*, an academic journal. In addition, we will profile "black press" outlets originating online that share an ideological connection to the historic black press such as *One* Magazine, *Blacknet UK News*, and *The Conduit* (now defunct). Illustrative of online "black presses" of questionable racial situatedness are *Keep It Real* and *dailydiva.com*. "Black press" outlets originating online that share an ideological connection to the historic black press such as *One* Magazine, *Blacknet UK News*, and *The Conduit*,[6] to name but three, are included as concrete examples of the black press legacy transformed in cyberspace. *Keep It Real* (a hip-hop inspired e-zine—now defunct), and *dailydiva.com* (a type of e-zine seemingly targeted at black women and patterned after *Essence* Magazine) could be considered forerunners to MySpace, Facebook, and even Twitter. Still, the contents of these two latter electronic magazines in the late 1990s evince a strong undercurrent of pernicious and anti-black rhetoric so reminiscent of white orthographic dissimulations of southern black dialects. In effect, most of the written texts evoke a sense of failed simulated Ebonics. While it is difficult to know for certain about the veracity of race and gender claims authorizing these content providers, sites of this ilk are worthy of scrutiny, least of all for the lessons they suggest about the increasingly unstable nature of identity politics in the age of digital reproduction.

ESTABLISHED BLACK PRESSES MIGRATE TO CYBERSPACE

African Americans' long-standing quest for racial equity and due process in the United States is marked by a series of epochal migrations. During slavery it was the clandestine migrations following the "North Star" to Canada and American cities above the northeastern border infamously known as the Mason and Dixon line. Following the postwar Reconstruction era, African Americans migrated in large numbers to nonsouthern states, if not necessarily in search of the American dream, then certainly in search of escape from the southern region's unrelenting and pervasive racial persecutions.[7] For most African Americans fleeing the South's degradations and repressions at the beginning and during the middle of the twentieth century, destinations such as Washington, D.C., New York, Chicago, Oregon, Seattle, California, Iowa, Colorado, and various locales in between represented real world equivalents to the scriptural promised land.[8] More recently, however, the cumulative effects of economic stagnation in the urban northeast, attacks on and recisions in civil rights gains, and increasing interethnic conflict above the Mason and Dixon line in the wake of the racially polarizing Reagan-Bush 1980s have contributed to a notable reverse black migration southward. This return signals a sort of black acquiescence to the intractability of America's politics of privileged whiteness that erases any doubt that, indeed, the struggle continues.

In charting the contemporary black press' migratory patterns to cyberspace it becomes abundantly clear that predictions and lamentations about the inevitable demise of the nation's black newspapers continue to prove unreliable. And while it seems fashionable in some intellectual circles today to assign blame for the diminution of the significance of the black press and other social setbacks to the real and perceived failures of integration in this post–civil rights era, it is important to remember that black suspicions of integration are not merely contemporary conceits.[9] As far back as 1949 Thomas W. Young presciently connected integration with the "prospective death of Black newspapers" (Pride and Wilson 261). In *A History of the Black Press*, Armistead S. Pride and Clint C. Wilson II quote pertinent statements released by Young, who was then the president of the Negro Newspaper Publishers Association (NNPA), on the occasion of a 1949 National Negro Newspaper Week observance. According to Pride and Wilson, Young believed that

> once the general press [mainstream white press] routinely reported the Negro's personal and group news, crusaded against injustices and inequalities, and chronicled the achievements of the race, the foundations for Negro organs "would cease to be." . . . "The more closely it approaches success, the nearer it propels itself to the brink of oblivion. And if it should eventually succeed in helping to create the kind of society for which it strives, the Negro Press will have contrived its own extinction. . . . Self-liquidation is in the final analysis what we are really striving for." (261)

By contrast, *Louisville Defender* city editor Fletcher Martin, a contemporary of Young, "saw no occasion for all Black publishers to close up shop following some long-awaited gains in civil rights, education and living conditions. 'The Negro press won't die'" (262). Even if Young's "self-liquidation" thesis carried a ring of noble sacrifice and sober pragmatism, given the civil liberties advocacy and crusading mission that gave birth to the black press, Pride and Wilson report that most black publishers rejected this assessment. Instead, most were inclined toward Carl Murphy's view that extinction or "self-liquidation" were not on the agenda. Murphy, the publisher of his family's *Afro-American* chain of newspapers, expressed this counterview in his 1954 presidential address to the NNPA, wherein he proclaimed, "We have the facility to change with the times"

(263–64). Clearly, Murphy could not have envisaged the formidable developments on the horizon, which would thwart even the most venerable of the black presses' efforts to adapt and persevere as the civil rights movement gained momentum at the decade's end. Several challenges roundly tested the black press' facility to adapt amid the vicissitudes that marked the volatile civil rights era and beyond:

> The competition from mainstream media, the papers' failure to maintain relevancy for a younger and more strident Black population, and a conservative business posture made the traditional organs less viable as advertising vehicles. They could no longer deliver the readers coveted by national advertisers. The relationship that had been so painstakingly developed and nurtured over the previous 30 years appeared to disintegrate overnight. Negro newspapers went out of business at an alarming rate throughout the 1960s, 1970s, and 1980s. Of small consolation was the fact that numerous white dailies were suffering the same fate, along with some slick mass circulation magazines such as the *Saturday Evening Post, Colliers,* and *Look.* (Pride and Wilson 246)

A retrospective look at the predicament of the historical black press in our post–civil rights moment suggests that although seemingly diametrically opposed, both Thomas W. Young's "self-liquidation" thesis and Carl Murphy's belief in the press' "facility to change with the times" were largely correct as indices of black press survivability. What Young and Murphy's dialectic attests to is the tremendous calculated risk that the black press took on behalf of its constituency in its often successful negotiations that pushed for a more inclusive democratic reality in U.S. civil society. The enormous cost was the "liquidation" and/or diminution of influence and viability of the very black presses that agitated for the conditions most responsible for its own demise, as Young foretold. At the same time, it is difficult not to regard the black press' new guard as the proverbial Phoenix arisen from the ashes of that portion of the black press old guard that it eulogizes. By 1989, one of the legatees of the historic black press, *Black Enterprise* magazine, tallies the cost of the changed order in black journalism:

> Gone are the many thousands of subscribers who faithfully read the *Afro American* papers in Washington and Baltimore, the *Journal and Guide* in Norfolk, Va., and the highly regarded *Pittsburgh Courier.* Today, these legends only reach a fraction of the readers they used to. . . . The end of the

civil rights era and the advent of integration appear to have spawned a generation of young black adults who are unimpressed with black papers that
don't display the spit and polish of mainstream newspapers. (Pride and
Wilson 246)

This disquieting shift clearly bears out Young's old-guard self-liquidation
or disestablishment scenario, almost too uncannily, while simultaneously
calling our attention to the emergence of a new black press vanguard
ready and capable of confronting the new media landscape. With integration's apparent devastation of the historic black press, and the surviving presses' refusal to be forced into oblivion by the mainstream media
and new digital media technologies—replete with high-tech "spit and
polish"—it is remarkable that today's black press is yet again at the forefront of a bold new migration. Only this time the migration is to the digital promised land of cyberspace. It is fitting, indeed, that Carl Murphy's
own enduring *Afro-American* newspaper organization fulfilled his prophesy of adapting to the times by becoming the first established black newspaper to go online. It actually beat the *New York Times* to the cyberspace
distribution and publicity trough.

AFRO-AMERIC@WWW.AFRO.COM

In 1995 when the *Afro-American* newspaper began its "homesteading on
the electronic Frontier," to borrow a phrase from Howard Rheingold, it
was the first of the established black newspapers to do so. It even predates
most mainstream establishment papers' notice of the nascent technology's
imminent threat and competitive positioning, not to mention these
entrenched media's delayed plunge into this new media abyss.[10] Two years
prior to the *Afro-American*'s bold migration to the Internet, Rheingold
observed: "The Net is still out of control in fundamental ways, but it
might not stay that way for long. What we know and do now is important
because it is still possible for people around the world to make sure this
new sphere of vital human discourse remains open to the citizens of the
planet before the political and economic big boys seize it, censor it . . . and
sell it back to us" (Rheingold 5). Obviously, aiming to take advantage of
the wide-open, frontierist ethos typical of the Internet at that juncture, the
Afro's pioneering move to establish itself in cyberspace is telling of black
press entrepreneurs' resilience and their often-unacknowledged historical

technolust. What the *Afro's* early presence in cyberspace recalls is earlier instances of vital and significant black involvement with former new media technologies such as film (before the advent of sound), radio, and TV.[11] This was particularly the case prior to the hegemonic stranglehold on access to these older mass media industries exerted by global conglomerates making up what Ben Bagdikian describes as the "media monopoly."[12] As the big-money media monopolies now lasso the maverick spirit of the Internet, corralling this upstart communications rival, black press early adopters of the technology such as the *Afro* tenaciously preserve their online niches while the swell of newcomers stake their claims on remaining and yet-to-be-developed new ones. The recent advent of the web logs or "blogs" (usually described as an online diary) is just such a new online niche that challenges dominant media's reactionary new media power grab. (More about black blogs later.)

Since a comprehensive investigation of *The Afro-American* organization's online presence from 1995 to the present is beyond the scope of this work, I have opted for a discussion of the *Afro's* website (site) contents for the week of 21 December 1998. This moment-in-time critique, while necessarily incomplete, does permit a manageable and representative sample of the site's earliest form and function. And although this analysis is directed toward a particular week's offerings, references to data located on the site's extensive archive will be incorporated. Primary among the *Afro's* many distinctions (at that point in time) was its design configuration. In contrast to other print newspaper organizations whose online presentations replicate their traditional print-based looks, the *Afro's* design features were more aligned with and attuned to the new visual aesthetics and interactive functional imperatives of the graphics-driven, digital communicative cues of the World Wide Web in the 1990s. As if becoming a materialization of the ancestral Murphy's injunction to change, the *Afro-Americ@online* was and remains an effective digital text ("digitext") that conformed well to the specificities of the emergent easy-to-navigate hypertext systems of the Internet. Moreover, this digitexual format enables an efficient administration of the site's multitasking, which is essential to a national database charged with centralizing vast amounts of information, disseminating it to readers, and instantaneously publishing reader responses. From the outset, this site did not evoke a virtual copy of a print original, as do some black newspapers with online versions such as the *Indianapolis Recorder* and the *Charlotte Post.* Even the *New York Times online* (figure 3.2) was tethered to the old print media look. By contrast,

FIGURE 3.2. Screen shots of *The New York Times* © in 1998. *The New York Times* also kept to the old media print style online.

the front page of the *Afro* site is a graphically sophisticated yet very under-stated splash page containing text and Afrocentric image icons that function as the navigational gateway to the rest of the site (figure 3.3). Some-what reminiscent of a print newspaper's masthead, the site splash page's title banner contains the text "*AFROamerica@*," with a three-dimensional drop-shadow effect that is positioned over a familiar cyberspace image—a cloud-laced, blue-sky background or wallpaper graphic. The site's creative deployment of these digitally manipulated images and fonts is but one example of its departure from the often conservative traditions of print journalistic style. This virtual frontispiece is further organized around four fixed or permanent topic divisions termed "Culture," "Information," "History," and "Kid's Zone." These recurrent topic buttons (graphics linked to other site locales) are strategically situated in the center of the site's splash or "home" page. Flanking the right and left sides of this image bearing the permanent topic areas are two graphic text buttons linked to the weekly content changes of news, features, general information, and special topics. Across the bottom of the page are text and icon

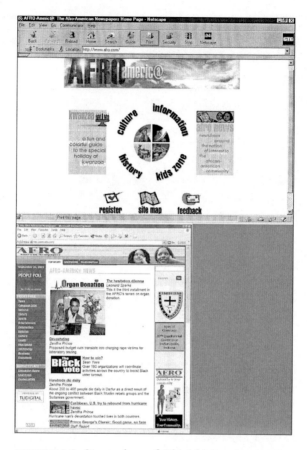

FIGURE 3.3. Screen shots of *The Afro America* newspaper in 1998 and 2004. ©The *Afro Americ@* online press as it appeared circa 1998 with its new media, splash page aesthetics. Although the later *Afro* online still adheres to a largely new media visual style, its home page has become more standardized.

button combinations entitled "Register," "Site Map," and "Feedback." These fixed or regular subject categories are all index-hyperlinks that connect visitors to the site's vast information reservoir by simply clicking on the desired text or image. Not only is the *Afro*'s site visually inviting, but it achieves a high level of user friendliness and intuitive utility. For African American masses who might lag behind the general populace in computer literacy, the site's professional construction, ease of access, navigational clarity, and rich interactive allure serve as an effective primer for learning the basics of Internet use. Moreover, it suggests the press' understanding that bridging the ever-widening technology gap requires all manner of interventionist strategies, including a relatively transparent and intuitively navigable site design.

During the week of 21 December 1998, a click on the "afro news: news from around the nation of interest to the african-american community" text button connected online readers to its national news department. Structurally adhering to a literal table of contents or index function with its three-column newspaper formatting, the e-news page provides both national and regional headlines or capsule descriptions of events and information for the current week. Among the regional stories covered that week were "Western—Black Community Celebrates Cancellation of *Desmond Pfeiffer*, Los Angeles, CA"; "Central—Group Sues Top Communications Co., *Michigan Chronicle*"; "North-Eastern—Transvestite's Mother Gets $3 Million Judgment, Baltimore, MD"; "South-Eastern— Race Relations Dim according to Study, Nashville, TN"; "National—The Booker File: Services for Boxing Legend Archie Moore; Mayor Wellington Sought by Hitman"; "Capitol Hill—CONGRESSIONAL ROUNDUP: Thompson wants reimbursement for Espy; Jackson, Meeks Sponsors Bills for Supreme Court Hiring; Spingarn Medal Nominations Accepted." Headlines from the sports, entertainment, commentaries, and editorials sections also appear on this page, as well as the *Afro*'s "National News Archives," a database of past editions of the press' e-news coverage. To access the stories promoted on this contents page, and other items not previewed here, readers simply click and scroll.

While overall layout, design, news, and information features of the *Afro-American* online invariably pose questions about analog to digital adaptation and medium specificity, the site represents an effective and audacious amalgam of old and new technological mesh. Put another way, the *Afro* online seems comfortably positioned astride the historical traditions of the venerable newspaper's past and its ambitious future quest for black press endurance in the age of global multimedia behemoths. Notwithstanding the site's forward-looking visual and structural formations, its discursive trajectory often remains committed to the need to report on news, information, and editorial content that seems little changed since Carl Murphy ran the paper at midtwentieth century. For example, in his "Congressional Roundup" column, Washington *Afro* staff writer James Wright reports on Congressman Bennie Thompson's (D-Miss) introduction of legislation designed to lessen the financial hardship of black public servants who are victimized by power-hungry, vindictive, and racist independent counsels. The push by African Americans in Congress to introduce "legislation to pressure Congress" and the Supreme Court to improve their hiring of minority clerks is also reported. In other national news for the week, the accomplishments of members of the community are highlighted, fundraising activities for the Metropolitan Police Boys and Girls Clubs are promoted, United Way fundraising records are acknowledged, and Rosa Parks sets the record straight about her civil rights activities at a gathering organized by "College for Kids, a Program aimed at youth ages 9–12, held every Saturday at the George Washington University." Having noted the site's all-too-familiar task of having to disabuse most white Americans of the belief that black Americans have attained first-class citizenship in a new and improved color-blind society, it becomes necessary not to blame the new high-tech messenger for reporting the continuing practices of low-tech and no-tech racism that still wound the nation.

Where the site's information content parallels its progressive visual form, however, is in its domains of "Culture," "History," and in the variety of unrestricted, and real-time interactive opportunities made available online. In that portion of the *Afro*'s site designated as "Culture" are links to a diverse array of content, including "Community Discussions," "Weblinks to Africa," "Art Gallery," "The Polling Place," "Every Wednesday: A Weekly Culture Magazine," "Black Greeks across the Country," and "Your Cool Links." Each of these autonomous categories is self-evident. However, I want to address briefly the progressive vision of this particular element of the site. In the first place, the "Culture" domain functions to massify, instantaneously, black cultural production via global exhibition and distribution channels systematically disallowed to African Americans by the vested, big-money interests of traditional mass media oligopolies. Moreover, the *Afro*'s appropriation of the Internet's virtual gallery feature for the celebration of black art and artists speaks to the publisher's' ability to seize the technology for cyberspace promotional and entrepreneurial discourses that counteracts African Americans' ongoing race-based exclusions in real space. In terms of interactivity, the *Afro*'s "Culture" page successfully rearticulates the necessary two-way communication process between ethnic/race presses and their constituent readerships for the changed exigencies of the new digital realm. The print model of reader-to-press interaction rested largely on a press' ability to induce reader responses to published information and then (following established gatekeeping practices) to publish selective feedback therefrom. The website, on the other hand, permits uncensored, unmediated, real-time posting to specific areas of the *Afro* site's "virtual" public or cyberspheres. That there has been a concerted effort by the mainstream's traditional media to delegitimate and delimit the scope and influence of the Internet's hegemonic potential is a matter of public record.[13] But despite the old media's schizophrenic alarmist and consumerist rhetorics, many (particularly African Americans) are drawn to the uncensored stream of underreported news, novel information, and free form chat that exists online precisely because the influence gap between producer and consumer that characterizes traditional media is lessened significantly. Also, the prominence of links to other sites endows online black presses with a new and important dimension not possible within the materialist strictures of print publishing. Through the hypertext link or digitextual feature of webpublishing, each press offering a "drum list" on its site reinvents the traditional media's influential wire and syndicate services. Instead of sharing select and limited stories among members or subscribers, those cyberpresses featuring links (or "drum lists" as several Afrocentric sites rechristen web rings) to all manner of African diasporic sites become virtual global media distribution relay networks. In this way, site readers, producers, and lurkers are instantaneously transported to and from other national and international "black presses" in one seamless online flow. This virtual erasure of national borders and ideologies has the potential to strengthen the bonds of African disaporic unity in the global struggle for liberation and self-determination in ways that no other modern tool of communication has yet achieved. We must wait, of course, to see if this phenomenal potential will be actualized.

In terms of the liberation struggle on the American homefront, the *Afro-Americ@* site necessarily must detail African Americans' continuing racial oppression, particularly given the mainstream press' displacement of institutionalized racist practices onto so-called rogue elements or isolated individuals and events in the "democratic" culture. Consequently, the black press' journalistic mission rarely moves beyond the pull of what James Baldwin terms "protest literature." Be that as it may, one key aspect of the *Afro*'s online ability to redirect the terms of the text/reader interface is that reader responses to the news are less marginalized; instead they are welcome, instantaneous, and widely disseminated. The site's webmaster trusts the site's readers or "end users" to proof and police their writings and to abide within the code of the honor system where truth, decorum, and accuracy are concerned. Once you "send" your data to the "Culture" page's domain entitled "Your Cool Links," it is automatically cybercast. This is the equivalent of network television's live broadcasts, without recourse to the three-second delay. This decidedly antigatekeeping feature of the site is in keeping with a neoidealist spirit of the Habermassian public sphere.

As the black press writings online illustrate, it matters little whether or not societal assumptions about black second-class citizenship are myth, fact, or somewhere in between; the real consequences of black Americans' continuing repression under white supremacy in American civil society too often are deadly and incontrovertible. How else to explain the recent horrors of high-profile human and civil rights violations visited upon Abner Luima, Amidou Diallo, and Taisha Miller by white law enforcement officers (and there are many more such instances) at the close of the twentieth century. It seems that W. E. B. Du Bois's Victorian era prognostication that the problem of the twentieth century will be the problem of the color line continues to resonate in the new millennium as well.

Clearly, the *Afro* is a trailblazer caught up in all of cyberspace's semiotic ambiguities and vicissitudes. The site can symbolize the idea of bounding the obstacles to progress in an eagerly awaited black future vision; or it can symbolize the retrenchment of the old in the new technological garb. The danger of the latter is a tendency to limit even the desire to explore the outer limits of the new digital media's communicative possibilities. The *Afro*'s developmental trajectory follows the progressive promise of the former.

THE *CHARLOTTE POST, PHILADELPHIA TRIBUNE*, AND *INDIANAPOLIS RECORDER* GO ONLINE

Joining the *Afro-American* newspaper in the migratory trek to cyberspace are such venerable and long-standing black presses as the *Charlotte Post* (publishing since 1878),[14] the *Philadelphia Tribune* (since 1884), and the *Indianapolis Recorder* (since 1895). What these presses' online publications share in addition to a decided emphasis on "data that is both informative and entertaining" (Downey) for its black clientele, as the *Charlotte Post* puts it, is a visual style consistent with its print progenitors. Where the *Afro*'s site deploys then-contemporary online aesthetics, defined by visually striking splash pages, colorful and fresh "imagemaps" ("an image that is treated by the browser as a link or navigational tool"),[15] and text links, the *Recorder* and the *Post* do not. Rather, they employ for their home pages traditional print structures and designs. For the most part, however, this design carryover from print newspapers is abandoned when users click on links to full articles. The *Post*, though, does achieve a more contemporary website design with its large-scale photos. All the presses, including the *Afro*, present their articles in full-page formats with perhaps a left menu bar to navigate around the entire site.

As these later arrivals to the Internet became more net savvy by the year 2004, it was interesting to observe how all these presses' artistic form and content developed along a more standardized look for contemporary news and information sites—as illustrated above. Turning to the early content of these sites, it is the case, as Roland Wolseley notes, that black readers look to their presses "to find out 'what really went on' when a news story about blacks breaks, even though it may be covered by the white media . . . they must turn to their own press for details" (198). Since these online presses publish weekly, their readers likewise could expect "details" about *general news* stories (that may or may not directly affect black people) as well but usually with a black angle or point of view. And given the marginalization of black concerns in white mainstream news organizations, it is hardly surprising that the politics of black online journalism continues the practices of agitation and advocacy for racial justice begun in 1827 with *Freedom's Journal.*

Indeed, Frederick Detweiler observed several characteristic themes of black newspapers in the 1920s that pertained to racial struggles, such as "unfair laws, discriminatory acts of whites, such crimes against blacks as lynchings, and the positive achievements—new businesses begun, political offices gained, educational honors or progress made by individuals" (quoted in Wolseley 197). In the 1950s, another scholar of the black press "published a system of classifying the contents of black newspapers. . . . First was what he called the characteristic Negro Story; it began with the escaped Slave Story, then the Lynch Story, the Protest Story aimed at Jim Crowism, and the Integration Story . . . the Black Power Story, and Separatism Story, and the Black Revolution Story . . . the Negro Angled Story: news of blacks taking part in white news events . . . [t]he Gossip Story [and finally] the African Story" where African Americans began to identify more personally and politically with the land of their forebears (Wolseley 198). It is worthwhile to note that any survey of black presses in cyberspace manifests the persistence of these themes and stories mainly because the conditions that necessitate these journalistic preoccupations have not abated.

Beginning with a sketch of the online content of the *Philadelphia Tribune* for the week ending 11 December 1998, that ranged from that city's plans for 1999 King celebrations to City Council news, to editorials on President Bill Clinton's impeachment saga, we ultimately are confronted with the undeniable glacial rate of social change in the black experience. In his 1891 seminal history of the black press, I. Garland Penn notes the nineteenth-century *Philadelphia Tribune*'s reputation as "one of the leading Afro-American journals of this country." Attributing the paper's excellence to the skill and dedication of its proprietor and editor Christopher J. Perry, Garland quotes Perry's self-articulation of the press' mission on its fourth anniversary:

> *The Tribune* is a paper of the people and for the people. It is the organ of no clique or class. As its name indicates, its purpose is to lead the masses to appreciate their best interests and to suggest the best means for attaining deserved ends. . . . Our past year has been a complete success. We believe that it has been due to our effort to please our patrons and to be worthy of their confidence. It shall be our purpose in the future, as it has been in the past, to maintain *The Tribune*'s reputation for consistency, reliability and news enterprise. (Penn 147–48)

Many of founding editor Perry's concerns, expressed more than a hundred years ago, appear to be among the guiding principles of this enduring press even in its digital configuration. In fact, of the three online presses under discussion here, it is the *Tribune*, with its refusal of high-tech "spit and polish" graphics and digital animation software (Java and Flash applets) that most closely adheres to the historic black press zeitgeist. The site is text-dominant with a striking absence of photos, graphic arts, and advertising. Unquestionably, the *Tribune*'s site upholds Perry's ethos of black press consistency, reliability, and enterprise.

The *Indianapolis Recorder* is another journalistic website with a historical black press pedigree. Founded in 1895, within an already vibrant black press culture that included the *Indianapolis Leader* (1879) and the *Indianapolis World* (1888), the *Recorder* was considered Indiana's "'flagship' paper."[16] Darrel E. Bigham, a scholar of Indiana's black press, has noted:

A black press has existed in Indiana since 1879, and its development . . . was "typical" of the evolution of the black press in America. Fifteen black Indiana presses, about 37 percent, surfaced before 1900, twelve between 1900 and 1920, and nine between 1921 and 1960. Thus, over two-thirds of the presses began after the great migration of Southern blacks to the North. . . . [L]ike its counterparts in the South, [the modern press] established its roots during "a time of crisis." (65)

What distinguishes the online *Recorder* from its print press progenitor is the fact that it was established during a time of phenomenal opportunity in a new media age. A part of its history not lost in the migration to cyberspace has also been a key element in its formidable longevity, an editorial policy that celebrated the accomplishments of blacks nationally and locally. Bigham points out: "A front page in the *Recorder* . . . typically contained a mix of local and national items, and often the lead story dealt with a matter of significance on the local level" (65). In the last week of December 1998, Amos Brown's column for the "'Just Tellin'" page of the *Recorder* site, entitled "A last look back at 1998," is exemplary of this national and local news mix. Brown writes:

The best thing about 1998 was Mark McGwire and Sammy Sosa demonstrating that Blacks and whites [sic] can be competitive while exhibiting respect and mutual admiration as both shattered one of sports' hallowed records. The worst thing about 1998 was the yearlong Dynasty on the Potomac: the political soap opera involving the President and his cigar, the obsessed special prosecutor, Monica, the devil with her blue dress off. . . . A story with sex, lies, videotape and more hypocrisy, fussing and fueding than a year's worth of Jerry Springer shows. The best thing about 1998 for our Indianapolis African-American community was the economy, or as Smokey Robinson once sang, "There's plenty of work and the bosses are paying." The worst thing about 1998 for our Black community was continued escalation of Black-on-Black murders.

Whereas Brown's retrospective glance illustrates well the press' commitment to its historical legacy, Brown's vernacular articulation of serious news issues is well suited to the discursive tone and tenor of everyday Internet speak. In contrast to the *Tribune*, the *Recorder* adapts its website visuals a bit more to accommodate both its digitextual and print-based media systems. The *Recorder*'s homepage (also termed an "index page") combines vivid colors in its masthead, kinte clothlike horizontal page divider, and text tables. The site features photos of local events and Internet service advertising. The site also provides an interactive email feature encouraging reader feedback and commentary posting that updates the all-important letters to the editor component of black press publishing. Online departments such as "Business Briefs," "Entertainment Briefs," "Education Notes," "Local Briefs," "Lottery Results, "Political Notes," "Recorder Web Links," and "Religion Briefs" ensure that readers have ample topics with which to interact. Although it is difficult to know whether or not the *Recorder* maintains its reputation as Indiana's flagship black press, its presence online suggests so. As of December 2004, the website's masthead continues to assert that it is "Indiana's Greatest Weekly Newspaper."[17]

The last online newspaper surveyed here with claims to the historic black press lineage is the *Charlotte Post*. The site lays out its credentials on its "About Us" page: "The *Charlotte Post* has served the African American community of Charlotte and the metropolitan area for more than 115 years. Each week the *Post* is read by thousands of Charlotte and surrounding area residents interested in the most in-depth coverage of minority issues. For providing this service, the *Post* has continually been awarded national and local awards." Distinguishing this site from the others is primarily its liberal use of text-related photos, navigational frames that provide an important place-keeping function as you surf, and a threaded chat/discussion feature connecting reader responses to specified topics.

Typifying this site's more interactive aspect are the two provocative email discussions hosted by the *Post* at years' end. During the last week of December 1999, "Should the Census Bureau Establish a 'Multiracial' Category to Allow Individuals of 'Mixed Race' to Legally Identify Themselves?" and "Has Affirmative Action Outlived its Usefulness?" ("About Us") were the hot topics prompting reader feedback. Of the five reader posts to the former question, all but one reject the idea of legislating a "multiracial" category for mixed race people, citing deleterious political implications. One reader sees this simply as a divisive tactic threatening black solidarity and what Gayatri Spivak terms "strategic essentialism": "I think that this movement will further divide the black population. I also think that this issue is being used as a buffer between us and white folks. After all, he is not trying to re-classify himself but if he sees any benefit (political), he will sanction it? I want those involved in this issue to think about it!" Another corroborates the sentiment with this perspective: "I think this is and has always been a way to keep America segregated. . . .

[T]he government should spend more time and money in finding ways to end segregation because it still exists. We are all Americans!" ("About Us"). The most in-your-face condemnation finds troublesome identity politics at the root of this dilemma:

> I clearly see this as some more of our modern day "Political Correctness" gone amuck. I sit back and watch people try to put their "Black" heritage behind them because it seems to be trendy to be mixed . . . I remember when people were proud to be "Black." . . . [Now they] want to switch, and place their "Blackness" in a closet. But just like Michael Jackson, they too will find out, no matter how light you think you are, how dark you are, who your grandmother was, or if your grandfather was white or not, all the man behind the sheet sees is something to swing on the end of his rope. ("About Us")

This paraphrase of Michael Jackson's hit song "Man in the Mirror" is the email respondent's reminder that America's one drop of black blood litmus test for white racial purity still has cultural currency,[18] still with deadly consequences for blacks, no matter how rich and famous.[19] Even the one reader who dissents posts an ambivalent reply. While this emailer answers affirmatively that "mixed race" persons should be legally identified, because "[i]t is becoming harder and harder to identify persons by race," she confuses her position by asking, "What would be the purpose?" ("About Us").

Regarding the site's question, "Has Affirmative Action Outlived its Usefulness?" the feedback was unanimous. None of the three who replied thought so. The primary concern of these site users was the eradication of employment discrimination too often maintained through "good-old-boys" networks and "glass ceilings," as one of the email respondents quips. This person refuses the historical amnesia of affirmative action foes and offers this memory jog: "One of the main reasons this country was settled was to find opportunities (land ownership, etc.) where there were none in the places they fled. The 'good old boys' then were Kings and the glass ceiling was established by royalty. How easily conditions are forgotten when you are on top." As this thoughtful email post indicates, talking back against the new world race and gender oppression at the hands of the formerly oppressed is one important black tradition that finds new momentum as African Americans carve out an alternative black public sphere in cyberspace. Now that the email function of black press online sites serves to contemporize the letters to the editor mainstay of the news-paper-reader interface, replete with an instantaneity so crucial to topical news interest, it is likely that a formidable sea change is in the offing that augurs well for publishers and readers of journalism alike. The ease and spontaneity of email submission and delivery encourage a more democra-tizing ethos in both the consumption and production of journalistic dis-course across the board. Whereas the expense of reams of newsprint might have curtailed the available space for publishing all reader feedback, it is conceivable that the virtual spaces of electronic publication are not so restricted and thus are capable of accommodating voluminous instances of logging on and weighing in, depending, of course, on the issue at hand.

One *Post* online issue that likely would yield numerous reader emails, if so elicited, was its Christmas week news story entitled "Dolls Reflect, Shape Cultural Identity," by Archie T. Clark II. Clark's article, which revisits the issue of young black children's ongoing preference for white dolls over black ones, makes the case that even today such con-sumer choices are symptomatic of a persistent "lack of self-esteem and racial identity" in segments of the black community. Raleigh, North Car-olina, doll merchant Kamau Kambon reveals a little-known casualty of this particular aspect of cultural disconnect when African Americans are confronted with the dilemma of purchasing the traditional white Barbie, or its ethnic simulacrum, and the question of whether or not it matters.

> "You better believe it matters," said Kamau Kambon. . . . Two years ago Kambon, who owns Blacknificent Bookstore in Southeast Raleigh, observed and read about consumers, some of them black, snatching up white Barbies while black Barbies remained on the shelves. He was disap-pointed at what he was seeing. "I don't carry too many black dolls because people don't buy them." . . . "In 1996 about 96–98 percent of the black dolls manufactured that year were left on the shelves and black people were buying dolls—the white ones." (Clark)

Besides confirming a suspected fiscal disincentive for reluctant white manufacturers to invest in and promote nonwhite dolls when lucrative sales receipts show "that people, regardless of color, wanted a doll named Barbie" (Clark), Kambon reveals the near impossibility of black entrepre-neurs merging sound business practices with the promotion of a "posses-sive investment"[20] in black racial identity and self-esteem. (Kambon quoted in Clark).

The value of Clark's investigation, aside from its timely correspondence to the rise in e-commerce, is its historical research into the destructive potential of identity politics in some forms of child's play. Since late 1997 online business news has moved from the high-tech specialty trades and business sections of mainstream presses to the front pages of national dailies and monthly magazines. In fact, e-commerce is responsible for both elevating and lowering the American stock market to unprecedented levels in recent years. One important feature of black websites, in advance of e-trade hysteria, has been the marketing of black arts and other Afrocentric commercial goods because the new electronic marketplace affords enterprising black firms, start-up organizations, and even mom and pop operations unparalleled access to a more level economic playing field despite the emergence of global oligopolies and media monopolies. And whether or not Clark intended his story to revivify a spirit of black critical consumerism that defined such effective segregation era boycott campaigns as "don't shop where you can't work" is unimportant. The important part is the historical and scientific basis of his argument that suggests *Post* readers not forget hard-fought gains from the past nor fail to appreciate the psychosocial as well as financial benefits of buying black.

Among the historical proofs that Clark revisits are Kenneth Clarke's seminal study and Dr. Darleen Powell Hopson's 1988 replication. For Archie Clark, the journalist, it is central for black families to understand that more than "beauty is at stake when a child prefers a doll of a different race." He writes:

In the late '40s and early '50s, Kenneth Clarke took black and white dolls to schools throughout the South. With the consent of the faculty, Clarke studied responses to simple questions as the kids observed the dolls. The results revealed a majority of children answered favorably towards white dolls, which was interpreted that kids did so because of a lack of self-esteem and racial identity. It was determined that kids in the study had these feelings at the age of 3–4. The results sent shock waves at the time and even had implication in the Brown vs. Board of Education decision that led to the desegregation of public schools. In 1988, Dr. Darleen Powell Hopson, a practicing clinical psychologist, replicated the doll study using drawings, and included children from the Caribbean. She found similar results.

Clark concludes by quoting Baruti Katembo, a math teacher and Raleigh community activist who started a Fourth of July celebration for local black people: "A doll is something the child plays with as an extension of themselves. . . . When a child owns a doll, they unknowingly idolize it and want to be like it. I don't think white dolls should be given to black kids." Katembo states further: "As long as we continue to see ourselves as extensions of white people, we will be further and further removed from being able to define ourselves." Clearly, this job of situating contemporary black cultural and business problems in historical precedents is a black press strong suit. For even if the mainstream press were to report on black youths and white Barbie dolls, it is extremely doubtful that they would angle this news in terms unfavorable to consumerism, let alone in terms of historically documented mental health issues. By foregrounding its information function in this way, the *Post* online lives up to its own published credo and its black press legacy.

Now, as much as the *Post* joins with the *Afro*, the *Recorder*, and the *Tribune* in upholding the best practices of the historic black press' uplift mission in cyberspace, one of publisher Gerald O. Johnson's planned "new features" for the *Post* returns us to a questionable blast from the print past. In his "What's New," page, Johnson promises to revive the cheesecake photo staples that dotted the pages of even the most venerable of black presses from around the 1920s onward. Johnson says, "As a new feature, we have added a 'beauty of the month' section. This section will profile some of Carolina's finest. Browsing this section will make you understand why nothing could be finer than being in Carolina" (Clark). Given the growing popularity of so-called voyeur sites featuring unrestricted visual pleasure and access to the quotidian life experiences of young, nubile girls and women, perhaps Johnson is only guilty of shrewd e-business acumen, or, to use Wolseley's terms, perhaps he is merely "putting in what sells" (Wolseley 204). Regardless of his motivation, this is one carryover of masculinist *visual pleasure*[21] from the historic black press that might be reconsidered. And by 2004, the "beauty of the month" feature was gone from the site's menu.

EBONY AND *JET*: THE POPULAR
MAGAZINES TAKE TO THE ETHER

Accompanying the newspapers to the digital outposts of cyberspace are the black general and specialty magazines such as *Black Enterprise, Black Collegian, Ebony, Jet,* and *Essence,* among others. And while these well-established, popular print magazines have not been in circulation as long as their newspaper counterparts, the significance of their relative longevity and continuing influence can be measured by their abilities to withstand the legendary instability and financial risk of the crowded magazine publishing field (Wolseley 168), black or otherwise. Furthermore, these national magazines have proven adept at keeping pace with the changing needs of their readers and the often capricious and competitive exigencies of the publishing world. That these magazines are now online reflects only the latest (and arguably most profound) shift in publishing trends and market fragmentation to which they have capably adjusted.

It is interesting that the magazines we will briefly consider here, *Ebony* and *Jet*, confine their online content primarily to narrative précis and attractive photographs from featured stories more fully detailed in the print editions. In contrast, then, to the information-driven function of content dominating most of the online newspapers, the magazine sites function as virtual publicity departments, virtual newsstands, and virtual or e-subscription channels for the primary business, the monthly print editions. As with the air-brushed photographic perfection necessary to compete successfully on the actual newsstand, the compelling photos of black celebrities on the *Jet* and *Ebony* home pages lure web lurkers and magazine loyalists to closer scrutiny, a scrutiny predicated on purchasing the print magazines promoted by the site. For instance, during the week ending 31 December 1998, *Jet* displayed three distinct photos of rhythm and blues superstar R. Kelly on its virtual cover page. A smiling and confident-looking Whitney Houston shared *Ebony Online*'s home/index page with magazine founder John H. Johnson. The news in that edition was that Houston was thirty-five years old and that Kelly won three 1998 Grammy Awards and solidified his crossover status with his hit duet ("I'm Your Angel") with white, Canadian singing sensation Celine Dion.[22] In keeping with the present aesthetic principles of the web, both *Jet*'s and *Ebony*'s home pages are big on photos and graphics and small on print textuality, as the printed text mainly serves a linking function directing users to other site locations such as its *Ebony South Africa* website.

SOJOURN TO THE DIGITAL PUBLIC SPHERE FOR THE MILLENNIUM AND BEYOND

This survey of select historic black presses' migration to the Internet clearly reveals their commitment to continue the struggle for black political, social, cultural, and economic survival and prosperity well into the digital age. What the online incarnations of the *Afro American, Indianapolis Recorder, Charlotte Post,* and *Philadelphia Tribune* newspapers represent, besides a corrective to a presumption of black technophobia, is African Americans' robust technological participation in the nation's postmodern public sphere or what Nancy Fraser more accurately sees as an agglomeration of many "counterpublics." These presses, in print and online, exemplify Fraser's challenge to Marxist critic Jürgen "Habermas's account of the bourgeois conception of the public sphere [that] stresses its claim to be open and accessible to all," when women and men of racialized ethnicities of all classes were excluded on racial grounds (56–80). Moreover, they seem to confirm Houston Baker's black revisionist notion of the Habermasian public sphere ideal. For Baker, the fact that blacks might find attractive or believable the notion of a public sphere, predicated on a system of property ownership and literacy, is difficult at best. But, following Fraser, Baker sees the potential for transcending these limitations, specifically for black communities. Baker recognizes that African Americans

> are drawn to the possibilities of structurally and affectively transforming the founding notion of the bourgeois public sphere into an expressive and empowering self-fashioning. Fully rational human beings with abundant cultural resources, black Americans have always situated their unique forms of expressive publicity in a complex set of relationships to other forms of American publicity (meaning here, paradoxically enough, the sense of publicity itself as authority). (Baker 13)

And it is the expressive, self-fashioning, and emancipatory potential of the Internet, at this still-nascent moment, that enables the historic black press to affect a structural transformation of publicity to disseminate widely black counterhegemonic interpretations of local and global events, thus bearing out Baker's black public-sphere thesis. For example, as the Clinton/Lewinsky affair and the subsequent impeachment trial became scandalous fodder for newsprint and the airwaves, the white mainstream presses tended to portray the African American community as an essentialized, pro-Clinton bloc of political lemmings, pathetically dispossessed of critical consciousness. It is true that the presses' online editions carried impeachment stories, but, as the *Recorder* demonstrates, this national story of political intrigue receded to the background as the paper's "Top Stories" were local ones. The home page's feature stories were "Madame Walker

Center Honors Business" and "NNPA [Nation Negro Publishers' Association] National Briefs," as Amos Brown's satirical engagement with the issue, discussed above, became one item among many in the 1998 year-end review of news. And though Brown's discourse of equivalence between "The Radical Republican Lynching/Impeachment of President Clinton" and the historic acts of Ku Klux Klan terror against African Americans conveys a nuanced sense of many black people's objection to the impeachment, Samuel F. Yette, columnist for the *Philadelphia Tribune*, puts a finer touch on the issue. In his article "Clinton's Attack on Iraq Shows He Is Out of Control," Yette gives voice to that independent segment of the black community that the mainstream press routinely puts under erasure in its essentializing discourse on blackness. Discussing Clinton's strained credibility following the political fallout over the Lewinisky matter, Yette expresses this skepticism about Clinton's ill-timed attack on Iraq:

> He said also that he acted to protect 'America's vital interests.' Being thousands of miles from the Persian Gulf, the president was hard put to explain how this nation's vital interests were threatened. A master of Orwellian News-speak, even as he made war, Mr. Clinton pledged to "stand strong against the enemies of peace."

Even though Yette's article bears the customary editorial disclaimer that accompanies controversial or polemical positions espoused by writers, the fact that the *Tribune* cybercast Yette's views at all bears out Houston Baker's views about the viability and legitimacy of a black public sphere. With the growing power and dominance of global media conglomerates, it is evident that the revolutionary digital public sphere developing in cyberspace represents the hope and promise for the ongoing survival of the independent black presses, established ones and upstarts alike.

Where established black cyberpresses such as the *Post*, the *Recorder*, the *Afro-American*, the *Tribune*, *Ebony*, and *Jet* (among others) provide a necessary link to the past and its lessons, newer ones such as the *Capital Times*, the *Conduit*, *One* Magazine, and even the journal *Callaloo*, became temporary autonomous zones or beacons lighting the pathways of progress to bright futures for black publishing online. As it stands, the black press presence in cyberspace is promising indeed; it remains to be seen, however, whether the Internet and this counterpublic will continue to coevolve in the new global information economy. Yet these examples represent a tiny fraction of online black presses to date, particularly, when

Yahoo put the number at more than two hundred thousand in 1999. If the history of the black press is its prologue, despite the demise of the *Capital Times*, the *Conduit*, *One* Magazine, and other newer black-oriented journalistic websites, then we can be confident that the story of the black press in cyberspace will persist and be regenerative.

CHAPTER FOUR

＿＿＿＿＿＿ ⠿ ＿＿＿＿＿＿

Serious Play:
Playing with Race in
Contemporary Gaming Culture

[W]ho would have predicted that young black and Latino males would spend enough time in Times Square video arcades during the late seventies to make those games the million-dollar industry that they are?

　　　　　　　　　　—Greg Tate, "Black to the Future"

In the '80s and '90s you never saw black characters. If there were any black ones, they would get beat up, really whumped so fast, before they had time to get into character.

　　　　　　　　　　—Orpheus Hanley, *Midway Games*

I hacked another game and created a game called Blacklash. . . . I was fed up with companies making black games that have got no relation to black people whatsoever. You'll have someone make a game, and one of their characters got dreadlocks—and it's like someone put a mop on his head.

　　　　　　　　　　—Richard-Pierre Davis, Mongrel.org

Machines have the morality of their inventors.

　　　　　　　　　　—Amiri Baraka, "Technology and Ethos"

When my preteen niece challenged me to a game of *Super Mario Brothers* during a family Christmas gathering a decade ago, it was my reintroduction to video game play following my casual initiation during the *Pac Man* and *Ms. Pac Man* craze of the mid-1980s. I was unprepared for the seductive and addicting qualities of this second generation of video games due, in part, to the striking evolution of gaming hardware and software packages, narrativity, and character designs from blocky, one-dimensional geometric renderings to the more technically accomplished Disneyesque animation standards featuring fully individuated cartoon character types. I am thinking here of Mario and Luigi, popular characters of the *Super Mario Brothers* game franchise that has been described as "one of the best selling games ever."[1] At the time, I found the hand-eye-coordination demands of interactive play (predicated on mastering the action keys of Nintendo's control pads) a welcome distraction from and counterbalance to the cerebral demands of my graduate school course of study. From that moment on, I became a fan of video game entertainment, unaware of how this seeming innocuous diversionary play would become an important part of my later scholarship and research interests.

Exhilarated by my easy mastery of relatively complex controller key commands and minimal "story" advancement demands, using intuition not manual instruction (although my niece talked me through the basics), I rushed out and bought my own Nintendo console and *Super Mario Brothers* game. Looking back on that pleasurably fateful Christmas break, I suspect the lure of video game play for me (a woman graduate student) was only differentiated from that of more traditional players to the extent that my pleasure inhered in a displacement of the high-stakes, immersive intellectual work of graduate study, temporarily, onto the no-stakes immersive play of the game. The work/play dialectic of intellectual growth at school and digital dexterity (fingers in this case) at home effected a balanced scale of my "transmedia"[2] mastery during the ensuing decade, which happened to coincide with the gaming industry's own development of interactive play designs.[3]

However, as the current research progressed, my efforts to dissociate my objective study of race in video games from my subjective experiences with and frustrations about enjoying gaming, despite its encrusted discourses of racial difference and otherness, seemed less crucial. After all, Hayden White reminds us that hoary or "outmoded conceptions of objectivity" do little to conceal the subjective nature of evidence and facts "constructed by the kinds of questions which the investigator asks of the phenomena before him" (White 43).[4] Moreover, I am convinced that White's observations about objectivity in discourse production in the field of history remain pertinent. About writing histories of History, White argues, "It is difficult to get an objective history of a scholarly discipline, because if the historian is himself a practitioner of it, he is likely to be a devotee of one or another of its sects and hence biased; and if he is not a practitioner, he is unlikely to have the expertise necessary to distinguish between the significant and the insignificant events of the field's development (83). As a practitioner and historian of popular culture, and a longstanding fan and foe of video game texts, I share White's estimation and easily recognize its applicability to my concern with examining race matters in the short history of computer and video games. (I will use the terms *video games* and *computer games* interchangeably.)

Because the video game industry privileges "boys in their pre-and early teen" years (Bolter and Grusin 91), I am acutely aware that my mature, black, and female body is marked and thus marginalized as a shadow consumer in the gaming industry's multibillion-dollar marketplace. Moreover, my informal surveys of video game cover art and game descriptions, print and online game reviews, manufacturer strategy guides, and popular media coverage of expert gamers uncover not only an essential and privileged male gaming subject but one who is "universalized" under the sign of whiteness. For me, this distinct racial discourse in gaming culture's dramatic movement from its second to third generation of sophisticated 3–D character designs, with various racial types in tow, begged the question, When and where does the racial problematic enter in contemporary culture's moral panics about gaming's potential dangers?

Until late 1999, most public concern about video games focused on presumed dangerous behavioral consequences for minors and impressionable teens due to excessively violent content[5] and, to a lesser extent, on gender bias.[6] Race was the structured absence in this latest iteration of generation-gap politics between parent and youth cultures. The present discussion addresses this all-too-familiar lacuna by interpolating race matters into the fracas. I situate my critique of gaming culture within a discursive ambit that includes select game titles, video game journalism, personal interviews, and formal and informal survey data that specifically engage matters of race and blackness in video and computer games. Finally, methodological approaches and precedents from influential and emerging scholarship on cultural theory, gaming, and other modes of contemporary popular culture are referenced here as hermeneutic touchstones or useful conceptual models in this interrogation.

RACIAL ENCRYPTION AND DECRYPTION IN VIDEO GAMES

> Encryption technology encodes computer files so that only someone with special knowledge, such as a unique secret "key," can read them.
>
> —Solveig Singleton, "Encryption Policy for the Twenty-First Century"

Most public debate about encryption technology revolves around the need to balance protections for e-commerce, law enforcement, and military secrets, with the preservation of individual privacy rights (a debate that has become exacerbated in the aftermath of the 11 September terror attacks). I propose a redirection of the encryption problematic to issues of computer game representations and iconography. What makes interrogating encryption strategies and practices an issue in gaming's address of race in its human characters and human-creature hybrid designs is the question of mastery. What "special knowledge," we ask, are gamers expected or encouraged to master (besides the arcane algorithmic architecture encrypted in individual game rules and protocols) in their pursuit of successful play? If we extrapolate from Marsha Kinder's observations about "the interrelated processes of assimilation and accommodation in the cognitive development" of children in recognizing gender differentiation in their own subject formations (6–9), "where traditional gender roles are increasingly reinforced rather than transgressed" (9), then surely racial differentiation becomes another important register of subjectivity.

What this suggests for our concern with gamers' mastery of the special knowledges required for effective game play is a need to understand how encrypted and encrusted racist ideologies in contemporary video games might function to interpellate gamers into what George Lipsitz describes as a possessive investment in whiteness. As "the unmarked category against which difference is constructed," whiteness, Lipsitz reminds us, "never has to speak its name, never has to acknowledge its role as an organizing principle in social and cultural relations" (1).[7] Nonetheless, then, as children and other gamers resort to their racialized cognitive processes of assimilation and accommodation, they easily recognize the significant returns on investing in whiteness. This issue of mastering the codification of gaming culture's own apparent purchase on the investment in whiteness warrants special interest and urgency in view of the position that ideologies of racial differences construct racial practices.[8] In other words, although we well understand the socially constructed nature of, say, gender and race hierarchies, they remain potent constructs "with sinister cultural causes and consequences" (2). The implications for gaming culture can be found in Justine Cassell and Henry Jenkins's discussion of the "girls' game movement":

> Violent games without positive representations of women . . . continued to dominate the field. Parents and critics began to suggest that if video games are a primary means of socialization for young boys in our culture, then feminist mothers and fathers needed to be concerned about their content. Some argued that games reaffirmed or reinscribed dominant and patriarchal conceptions of gender roles . . . or more frighteningly, that they foster a culture which sees violence, especially violence directed against women, as acceptable. (10)

Clearly, such concerns obtain for race matters as well. At the same time, it is crucial to be cautious about necessarily equating violent, misogynist, and racist gameplay with real-world behavioral effects, especially without regard for other important sociocultural influences[9] such as families, schools, churches, peers, and other interpretive communities. And even though researchers disagree about the extent to which gamers retain or reject dangerous stereotypical values and messages embedded in some video games (Kafai 295), it is incumbent upon us to address the risks and potential cultural injury inherent in the circulation of racist and sexist discourses in games and other mass media texts, particularly given what Carl Gutierrez-Jones calls "the legacy of racism in the United States" (3). Another significant element in this equation is gaming's valued status as "an easy lead-in to computer literacy," and the conviction that children who don't play games at young ages will be disadvantaged later and thus unable to compete in the information economy (Cassell and Jenkins 11). For unlike previous moral panics about the baleful influences of comic books, films and television programming, where parents and social influence leaders felt obliged to restrict children's access to these once-reviled texts, by contrast computer games elicit a counter tendency. Consequently, their sway can be more profound, particularly if we accept the view that interactive and fully immersive gameplay, unlike the putative passivity of film and video consumption, provide more intensely potent interactions with questionable ideas and discourses.

REPLAYING THE RACE CARD: GAMING'S "HIGH-TECH BLACKFACE" AND ORIENTALISM

On 21 October 1999 Michael Marriott broached the overdue issue of race, especially blackness, and video games in his *New York Times* "Circuits" article entitled, "Blood, Gore, Sex and Now: Race." This high-profile, high-tech article foregrounding racial representation in newer, more technologically sophisticated video and computer games was followed by an important and influential 2001 study by the nonprofit organization Children Now. Their study, "Children and the Media: Fair Play? Violence, Gender and Race in Video Games,"[10] garnered extensive national and international coverage, much of which was published and accessible online by entering the key words *race* and *video games*. (We will return to the Children Now study later.) Most likely this flurry of interest in race and video games was fueled by growing public interest in the digital divide question, most familiarly signified by images of computer-illiterate African Americans. Whatever the impetus, Marriott's article and the subsequent Children Now study were instrumental in positioning the issue of race in video games squarely alongside the gender problematic as an important matter in mainstream society's general anxiety about universal access in the new technological revolution. As important as the *New York Times*' venture into this important discussion was, it was not the first. In fact, two years earlier the *Village Voice* newspaper ran "Yellow Perils: Online 'Coolies' Rile Asian Americans," an article on race and video games by Athima Chansanchai.

Both Marriott and Chansanchai engage the volatile issue from the perspectives of game producers and consumers alike. Whereas the former's more optimistic tone suggests a bridgeable chasm between opposing factions if only each were sensitive to the other's position, the latter's tone conveys a more fundamental and intractable impasse. Apparently, the rhetorical differences in the articles are imbricated in their respective profiles of mainstream and independent gaming cultures. However, when

considered in tandem, they are quite revealing of the limits of "'just saying no' to all manner of race consciousness" (Gutierrez-Jones 48–49)
despite convictions that *democratizing* new technologies are uniquely
poised to advance an ethos and subsequent practice of well-meaning color
blindness. For example, Marriott reports the following responses from
black and Latino informants to the assumption that since "non-white
characters are [now] stars rather than bit players" this somehow represents
progress. Marriott begins by quoting African American gameplayer and
Midway designer Orpheus Hanley on his sense of estrangement from the
action of games that he played in youth, because no characters "looked or
behaved anything like him."[11] A Puerto Rican arcade games player, who
commented on condition of anonymity, was not impressed by games such
as the Midway company's *Ready 2 Rumble* boxing game, featuring the
popular, huge-afro-coiffed boxer Afro Thunder. "I don't think it's funny,"
this player asserts. "They just look like another group of silly stereotypes
to me." (qtd in Marriott D7).

But it is Adam Clayton Powell, III who gives the article its overarching "high-tech blackface" theme: Powell, the Freedom Forum's vice
president for technology and programs, raises the specter of game play's
intensities of cathect:

> Because the players become involved in the action of the character far
> more than sitting back and watching a character on television . . . they
> become much more aware of the moves that are programmed into the
> game. Any game has a certain stereotype, negative or positive, but a com-
> puter game is going to pass that message along pretty powerfully. (Valdiz
> quoted in Marriott D7)

As Powell correctly points out, generic stereotypes are part and parcel of
entertainment media's shorthand narrative structures and communicative
devices and thus are not inherently mendacious. However, it is video
games' and other new media texts' hot wiring to existing racist discourses
and negative racial stereotypes that causes concern.

In mounting a counterview to Powell's concerns about "the threat of
furthering racial stereotyping in computer games, which he called "high-
tech blackface," and arguing against other minority voices expressing similar reservations, Marriott juxtaposes less critical commentary in his article from minorities working in and outside the gaming industry. The
commentary is telling and bears quoting at length. Marriott writes:

Game makers like Emmanuel Valdez, who is Filipino, says a game with a nonwhite focus is a means of making the game stand out in an oversaturated markeplace that is warmed by almost 2,000 new games a year. "I think people are a little tired of the Aryan, Square-jawed, blond hero," said Mr. Valdez, a computer game artist for Midway, the company that makes *Ready 2 Rumble*. Mr. Valdez used Mr. Hanley as the model for Afro Thunder—the spindly-legged, gigantic-Afro-wearing trash talker, whom Mr. Valdez said was the game's most recognized character. Mr. Hanley also lent his voice to the character. (D7)

In addition to Valdez's less-condemning, more market-centered perspective, Marriott includes a positive perspective on the issue from a black scholar. Marriott adds:

Elijah Anderson, a professor of sociology at the University of Pennsylvania, said that the racial and ethnic shorthand behind these nonwhite characters might be intended for white computer game players. . . . "A lot of people living in the suburbs admire this fire and this spunk they see in blacks, a kind of aggressiveness a lot of them want, too. . . . A lot of these suburban, white-bread kids hunger for this kind of experience." Perhaps, he said, by inhabiting the *soul* [emphasis added] of the virtual black character in a game, they can safely get a taste of urban-inspired cool. Dr. Anderson said, "Another part of this is that we all live in a diverse society now, and these kinds of games play to that diversity." "In a certain sense," he added, "it's a positive." (D7)

The critique of white, suburban male youths' fascination with and consumption of a safe taste of urban-inspired cool has previously been made by vocal black and other opponents of gangster rap music. And given the paucity of African American and other minority executives in important decision-making positions, such rationalizations, predicated upon the mere presence of minority bodies working in these new culture industries, seem disingenuous at best and dangerous at worst in their failures to address the structural racism emanating from business' top-down values and practices. Marriott also interviewed Guy Miller, a white game designer of the *Shadow Man* computer game for the Acclaim company. This game features "a black cabdriver who has been turned into a 'supreme zombie-warrior slave.'" As a white designer responsible for the envoicement of a black game character, Miller's comments to Marriott are revealing. "We knew we had to get it right," is how Miller explains his racial authentication strategies. As Marriott puts it: "To give *Shadow Man*'s voice a certain authenticity, an African-American was selected to do the voice work. To give *Shadow Man* his catlike stroll, a black boxer's athletic stride was digitally captured and infused into the computer character, said Guy Miller, who designed the game" (D7). Is this fetishization of digital technologies' ability to render convincing representational signifiers of a limited and specific type of blackness what it means to get it right? And, dare we ask, for whom are we getting it right? After all, the early cinema eventually exchanged white actors in blackface for black ones without significantly changing demeaning and racist film representations of black life and culture.

As frustrating as Marriott's liberal-humanist take can be on mainstream gaming's newfound racial awareness and new market strategies for these "realistic new game characters," Chansanchai's report on the independent video game industry's discovery of racial diversity as a selling tool is downright scary. As Carl Gutierrez-Jones suggests, when contemporary racial identity politics collide with "the 'angry white male' backlash" (49), we are confronted with a dangerous alchemy. Like Marriott, Chansanchai's reportage is a polemic, of sorts, between opposing constituencies: those represented as other and those representing the other. After describing some offensive characteristics encrypted in a "bomb-crazy" Japanese zombie game character named Shadow Warrior, Chansanchai frames the discussion in less dissembling terms:

> Welcome to the high-tech world of deliberately revolting online interactive video games. 3D Realm's *Shadow Warrior* and its predecessor, *Duke Nukem 3D*, run the gamut of blood and guts, foul language, and outrageous stereotypes. "Our games are anti-p.c. by design," brags Scott Miller, president of Apogee Software, 3D Realms's parent company. "We do not shrink away from issues that would send p.c.—anal companies running with their tails between their legs." And they sell. Armed with top-of-the-line 3D graphics, they draw players like blood draws flies, making them instant hits.[12]

Accompanying the article "Yellow Perils: Online 'Coolies' Rile Asian Americans," are two illustrations of the contested images. One features a close-up, facial, two-shot portrait in a faux-wooden frame enclosing a slender, square-jawed Aryan male figure wearing a baseball cap (in the foreground), paired with an obese, buck-toothed Asian-looking male character (in the background). The text overlain on this image reads "All the Killin,'" "Twice the Humor," and "Half the Intelligence" (25). The caption of this image states, "Good ole boys wreak havoc on the net." The second illustration presents a full-body, Asianlike robotic figure wearing a familiar "coolie" hat and grasping a box marked with a prominent "TNT" label. These striking markers of difference and otherness underscore the troubling racial economies at work in new media discourses against which injured groups are compelled to protest. Indeed, Chansanchai notes that vocal Asian critics were unswayed by Apogee's claims that the game *Shadow Warrior* "was intended as an innocent parody of bad kung fu flicks." Underlying Asian opponents' condemnation of the game is a resistance to what could easily be viewed as an Orientalizing discursive logic structuring the production and reception of these game images.

When *Computer Gaming World* columnist Elliot Chin remarks incredulously on white games producers' conflation of Japanese and Chinese stereotypes, we glimpse a retrofitted Orientalist critique of *Shadow Warrior.* "'For Pete's sake,' wrote Chin, 'coolie hats are associated with Chinese, not Japanese, immigrant workers. It's bad enough to use the blatant stereotypes in a game's design, but 3D Realms can't even get their own stereotypes right'" (qtd in Chansanchai, "Yellow Perils" 25). Not only do Chin's objections point to the persistence of Orientalism and its homogenization of Asian diversity in the Western imaginary, but game designer Chris Miller's response "We're not trying to be *National Geographic* here. . . . We are having fun with the whole Asian Culture," underscores the ongoing need for Chin's and others' critical vigilance. It is telling that Miller is comfortable reducing the complexities of Asian cultural pluralities to a convenient one-dimensional whole. No doubt buoyed by his game's financial success, Miller arrogantly concludes his reply to critics by asserting, "Anyone we've offended has probably taken this game too seriously. If this game offends you or anyone, go play another game. We won't mind" (25).

Miller may not have minded Asian critics' refutations. However, *PC World Online* games reviewer Amy Ng encountered outspoken fans of the game who did mind and posted their dissatisfaction with her column in email responses that "ranged from flat-out disagreements to racial epithets." And despite alerting Asian advocacy groups to *Shadow Warrior's* racist affront, Ng, like Miller, ultimately defers final judgment to consumer tastes and preferences. "As a game," Ng states, "it's worthy of consideration . . . but I wouldn't play it or advocate playing it" (qtd in Chansanchai, "Yellow Perils" 25). Unlike Chin's unmitigated disdain for the game, Ng's opinion of the game as worthy of consideration appears conditioned by professional standards of journalistic objectivity and a strained critical distance, which contrasts with her personal rejection of the game's racism as evinced in her lobby of Asian advocacy groups. Nonetheless, Chin, Ng, and Miller's conflicting interchanges play out and enliven Edward Said's cogent analysis of Orientalism's hegemony that "is more particularly valuable as a sign of European-Atlantic power over the Orient than it is a veridic discourse about the Orient" (Said 6). As Said puts it further, and as the foregoing attests, "Orientalism depends for its strategy on this flexible positional superiority, which puts the Westerner in a whole series of possible relationships with the Orient without ever losing him the relative upper hand" (6).

This case of relational superiority works well to contextualize Miller's symptomatic utterance about "having fun with the whole of Asian cultures," within a signifying chain of Orientalist discourses that manifests itself in gaming culture's contradictory desire for and loathing of images of the Asian other. At one extreme is the familiar fetishistic encoding of superior Asian martial arts skill in sports genres, and at the other are derogatory codifications of Asians as undesirable "coolies" and "bomb-crazy" Japanese kamikaze zombies in other genres.

Stuart Hall reminds us that dominant discourses, such as Orientalism, do not constitute a closed system of meaning in the sender-message-receiver feedback loop, because audience receivers' interpretive processes are subject to distortions (Hall, "Encoding" 134–35). So we must not underestimate the lure and "textual erotics" that certain representational possibilities promise over others. In other words, while it certainly is the case that readers/audiences, and for us, gamers, can and do actively resist and often misread dominant plot structures, Peter Brooks's assertion that "the reading of plot [is] a form of desire that carries us forward, onward, and through the text" (37) is instructive. Thus, we see that part of the pleasure is reading the plot "correctly" and as intended, which Brooks's notion of "textual erotics" illuminates. In this way, gaming plot structures that posit an occidental *self* in conflict with an oriental *other* structure in a narrative pleasure principle predicated upon Orientalism's binary logics. Moreover, Ng's experience with the racial epithets hurled against her critique of *Shadow Warrior* illustrates the point quite convincingly.

Even as this investigation uncovers the disquieting fact that Scott Miller's *Shadow Warrior* is the progenitor of "equally crude imitations, like

Interplay's *Redneck Rampage*," Chansanchai finds critics who claim that "it is possible to play off popular stereotypes without being racist" ("Yellow Perils" 25). Ostensibly, this sentiment suggests a countervailing perspective to the foregoing. However, when revered game programmer John Romero's views are expressed, they seem to confirm rather than contest the Orientalizing circuit of meaning outlined above. Chansanchai writes:

> John Romero, the lead programmer for the legendary shooter games *DOOM* and *QUAKE*, is about to come out with *Daikatana*, a game set in Japan, circa 2455 AD. In this predominantly Japanese game, one of the characters is a well-muscled African American, Superfly Johnson. Romero says he wanted a "large, menacing character" who wasn't "snow white." "I won't be sitting down doing hardcore research on Asian or African culture," he says, "but I will avoid doing characterizations that demean the character's culture. You won't hear Superfly say, 'That's a bad mofo!' Likewise, you won't hear Mikiko say, 'Me love you long time!'" (25)

Positioned alongside Miller's cultural chauvinism, it would be easy to applaud Romero's seeming circumspection. Upon closer inspection, however, Romero's alternative rings an insidious alarm on another register. It is not enough to eschew racist linguistic denotations when, for example, damaging stereotypical connotations are smuggled in through "large, menacing" characterizations of blackness already sedimented with society's reified imagery of the criminalized black, male brute, to say nothing of the game character's blaxploitation moniker "Superfly" (figure 4.1). Given the potent racist significations at work in these Orientalist and Blaxploitation allusions, Romero's claim is hollow indeed. After all, as Marsha Kinder warns in *Playing with Power*, the danger in gaming's "cultural reinscriptions" is that, "[w]ithin particular social and economic contexts, the recognition of specific allusions makes certain intertextual relations payoff—especially at the point of purchase" (45). The payoff in these games' intertextual relations is their reinforcement of dominant culture's racist hegemony, and their redeployment and reification of specious racial difference for new generations and their new media culture industries. In his study of Asian American representations in American televisual discourses, Darrell Hamamoto stresses the fact that we must recognize how race is a fundamental organizing principle of America's pluralist society and that we cannot afford to ignore the real consequences of this reality for nonwhite Americans (x). We know that popular culture texts

FIGURE 4.1. Screen grab, *Daikatana* game. Daikatana ©
Ion Storm. Image features "large menacing character,"
Superfly Johnson (center foreground), arguably illustrative of what Adam Clayton Powell III calls "high-tech
black face." Also Marketing and packaging race: Cover
photos including: *Prima's Official Strategy Guide* for Midway's game sequel *Ready to Rumble: Round 2* and the
game *Tekken Tag Tournament* © Midway Games.

are effective conduits for the transmission, if not preferred reception, of
privileged sociocultural-political messages and ideas. However, we should
not presume some a priori value neutrality when narratives find novel
expressive appratuses, such as with computer games.

   Returning to the Children Now study, "Children and the Media: Fair
Play? Violence, Gender and Race in Video Games," we take up several antinomies and contradictions that complicate our investigation. Of concern here
is the best way to characterize the changing representational practices of

crafting human characters in gaming culture. At stake is the way in which video and computer games reinscribe, refuse, or alter racist stereotypes and iconographies from traditional media texts in Western society. In terms of gaming's reification of racist discourses, we are confronted with the way gaming's interactive function might be thought to intensify attitudes about racial difference and thereby represent an even more insidious strategy of interpellating gamers as racial subjects, as the Children Now study suggests. However, given cultural studies' paradigmatic revisions of reception and spectatorship theories, we also must consider gaming culture's potential to subvert and refuse racist stereotypes in character designs and functions that are more aligned with the new realities of our unpredictable and shifting multicultural identity politics and cultural practices.

If the Children Now "Fair Play" study is vulnerable to charges of reasserting debatable media-effects determinism and empiricism's "scientific evidence,"[13] it is also valuable for its sustained focus on gaming culture's capacity to habituate gamers (designers and players) to sexist and racist narrative structures. And although our project aims to balance the tensions existing between media influence and media reflection approaches, it is the case that these theoretical and methodological assumptions often are not equal in their explanatory potential regarding how games are actually consumed. The reality is that capitalist market strategies and imperatives oblige us not to underestimate the seductiveness of racist narrative appeals for mass audiences even as we celebrate ideals of negotiated readings, interpretive communities, and fandom's poaching practices. Accepting Hall's notion of an open system of signification does not foreclose our understanding that race is the point of reference against which resistance and alternative readings proceed. Again, it is instructive to recall that white patriarchal structures of media production and dissemination control the flow of ideas in both new and traditional media images and representations that do not accurately reflect contemporary society's complex demographics and cultural heterogeneity.

Not surprisingly, as the Children Now study asserts, "Children of all races want to see themselves represented in the media." In their study's extension of traditional media analyses to include video games, Children Now found significant problems in gaming's address to racial diversity, especially in terms of the raw numbers:

> More than half (56%) of all human characters in the study were white. African Americans comprised the second largest group, representing about

one fifth of all characters (22%). While Asian/Pacific Islanders accounted for 9% of all characters, Latinos comprised 2% of the population. Native Americans and multi-racial characters each accounted for .2% of the characters. White female characters outnumbered female characters of every other racial group. Over half of all female characters were white (61%), followed by Asian/Pacific Islanders at just over one tenth of the total female population (11%). African American and Native American female character portrayals trailed behind at 4% and 1% respectively. Latina characters were non-existent. . . . Games especially created for young children featured only white characters.[14]

Not only do these demographics foreground the lack of representational parity in gaming culture, but the study's content analysis raises even more troubling ideological concerns. For example, in their subsection "Stereotypical Roles," Children Now found that at 87 percent "nearly every video game *hero* was white [emphasis added]."[15] Among their findings also was the troubling revelation that gaming culture's new multiracial, multiculturalist ethos amounted to familiar characterizations of Latinos, Asian/Pacific Islanders, and African Americans as sports figures, antagonists, and bystanders. Most striking, and generative of a separate online response, was the fact that African American women "at 86%, were far more likely than any other group to be victims of violence. Their victimization" was almost twice that of white females (45 percent) and nearly four times the rate of Asian/Pacific Islander females (23 percent).

By calling attention to gaming culture's encryptions of a seeming logic of black female victimization and punishment, the Children Now study enables us to see gaming culture's apparent redeployment of dominant culture's distillation of racial blackness down to criminality, violence, and victimhood.[16] Clearly, encryption message senders presume decryption message receivers, otherwise the attempted communication exchange process is futile, and more important, cost-ineffective. And given the importance of the profit motive in the gaming industry, we likewise can presume a correlative if not a cause-effect dynamic at work here. Even taking into account poststructuralist deconstructions of the signifier-signified meaning loop, cinema studies theories of excess that destabilizes certitude in image construction, and cultural studies' advancement of resistant spectatorship and reception, these recognitions of the polysemous nature of signs and signification do little to dislodge the fact that privileged cultural ideologies are the "transcendent signifiers" or points of reference from which they all depart. It is in such racialized and Orientalizing discourses that Roland Barthes's assertion that there is no "zero degree of meaning" gains some material force. As Barthes cogently puts it, "discourse scrupulously keeps within a circle of solidarities . . . in which 'everything holds together'" (156), for gaming's readerly participants. In other words, we are confronted with the resilience and tenacity of ideology and its stranglehold on a particular circuit of cultural meaning. Terry Eagleton further clarifies the solidarities of how ideology holds together: "It is one of the functions of ideology to 'naturalize' social reality, to make it seem as innocent and unchangeable as Nature itself. Ideology seeks to convert culture into Nature, and the 'natural' sign is one of its weapons" (117). These analyses remind us that resistance to what Wolfgang Iser calls an "ideal meaning" and its corollary the "ideal reader" are predicated upon, in this case, an understanding of encrypted (or encoded) meanings that represent desirable gaming heroes naturally as predominately white and victims and antagonists naturally as nonwhite others.

What, then, are the means by which we can explore effectively this racialized meaning-encryption-decryption feedback loop in popular and alternative video games? To the extent that video games' readerly and writerly narrative structures draw upon and are imbricated in such traditional meaning-making media as literature and other print sources, theater, film, and television, influential and emerging work on race in literary and popular culture criticism, and critical race theories represent especially productive epistemological lenses for viewing the racial discourse in gaming's parallel and support industries, computer magazines and specific game tie-ins, the strategy guides.

"READING RACE" IN VIDEO GAME USER
MANUALS AND STRATEGY GUIDE TEXTS

Because video game magazines and strategy guides increasingly constitute a significant element of gaming culture's specific narrative dispositions and logics of mastery, how they engage the racial problematic becomes a key concern in this study. Any excursion into computer superstores, or perusal of retail store magazine isles and magazine stands conveys well the sophisticated nature of these specialized texts' visual appeal. To compete in an oversaturated marketplace, gaming magazines, like the others, attract their readers with splashy and visually sumptuous cover art, usually featuring recognizable game characters in striking and vibrant photo-realistic renderings. Other visceral lures in cover art feature celebrity images and interviews; film or TV show tie-ins to games; samples of "free games"; scantily clad, buxom young women; and most important, text promising "cheat" keys to mastering game play such as "the latest tricks, tips, and game shark codes"[17] or "how to unlock each character."[18]

Although the gaming magazine and strategy guides' cover art warrant detailed analyses of their own, we are most concerned with the textual discourses and meaning assumptions between the covers. To investigate the racial discourse of these specialized texts, I have selected as exemplars *Next Generation* (October 1996), *Computer Player* (October 1996), *Playstation* Magazine (October 1999), *Incite* (2000, both video and PC gaming editions), and *Prima's Official Strategy Guide* (2000, both their *Ready 2 Rumble Boxing: Round Two* and *Tekken Tag Tournament* editions).

That there are certain generic, ideological, and representational coherences unifying these different texts is granted and thus not at issue. However, it is the photographic confirmation of an unbearable whiteness of being underpinning the editorial hierarchies and advertising copy of these magazines that suggested this particular line of inquiry. For instance, the investigative journalism discussed above alerted us to the dominance of white males in video game design and production; but it was these magazines' own practices of including photos or drawings of their editorial teams, ad copy featuring young white males as ideal consumers, and the strategy guides' rhetorical privileging of white game characters that struck me. And although *Incite's* PC gaming magazine features photos of its lone black and two Asian males and one white woman, among its nine-member editorial team, I would argue that this racial inclusiveness, though important, does little to balance the magazine's overriding narrative ecology of whiteness. Another ideological touchstone informing our concern with the intersections of race, representation, and gaming interactivity is the matter of new media commercialization. Along this critical axis, the editors of one *Next Generation* (*NG*) article sum up the limitations of the gaming industry's ability to break out of dominant culture's discursive formations because of their commercial imperatives. In its special feature article "Money Makes the Games Go Round," the *NG* editors admit:

> From Silicon Graphics to 3DO, the world of gaming comes with strings attached, held in the hands of a coterie of venture capitalists. . . . You might

think that the game business is driven by creativity, which it is to a greater degree, but the barriers to entry get higher every day. . . . The costs of distribution, marketing, and of course, development for games are reaching Hollywood proportions. . . . You end up paying the stores all kinds of marketing money to get them to put your product on the shelf. On top of all this, you have to make sure that people know your software is out there. Now, what developer can afford to do all that? (59–63)

The answer, of course, is that gaming magazines are tapped to share the financial burden of marketing games to this very lucrative target market. Unquestionably, then, our analysis must encompass this commodification of gaming narrativity and iconographical representations, which we know from other media texts are difficult to disaggregate from dominant cultures' institutional racism or what Aldon Lynn Nielsen discusses as the "frozen metaphors within American speech" (3). As we move on to specific instances of gaming magazines' racial discourse, Nielsen's groundbreaking book on whiteness, *Reading Race: White American Poets and Racial Discourse in the Twentieth Century*, helps us better read the linguistic markers and structures of meaning at work in gaming's magazines and "strategy guides."

Since Nielsen's *Reading Race* concerns racial significations in poetry, his observations are most fitting to our attempt at nuanced readings of gaming culture's own generic narrative shorthand and specific language condensations. In his analysis of how poetic language often constructs representational blackness within a "white discourse as a set of self-confirming propositions," we find a useful approach for avoiding essentializing positions. As Nielsen correctly points out:

> Through the power of white hegemony, the signifiers of that system have been placed into circulation within society such that they are distributed fairly evenly across the population. It is thus not necessary that the full discourse appear each time that its operations are to be manifested. It is required, as [Hans Robert] Jauss has pointed out, only that one element of the system be presented. . . . Only one small portion of the imaging system, only a suggestion of blackness need appear for the entire structure to be articulated. (6)

If we have learned anything from semiotics, structuralism, and poststructuralism's influential critical demystifications of linguistic and imagistic signifying functions, as Nielsen illustrates, it is that cultural inscriptions acquire meaning only as part of intact language systems that more or less rely on readers' varying fluency in various media literacies. To reiterate a previous point, this presumptive media literacy thesis does not foreclose what cultural studies' proponents advocate as readers' negotiated and oppositional reading practices against such ideal meaning—reception structures. So, despite the fact that gamers might read against, say *Prima's Official Strategy Guide*'s penchant for positioning *Ready 2 Rumble: Round 2*'s white characters as first-person avatars, against the second and third-person address for players opting for the game's nonwhite characters, Nielsen 's analysis reminds us not to ignore the political economy served by the games and game magazine editors' abilities to draw upon only a small portion of racial difference signifiers to shore up a strategic privileging of white characters in the pursuit of maximizing game points.

Let's now shift our focus to some rhetorical contours of these magazines' and strategy guides' racial discourses on specific video game titles. Of particular concern are *Prima's Official Guide*(s) to Midway's *Ready 2 Rumble: Boxing Round 2* (2000) and Nameco's *Tekken Tag Tournament* (1996), *Computer Player*'s "Strategy Guide to Interplay's *Conquest of the New World*" (1995), and Mindscape's user manual for *Imperialism: The Fine Art of Conquering the World* (1997). (Of interest as well, but not discussed here, is *Incite*'s PC gaming review of Eider's *Urban Chaos* [1999], a computer game produced in England.)[19] Additionally, we will look at the deployment of racial signifiers in the news and advertisement features that appear throughout the entirety of the gaming magazines and strategy guides under analysis here. We have already referenced gaming culture's debt to or extrapolations from traditional media's narrative cues and economies of representation. As we begin our critique of Prima's and *Computer Player*'s strategy guides' rhetorics of race, we are confronted with the ongoing tensions that complicate any attempt to balance simultaneously issues that transverse both ideological and formal critiques of traditional and new media texts. In many ways, some Russian formalist criticism further clarifies the stakes involved in our deliberations. For example, Nielsen, like Victor Shklovsky, speaks to the imaging functions of poetic language, with Shklovsky focusing specifically on poetic formalism's ability to disrupt the notion that "art is thinking in images," especially when that "thinking" relegates images of the unknown to "terms of the known" (4). It is this problematic that seems to trouble video games' emergent formalist aesthetics at its point of contact with the discourse of race. *Computer Player* magazine's elaborate strategy guide for the CD-ROM computer game *Conquest of the New World* (*Conquest*) is an amazing case in point with its striking assemblage of instructional textuality, old world cartographic and maritime iconographies and drawings, and new media screen shots of pixelated digital images from the game itself. This old media, new media reflexivity, rather than constituting what Wheeler Winston Dixon describes in another context as a "contemporary transgressive hypertext" (79), instead relegates the new medium's inchoate imagistic properties to terms of the known and discredited language forms of colonial racism.

Before we delve into the specific colonialist rhetorics of *Conquest* and another game of empire simulation, Mindscape's *Imperialism: The Fine Art of Conquering the World*, it is useful to outline a few computer/video game genres that delimit somewhat such games' generic metalinguistic or overarching discursive frameworks and terms of reference. Even making allowances for the particularities of computer and video game genres over, say, those of literature, film, and television, it is important to bear in mind David Crowley and Paul Heyer's statement: "Despite the dramatic implications of the computer we must not forget that some of its aspects have been formed from traditional ways of structuring information found in previous media. The computer program is a case in point" (308).

And the gaming industry, with its myriad adaptations of and tie-ins with popular literature, films, and television shows (*Star Trek*, *Star Wars*, *Harry Potter*, etc.) benefits significantly from its generic ties to these traditional media's "standardized classification systems of knowledge" (Crowley and Heyer 308). It remains for us, however, to point up their new media perpetuations, permutations, or disruptions of dominant ideological assumptions where they surface.

International Hobo (*ihobo*), an online site that provides a useful "Guide to Computer Game Genres,"[20] specifies several of the most recognizable categories of games. It lists and summarizes these categories as Shooter, Bat and Ball, Racer, Collector, Video Pinball, Puzzle, Strategy, Adventure, Video Boardgame, Fighting, Sim, Computer RPG (CRPG) or Computer Role Playing Games, Platform, Sports, Arcade Adventure, and Rhythm-Dance. It also discusses what it terms "pseudogenres" and "subgenres." *Conquest* and *Imperialism*, the games presently at issue, most accurately fit *ihobo*'s description of the sims genre's preoccupations as simulating the conditions of real or imagined environments; structuring game play primarily around "resource management;" and challenging players to master and control "multiple entities or resources, rather than a single character."

Maximizing gamers' abilities to achieve these goals is precisely what Zack Meston, the strategy guru of *Conquest*, seeks to accomplish in his promise to unlock the game's coveted conceptual keys or rules of engagement and strategic parameters in his article's opening address to the magazine's apparent ideal gamers. And, as the guides' character descriptions, skills, functions, motivations, and their all important races and ethnicities will reveal, white masculinity remains gaming's predominant ego ideal or avatar of the realm. This is despite the high-profile nature of its emergent nonwhite male character stars (i.e., Afro Thunder et al.) and capitalizing on girl-inflected games such as *Where in the World Is Carmen Sandiego*, and *Lara Croft, Tomb Raider*, wherein white femininity comes in as a strong second, but we get ahead of ourselves.

Our present focus on these examples of the sims genre and digital mythologies of neo-empire concerns gaming's narratological and ideological recrudescence of Western colonialism and imperialism's white masculinist hegemony. Both Meston's 1996 strategy guide to *Conquest* and *Imperialism*'s user's manual betray a worrisome tendency in gaming culture to reinstate and reinscribe such anachronistic prerogatives, even in the form of play. Consider how Meston's "strategy" from the start structured absences and latent presences that reinforce Eurocentric racial differences. To begin, Meston writes:

> Because of *Conquest* of the New World's spiffy, *open-ended structure*, I haven't given you a walkthrough, but 2,000 words of advice on the game's most crucial aspects: how to allocate your special abilities, how to win the very tricky combat sequences, and how to win the game in the one-player and multiplayer modes. (92; emphasis added)

If *Conquest*'s gameplay is defined by a spiffy, open-ended structure (whatever that means), Meston's advice and descriptions are not. They are carefully enclosed within a Eurocentric colonialist literary tradition wherein the racial other is constructed in binary opposition to the imperial (read white) self. As Abdul R. JanMohamed would put it, "in the 'imaginary' colonialist realm, to say 'native' is automatically to say 'evil'" (19). If the game strategists do not explicitly posit an "evil" racial other, they certainly do construct the game's native other as an antagonist in the diegesis, which Meston's taxonomy strongly makes clear. Within his four-part categorization defined as: (1) Special Abilities, (2) Combat, (3) One-Player Tactics, and (4) Multiplayer Tactics, Meston's rhetoric sets up a fetishistic scheme consisting of what JanMohamed describes in another context as a "nondialectical, fixed opposition between the self and the native," or more accurately in Meston's terms, the "High Native."

It is interesting that Meston's ideal reader/gamer address is bifurcated according to an "identification and difference" meaning split whereby imperial agents (protagonist-Self) are encrypted with special abilities allowing game-point advantages not equally available to the High Native (antagonist-Other). Through a selective rhetorical use of the second-person narrative address, Meston alerts readers that maximizing *Conquest*'s game play is bound up with gamers' necessary identification with the various imperial agents to defeat and conquer the High Native and its material resources. Some of Meston's strategic recommendations and descriptions not only skew the tactical point advantages but the rhetorical address to gamers as well. Meston begins his strategy recommendations and hints for "Victory Points" with a "Special Abilities" category, including the eight central characters and two important maritime skills, which I have diagrammed below. In Meston's articulation *Conquest*'s victory point advantages do not accrue evenly for game play between protagonists and antagonists, which obviously is typical of games' binary logics of pitting characters in opposition. However, what is particularly remarkable here is not so much Meston's denotation of eight separate character types for agent avatars aligned with the game's goals of empire but his connotation of the game's antagonists as two essential types, "High Natives" and other "tribes." More important is Meston's positioning of the High Native in the One-Player Tactics category that is subdivided into a functional triptych of strategies; namely, "Strategy 1—Peace," "Strategy 2—War," and "Strategy 3—High Native."[27] In this way, Meston's strategy guide arguably redeploys colonialist discourses' imperative of dehumanizing the native Other in comparison to the imperial Self. In Meston's schematic, the High Native is constructed as a condition rather than as a human agent acting upon a condition or strategic situation. To be sure, Meston's strategy guide does give the High Native certain game play advantages. Nonetheless, those advantages are thematically and ideologically coded to provide rhetorical cover, or an acceptable alibi, for the game's imperialist agenda of mastery and tropes of conquest and victory. Not surprisingly, mastery is measured by the game's accumulation of weighted "Victory Points." For example,

Special Abilities	Victory Point Advantages	
	Imperial Agents	High Native Agent
1) Admiral	X	X
2) Cartographer	O	O
3) Colonialist	X	
4) Conqueror	X	X
5) Craftsman	X	
6) Discoverer	X	
7) Miser	X	X
8) Missionary	X–	
9) Navigator	X	X
10) Pacifist	X–	X+

High Native and Imperial Agents do not possess equal victory point opportunities.

in Meston's Combat category, he sets the terms of weighted victory points for Imperial Agents and High Natives alike. As a category description, and its explanatory logic, it bears quoting in its entirety:

> **COMBAT:** Always start by using experience points to increase *your* leaders' number of attacks to at least five: anything less would be *uncivilized* (and fatal in battle). Worry about a movement bonus for slow (and low-level) leaders; don't bother with charisma. A Level 1 leader should have six or seven units and four attacks; a Level 2 leader should have eight or nine units and five attacks; and so on. *For the High Natives* [emphasis added], a Level 1 leader should have 10 units and six attacks; a Level 2 leader should have 12 units and eight attacks (along with two charisma points to get help from other tribes). (93)

Now at first glance the combat category appears to privilege the High Natives, with its level 1 leader enjoying a specified three to four units and two attacks advantage spread. However, upon closer inspection we realize that game players (as ideal textual readers), are positioned discursively, via Meston's second-person address, as the game's narratological underdogs against the High Natives as superior combat adversaries. My added italics are meant to highlight *Conquest* gamers' presumptive identification with Meston's second-person designation of "your leaders" as themselves, against his third-person designation of "the High Natives" as the racial other in this game's combat mode. That Meston's "You" versus "Them" binary address to ideal players is a standard functional motif of game magazines and strategy guides is understood. The problem is that such standardization practices increasingly reify or naturalize nonwhite characters as objectified third-person others whose alterity is so irremediably different that ideal players would have little to no incentive to adopt[21] them as avatars or skins. Indeed, the welcome diversification of game characters is significantly delegitimated when minority characters function primarily as objects of oppression, derision, or narrative obstacles to be overcome or mastered. For they are never heroes even in their own lands.

If Meston's "tips" hint at *Conquest's* differentially structured game play based on racialized characters, then programming designers of *Imperialism: The Fine Art of Conquering the World* convey explicitly gaming's colonialist remythologizing aspects along the lines of what Abdul R. Jan-Mohamed and others refer to as "The Economy of Manichean Allegory." Like *Conquest*, *Imperialism* is a neocolonialist strategy-sim game that bears out the racist logic of colonialist power relations that postcolonial theorist JanMohamed describes.

> The colonialist's military superiority ensures a complete projection of his self on the Other: exercising his assumed superiority, he destroys without any significant qualms about the effectiveness of indigenous economic, social, political, legal moral systems and imposes his own versions of these structures on the Other. (20)

In the manual's section called "*Imperialism* Basics," the "Countries in Imperialism" articulate not only how certain racialized characters are programmed at a strategic disadvantage but also how the game structures in biased advantages. As if a complete confirmation of JanMohamed's charge, the manual states:

> In *Imperialism* there are two types of countries. The first type, Great Powers, are actors in the game, each ruled by a human or by a wily computer

foe. The second type, *Minor Nations, serve as regions for exploitation and battle by the Great Powers.* A Minor Nation in *Imperialism cannot* develop into a Great Power, *nor can it win the game.* . . . In *Imperialism,* colonization refers to a "*peaceful*" takeover. (Emphasis added) (13)

It is telling enough that *Imperialism* programs a nineteenth-century colonialist military ethos into contemporary game play, as it states, "modeled on the real world of the nineteenth century" (1) yet recasting colonialism as "peaceful." But coupled with the game's striking cover art displaying an illuminated white-skin hand grasping a globe, such representational economies advance a worrisome yet unrepentant ideology of neocolonialist Eurocentrism that posits imperialism as spreading the necessary light of Western civilization. And given this game's obvious Eurocentrism, it might be reasonable to presume its relative lack of appeal for nonwhite gamers interested in mastering strategy-sim games. However, one gamer informed me that this genre does not necessarily foreclose participation and mastery from those gamers not necessarily considered the industry's ideal or targeted end user.

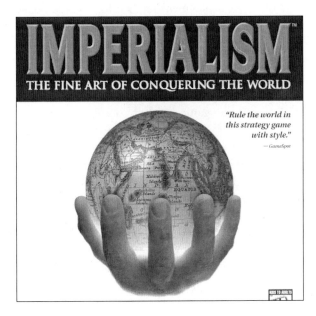

FIGURE 4.2. *Imperialism's* game box cover design, © Strategic Simulations, Inc., depicts a white male hand grasping the globe.

CIVILIZE THIS! OR IN GEEK-SPEAK: RTFM!

Despite game designs' restraint on users according to what Jean Francois Lyotard suggests is the tyranny of the computer bit, the basic unit of information regulated and circumscribed by the programmer (34), one Afro-geek lets us in on some subversive tactics and strategies to avoid such gaming circumscription and frustration. This geek, University of California, Santa Cruz, doctoral candidate Rebecca Hall, informed me that the first rule of geekness is to RTFM (read the fucking manual), and for games it is essential for circumventing the game's prescriptions, understanding its Byzantine rules, and mastering the gameplay of any genre. Hall finds it important to read closely and thoroughly any game's manual before attempting to play because she hates having an information deficit when her goal is to overcome some games' discursive tyranny. Hall became a video game fan in the mid-1980s. A favorite game was Avalon Hill's *Civilization*, a precursor to such strategy sims as *Imperalism*, for example. What is interesting about Hall's approach to *Civilization* and what makes it pertinent to our study is her example of how people actually play these games. In addition, her deployment of a stealth essentialism strategy that allows her to win games by playing against the norm speaks volumes about gamers' willingness to refuse and reject games' privileged narratives while still finding hours of challenging and pleasurable play. Hall's own description of her gameplay makes the point convincingly. It is important however to note that *Civilization* is not a war game (war games do not generally appeal to female gamers), but according to one website, FunagainGames, "The object of the game is to gain a level of overall advancement to which cultural, economic, and political factors are important. The winner is the player who maintains the best balance between activities of nomads, farmers, citizens, merchants and adventurers."[22]

Hall's game play is a novel enactment of this ideal scenario. And how she describes her stealth essentialism approach is revealing. The game begins with the dawning of civilizations somewhere between 4000–8000 to 250 BC. And what she appreciates most about the game is that game players set the condition for winning, whether it is through world conquest, being the first to launch a successful spaceship from earth, spiritual transcendence, or heading a world-class government. Where some of her acquaintances who play the game opt for traditional European civilizations as game avatars, she also notes that the game presents other options as well.[23] As she puts it:

There are ten-fifteen different peoples that you can pick from, and they have different characteristics, like the Zulu, who are militaristic and expansionistic. This means you go into the game with certain technologies and certain advantages, say military. And in this way it is coded. The Egyptians are spiritual and commercial, the Americans (I don't know why there are Americans and Abe Lincoln in 4000 BC right?). . . . And there's the Sioux and the Chinese. . . . They all have strengths and weaknesses, and anyone of them can win. (Hall interview)

As for Hall, it is important to play and win as an African civilization, which the game essentializes as Chaka Zulu (although sometimes she renames the character after an actually existing seventeenth-century African queen of Angola, named Nzenga). Hall continues:

When I play the Zulu . . . [with rules establishing that] you know how to build stone walls and you have the wheel. And then you've got to dedicate certain of your resources to research. Over time you learn more and more technology. If you pick a culture that is scientific you start out ahead of the game. But the Zulu are not scientific. So what I do (and this is where the resistance part comes in) is, I take the military advantage that is there, but then I focus more of the resources on the scientific. By the time I get to 1000 BC they are both the strongest militarily and the strongest scientifically, which positions them in a way that is stronger than the other groups. . . . There is also a telos. . . . After you've done enough research you go into different ages, like the Barbarian Age, the Premodern, the Enlightenment, whatever. And by the time you get to the 1800s, and the way I play it, the Zulus have the railroad by 1000 AD. You see Chaka in a suit, with the bone piercing in the ear—you know. So, its got the Western telos—right, but, it's a little bit subversive, and it is coded . . . I wonder how much I am deluding myself, but this game is different. (Hall interview)

Hall is not alone in her appreciation of *Civilization*'s various interactive modes wherein militarism is merely one of its many strategic foci. Other gamers, some hailing from Germany, England, and so on, who reviewed the game *Civilization* for the website FunagainGames, also find its non-wargame emphasis particularly appealing. As Lane Taylor from London writes, "*Civilization* is NOT a war game . . . or is it? The great thing about this game is that it can be different things to different people. If you want to play it as a war game, you can; if you want to play as a trading game, you can; if you want to play as a building game, you can" (Taylor). For Hall, it was finally a chance to "pick the Zulu and kick everybodies' asses" both militarily and scientifically in a popular video game not designed for that purpose. And no matter how opaque, incomplete, and generally incompetent the technical writing of the manuals, Hall's example reminds us of the necessity to RTFM before one can effectively resist or transgress programmers' tyranny of the bit!

PLAYING THE "SKIN" GAME

Where the strategy-sims marginalize the other, both qualitatively and quantitatively, gaming's sports and fighting genres, by contrast, foreground the other in their interactive fictions. Still, first-person games such as Nameco's *Tekken Tag Tournament* and Midway's *Ready 2 Rumble: Round 2*, for example, are in little danger of contributing to what Uma Narayan and Sandra Harding call "decentering the center." It is difficult to discern any progress between sports and fighting games' overrepresentation of racial minorities and strategy-sims' underrepresentation of these groups when white male characters (especially Americans) are continually privileged. For example, like real life (RL) sports, all of the characters in *Ready 2 Rumble Boxing: Round 2* (*R2R-2*) bear colorful names and nicknames that enliven and amplify their stereotypical "personalities" and delimited skills. The problem is that such charged enunciations appearing in strategy guides and manuals either fire or dull users' imaginations as they "select" these highly racialized game "skins." Writing for *Prima's Official Strategy Guide to* R2R-2, Keith Kolmos and his team reinforce heroic and sympathetic stereotypes of white game characters, while redeploying ridiculous and pernicious ones for black and other others.

Afro Thunder and his cousin G. C. Thunder as "arch rivals" not only evoke the discourse of black-on-black violence, but since the former "went Hollywood for a while" (Kolmos 22) and the latter uses "boxing as a vehicle for opening a chain of hair facilities" (62), and since each is "more of a performer than a boxer," these black skins are silly, malevolent, and trivialized dissimulations of black boxers' RL dominance of the sport. Furthermore, black skin Butcher Brown's King Kong look, "much-needed mental stability," and "banned . . . deadly knock-out punch" complete the familiar rhetoric of black male criminality and brawn over brains image.

FIGURE 4.3. Images of several of Midway games characters. Several of *Ready 2 Rumble: Round 2*'s stereotypically racialized game characters, © Midway Games.

(Interestingly, these characters' "special moves" and "combo moves" were programmed with too many skill deficits to be purely coincidental or insignificant.) Finally, *Incite*'s ad for *3DO*'s *Might and Magic: Day of the Destroyer* mytho-adventure game really betrays gaming's penchant for racist depictions of blackness. The ad consists of three characters in medieval dress and milieu. In the foreground is a diabolical-looking black man-beast figure together with a white, scantily clad, blond Amazon and her white knight dressed in armor from head to toe. Hovering above them is a requisite oversized dragon, in all its fantastic ferocity. The ad copy reads, "9 New Characters classes and races, 26 new skills, spells, and special abilities. New lands of heroic fantasy and adventure. Good. Evil. The

FIGURE 4.4. Image of characters from the game Might and Magic. The Medieval Squad? ©*Incite* magazine's retro-integrationist ad, with black man-beast hybrid avatar (left) together with two idealized Aryan "skins." Prefigures the mythological World of Warcraft (WoR) online gaming imaginary.

choice is yours." Let us reconsider this and the other games' representational economies in terms of Abdul R. JanMohamad's Manichean allegory. For him

> the imperialist is not fixated on specific images or stereotypes of the Other but rather on the affective benefits proffered by the manichean allegory, which generates the various stereotypes. . . . The fetishizing strategy and the allegorical mechanism not only permit a rapid exchange of denigrating images which can be used to maintain a sense of moral difference; they also allow the writer to transform social and historical dissimilarities into uni-

versal, metaphysical differences. . . . African natives can be collapsed into African Animals and mystified still further as some magical essence of the continent. (21–22)

Again, high-tech blackface and black "skins" are not the only representational casualties of the "joystick nation," to borrow J. C. Herz's terminology. As surprised as I was to discover Maori, Brazilian, Hawaiian, Taiwanese, Mexican, and Thailand "skins" also among Midway's *R2R-2* pugilistic ensemble, I was less surprised by the rhetoric and rendering that constructed them. Like the black American "skins," these other racialized others also were marked by such rhetorical differences as "Beast from the East," "Maori fighting ways are savage," "400–pounder . . . short on ring experience but long in the tooth," "lacking confidence," and so on. These are not exactly the skill levels that lure most users. These avatars are even more undesirable when white, ethnic "skins" representing Italy, Croatia, England, Canada, and America are described sympathetically, powerfully, and affirmatively, for example, "high tolerance for pain," "dedicated to boxing," "story is enough to bring a tear to your eye," "out to prove to the world that he'll be able to beat the best with just one hand," "although he's laid back, Brock gets pretty serious when he hits the canvas," "improved on his formerly rudimentary boxing skills, " "refined skills and superior knowledge of the sweet science" (Kolmos 34–73). With such visual and narrative inducements, and at costs ranging from five to more than fourteen dollars an issue, these texts and their alluring codifications of whiteness should not be underestimated. After all, stories of the comic book's strong influence on directors of films, music videos, and television shows are legion and legendary. To some extent, these guides seem more potent as imagistic ideals for the computer-literate net generation. And their discourses of racial difference can be subtle and disarming.

Tri Pham, Jeff Barton, and Michael Littlefield's *Tekken Tag* character rhetoric, while still privileging the white male characters, manages higher praise and aggrandizements for their other male counterparts than did *Ready 2 Rumble: Round 2.* For instance, the Japanese character Jin Kazama's attributes are outlined thus: "Power. Speed. Good looks. It's not hard to see why Jin Kazama is one of the most popular characters in *Tekken.*" But Jin's power is curtailed by "fewer moves than many of the other characters." Users are encouraged to "[m]aster the skills he does have, and you'll be tough to beat." Bryan Fury, *Tekken's* blond American kickboxer is the game's superman. "Unleash the Fury. Bryan Fury. This guy," the editors boast, "is a powerhouse. If you want a character with incredible power and the speed to use it, then *choose Bryan* [emphasis added]. . . . And with his long reach, your enemies will find it hard to hide from you." Even the black American avatar, Bruce Irvin, gets some props. They write, " Every fighting tournament needs a good boxer, and Bruce comes to this fight swinging. Power, speed, and a super juggling move make him a tough act to beat. He's got a lot of useful moves with plenty of variations. Mix and match his moves and go on the offensive to strike fear in your opponents" (31–65). It is noteworthy, however, that Bryan Fury is the only "skin" that readers are specifically recommended to select. This is particularly interesting in a first-person game of Asian martial arts, where the majority of skilled human characters are constructed as nationals of Korea, Japan, and China. In many ways the hidden assumptions of white supremacy, even in *Tekken Tag Tournament*, unproblematically suggest a superior interactive wish-fulfillment experience through white character ideals technologically enabled to out-master the mythic virtual masters from the East. *Tekken Tag Tournament* recodes the kung fu craze that swept through America in the late 1960s and early to mid-1970s and was captured in such television shows and films as *The Green Hornet, Kung Fu, Enter the Dragon*, and other Bruce Lee and Chuck Norris movies; it reinstalls the white male figure as the true master of these martial arts scenarios and functions to reinforce ideologies of white supremacy.

CONCLUSION: *ETHNIC CLEANSING*—THE GAME

> [Ethnic Cleansing is] the most politically incorrect video game made. Run through the ghetto blasting away various blacks and spics in an attempt to gain entrance to the subway system, where the Jews have hidden to avoid the carnage. Then, if YOU'RE lucky . . . you can blow away Jews as they scream "Oy Vey!," on your way to their command center. The Race war has begun. Your skin is your uniform in this battle for the survival of your kind.
>
> —*Ethnic Cleansing*[24]

In February 2002, analysts of the U.S. video game industry announced record-shattering retail sales of interactive game units in 2001 that topped out at $9.4 billion.²⁵ That same month, cybersleuth H. A. alerted our virtual community on the Afrofuturism listserv to the existence of the alarming, tour de force racist computer game *Ethnic Cleansing* by simply posting its URL, or web address, under the subject "*Ethnic Cleansing*: The Game!" Despite H. A.'s uncharacteristic lack of commentary in that initial post, the following few days were abuzz in thoughtfully passionate, detached, enraged, and engaged responses. For some, the question concerned whether or not black people should use the same "powerful open source game engine, Genesis 3D," used to create the racist game, to create games of retaliation or overdue reparations for centuries of oppression and legalized injustice against African Americans (Allen). Others, especially L.d.J, were unconvinced that the Internet could be "the great equalizer," given troubling developments in gaming culture as reported by the Anti-Defamation League (ADL). L.d.J. posted information from the ADL on hate groups' "manipulation of available technology to create violently racist and anti-Semitic versions of popular video games . . . with titles such as *Ethnic Cleansing* and *Shoot the Blacks*" (Johnson).

Clearly such use of the net for recruiting youths to the ideology of hate does not exactly embody the progressive revolutionary imperative of the temporary autonomous zone (TAZ) that Hakim Bey imagined when he spoke of data piracy and other forms of leeching off the net itself (*Temporary* 108) for "reality hacking" and "the free flow of ideas." But the fact remains that manipulated games began proliferating on the Internet to be "previewed, purchased or downloaded on the websites of the nation's most dangerous hate groups" including "neo-Nazis, white supremacist and Holocaust deniers" (Johnson). The ADL reports, "In 'Ethnic Cleansing,' the player kills Blacks and Hispanics (the game uses pejorative terms) before entering a subway. . . . [S]ound effects, described as 'Realistic Negro Sounds,' turn out to be 'monkey and ape sounds' that play when dark-skinned characters are killed in the game's first level" (Johnson). What struck me about this particular egregiousness was its eerie resonance with Lester A. Walton's 1909 essay, "The Degeneracy of the Moving Picture Theater," where Walton describes his encounter with the early cinema's profiteering on black pain and suffering. Walton writes incredulously that "several days ago, the writer was surprised to see a sign prominently displayed in front of the place bearing the following large print "JOHN SMITH OF PARIS, TEXAS, BURNED AT THE STAKE. HEAR HIS MOANS AND GROANS. PRICE ONE CENT!" (6). Most salient here is Walton's admonition that our failure to protest vigorously against such racist commodification of black victimhood would engender worse images in the future. Walton states: "If we do not start now to put an end to this insult to the race, expect to see more shocking pictures with the Negro as subject in the near future" (6). Certainly there has been a steady historical progression of pernicious representations of blackness in many film and television texts that bear out Walton's prescience. Unfortunately, video games such as *Ethnic Cleansing* only exacerbate the situation.

Exactly one month after H. A. posted *Ethnic Cleansing*'s URL to the Afrofuturism list, ABC's *World News Tonight* ran a segment on the game and its intergenerational group of hatemongers, revealing that the game's 20 January 2002 launch was planned to coincide with the nation's official Martin Luther King Jr. holiday.—I was watching and interrupted my chapter's conclusion on 10 July 2002, due to this serendipity. That evening, ABC's news show *Nightline* aired a program entitled "Just a Game: Playing *Grand Theft Auto 3*," (*GTA3*) which interrogates this game's excessive violence, incredible photorealism, amazing popularity, and staggering financial success. While I am interested in *Nightline*'s disclosure that *GTA3* has sold 3.5 million copies at fifty dollars each, and concerns about the game's "stunning realism" taking interactive gaming to a new level,"[26] I am more interested in how the discourse of race and gaming gets played out in *Nightline*'s latest moral panic and media rivalry episode, couched as news. *Nightline* points out the fact that the game's graphic violence has attracted both detractors and loyal consumers, that the U.S. Congress has denounced the game, and that *GTA3* has been outlawed in Australia, with other countries considering bans at that time. The program also highlights the debate about whether or not *GTA3*'s high-tech make-believe and ferocity might be considered cathartic, while others ask if *GTA3* and others of its ilk should be called games at all.

Obviously, this show has a general relevance for this chapter since it concerns video games and social values. However, certain aspects are especially pertinent as these issues intersect with race matters. First of all, *Nightline*'s in-studio panel of four, including host Ted Koppel, consists only of white males. And despite the show's packaged introductory piece featuring African American reporter Michele Martin, the all-white, male panel assembled to discuss the issue displays the still unbearable whiteness of being in mainstream media's future vision and current conceptualizations of new media technologies and gaming cultures' increasing cultural power and much-lamented societal influences. Second, I was struck by the fact that the only representations of "minority" (particularly black) characters in *Nightline*'s select video clips of *GTA3* were victims of the game's narrative violence meted out quite gratuitously by the game's white, male protagonist. At this point it is important to state that *Nightline*'s all-white and all-male panel is not the biggest problem here. The biggest problem is that *Nightline* anchor Ted Koppel and his fellow white, male guests—D.C. police officer Sergeant Gerald Neill, seventeen-year-old *GTA3* player Steve Crenshaw, and Cornel University instructor James Garbarino—find a way to evoke black criminality despite the obvious absence of blacks as gamers or participant agents in this story. Moreover, this panel constructs a narrative of normative suburban whiteness capable of neutralizing and policing video games' violent influences that, noticeably, hinges on conflating real life street-level violence in urban areas with the game's virtual urban violence.

Now, what angered me about this hyperbolic discussion of video game violence and the show in general was the fact that the show began with exculpatory rhetoric surrounding a white, seemingly middle- to upper-class female parent who purchased *GTA3* for her underaged, thirteen-year-old son and two of his same-aged friends to enjoy and master, despite the game's clearly labeled warning of unsuitability for children. *Nightline* continued in this vein by using seventeen-year-old Steve Crenshaw as a privileged *GTA3* native informant who could serve double duty. First, he signified an older, more age appropriate and mature white teenaged boy fan of *GTA3* (obviously one experienced with earlier iterations of the *Grand Theft Auto* game). Second, Crenshaw's apparent normalcy and reiteration of the thirteen year olds' statement that gamers understood the difference between real life and video game fantasy functioned to absolve the thirteen-year-old *GTA3* player, his irresponsible mother, and his two white friends of blame. And, as I have been arguing throughout this chapter, a significant transposition is effected around race, but in this instance *Nightline*'s Koppel, the white police officer, and the elite university instructor effectively displace *GTA3*'s social menace onto urban—read black—communities. Even though *Nightline*'s television viewers are shown powerful images of *GTA3*'s white, male protagonist's unprovoked shootings of police officers and prostitute characters (with graphic displays of blood spurting from their wounded digital bodies), and his hit-and-run vehicular massacres of black and other characters for extra game points, still Koppel, Sergeant Neill, and instructor Garbarino unproblematically inculpate blackness, or more accurately urban people, as the problem.

The consensus of the panelists is that *GTA3*'s narrative fantasy becomes a dangerous step toward reality for those who desire to act out the game's violent scenarios. *Nightline*'s experts do concede that most kids will not go out and kill. However, when Koppel asks Sergeant Neill to use his twenty-plus years of police experience to ascertain where *GTA3* might rank in comparison to "poverty, drugs, gang warfare," as a societal threat, he betrays a racist assumption about which groups are susceptible to gaming's putative corruptions, especially with such racially charged signifiers of urban decay and blight. Sergeant Neill's reponse is equally telling. He states: "This is a game. But it is a violent game. There is a thing called *urban terror*. There are some parts that are controlled by *armed youths who are urban terrorists*, and this game isn't a part of that for the average person. But for someone who lives in *that* neighborhood, *his reality is different from Steve's*" (Martin and Koppel; emphasis added). Again, the implicit racial opposition being constructed here cannot be denied. For young Steve Crenshaw not only functions in this rhetoric as the responsible, white face of *GTA3* fandom, but the sergeant is clearly positioning him as an average person in opposition to youthful urban terrorists that most *Nightline* viewers would presume to be poor black and other minority youths. Once again, the hegemony of white supremacy is interpolated here, and it only undermines sober and fair discussion about gaming culture and its uses and abuses. After all, the Colombine High School masacres were not perpetuated by criminal black youth.

Returning briefly to the Afrofuturism list's engagement with the racist video game *Ethnic Cleansing*, a few points should be made. Significantly, responses to the game were varied, cogent, passionate, thoughtful, and quite provocative. The discussion thread ranged from ideas about the creation of black-owned and operated video game businesses, including establishing manufacturing factories in Africa (Mr. B.); the development of black games and game consoles with the goal of replicating a movement much like "what the black comic book industry did in the early 90's" (C-Splash). Still others saw the issue in much broader global terms, and within a post–September 11 ideological context. For example, regarding historical racism in gaming, g-tech writes:

> In fact, if you really want to be technical about it games like this have existed for, oh . . . maybe 15 years or so since the first iteration of *DOOM* to be exact. Nothing new here. What has changed is the ability of propaganda pieces like this to garner attention, thus giving them a bit of legitimacy and free press. . . . In essence, we are doing the work for them. . . .

The gaming community isn't dumb, they aren't mindless drones who are being brainwashed or hypnotized. They are people like you, me, the guy across the street, etc. who are probably getting a bigger kick out of the competition of winning rather than the look of the toons (toons are the characters for you non-gamers). In fact, the subject of cheating is much more of a problem than racism. (g-tech)

For g-tech it is important not to buy into the alarmist hype surrounding *Ethnic Cleansing*, especially when the game is decontextualized and removed from larger geopolitical factors. G-tech continues:

> [I]n fact the most popular shooters are the patriotic ones. Take a look at the sales of *Soldier of Fortune, Rainbow Six, Counterstrike, Operation Flashpoint, Delta Force Land Warrior, Return to Castle Wolfenstein, Medal of Honor* and others if you want to see some really scary stuff. Teaching kids that it's OK for America to send covert operatives into foreign countries and assassinating or killing [leaders of] other cultures and getting points or rewards for it is probably the biggest problem we may face in the future. On their own the games are harmless, but coupled with a real war where you can mimic the actions of the real soldiers in a virtual environment, a President who supports these shadow wars and a patriotic state of mind in the country and you have a recipe for trouble. I can't begin to count how many "Get Bin Laden" scenarios are popping up all over the net.

Although I selected this particular post to highlight, some Afrofuturists participating in the *Ethnic Cleansing* discussion thread were not convinced by the arguments presented here and presented convincing counterarguments that I cannot elaborate in this space. However, one is particularly pertinent and makes a great concluding point because it addresses several issues at the heart of this essay. One of Mr. B's numerous responses to g-tech's commentary that is pertinent for us is his respectful yet counterresponse to g-tech's remark that "on their own the games are harmless." Mr. B. replies:

> I would never consider anything that structures the way people spend their time among a wide variety of options "harmless." They might not be causal or deterministic, they are definitely not neutral, and as a result, not harmless in my opinion. . . . Let's keep this discussion going. I don't think we're at odds here, but we do need to refine exactly what we are talking about."

We have been talking about the need to pay attention to how video and computer games, like other forms of popular entertainment, might be considered in relation to issues of identity politics, reproduction of racist ideologies, and hegemonies despite gaming's novel expressive hardware apparatuses. At issue here has been the concern over the politics of representation regarding race and the question about gaming culture's ability to replicate or challenge existing portrayals of specific groups in films, TV shows, and print media. We are talking about the ascendancy of a very powerful and technically evolving medium, and we want to be sure that race does not remain the structured absence or specious virtual presence in our societal concern about where the future of gaming is headed.

CHAPTER FIVE

·:·

The Revolution Will Be Digitized: Reimaging Africanity in Cyberspace

The degree to which consciousness will be digitized, corporatized, and consumerized in the future is already apparent in the Afrocybernetic videos of Puffy Combs, Missy Elliott, and Busta Rhymes, not to mention the Borg-like absorption of the Wu-Tang Clan by the American Mainstream.

—Greg Tate, "15 Arguments"

[C]yberspace offers "pure" discourse as a leveling playing field. But . . . do we, as authored subjectivities, bring our cultural baggage of marking to contaminate the playing field even before the games begin?

—Rajani Sudan, "Sexy Sims"

Charting any revolutionary movement can be confounded by the problem of situating and legitimating its origin narratives. Unfortunately, the present study is not spared this dread problematic. In fact, it appears particularly acute in the case of mapping a trajectory of African diasporic peoples' early involvement with cyberculture and digital information technologies. Nonetheless, what I have discovered through painstaking online searches of websites, home pages, listservs, and Internet databases is a wealth of information detailing black people's remarkable participation in the Internet revolution before and after its massification due to the 1993 advent of the World Wide Web's graphical user interface.[1] And despite mainstream media warnings early on about the notorious unreliability of "unfiltered" Internet content comprising "a data flow that bypasses institutions that have traditionally vetted the news—such as newspapers or scientific publications" (Thompson E1), I found the majority of my online case studies to be important and credible sources for alternative race and technology information.

At the same time, Tracy Thompson's 27 February 1996, *Los Angeles Times* article entitled "Net Fiction," which is a cautionary tale about the near impossibility of debunking inaccuracies "when urban legends hit the Internet," makes a good point. Moreover, Thompson's concern that "Netmyths are of great interest to sociologists and computer experts, who say they are creating new rules about distinguishing between truth and fiction"[2] because of their unfettered global information flows is well taken. Confounding my task even further is the difficulty presented by Internet hypertexts' production of the so-called readerless text. What this idea of the readerless text is getting at is the fact that mutable hypertexts, by their very editable, very random, and custom natures, ensure that critics can never read nor master the total text (Landow, "What's a Critic to Do?" 34), nor can the critic's ideal reader easily or assuredly access them. I want to add that the hyperephemerality of many of my online texts means that some have since disappeared from the net, thereby exacerbating the "readerless text" issue. My remedy from the beginning has been to download as many of the entire websites as possible for my own ongoing reference and future preservation, at least in print form. However, given the dearth of mainstream media interest in covering discomfiting race matters during the early stages of the Internet and the World Wide Web's growth, ethnographic information provided by black virtual communities homesteading in cyberspace necessarily becomes de facto origin narratives of black people's otherwise untouted entry into the digital revolution.

THE UNBEARABLE WHITENESS OF
CYBERSPACE AND THE DIGITAL DIVIDE

Since I began researching the African diasporic presence in cyberspace in late 1994, there has been a proliferation of scholarly and popular treatises on digital media and cyberspace's revolutionary impact on the brave new worlds of late twentieth- and early twenty-first-century societies. Many of these recent texts are marked by an ontological shift from a consensus delimiting the discussion in terms of theorizing and celebrating posthuman existentialisms and digital media formalisms, to engaging with the more vexing matters of race and ethnicity that persistently trouble our idealized "color-blind" new media technocracies.[3] In many ways, this contemporary work broaching some specificities of race in the evolving information economy supports my longstanding concern about and frustration with the unbearable whiteness of cyberculture during its earliest discursive formations.

What I have found is that despite the fruitful critical and theoretical advances that characterize the first wave of cyberspace studies,[4] an absence of focus on the complexities of race in the debates has, as Rajani Sudan warns, enabled "our cultural baggage of marking to contaminate the playing field even before the games" (71) began. For it is precisely the return of the repressed cultural baggage of racial marking in contemporary cyberspace discourse that concerns me. In recent years that marking has assumed the form of a potent trope of repressed racial difference in the information age, which we better recognize as the rhetoric of the "digital divide." Its cultural currency and global circulation inhere in its apparent distillation of intransigent racial stereotypes of certain groups in the West, especially that of black people as genetic intellectual inferiors. As I, mentioned in an earlier chapter, it matters little that specious sciences such as eugenics have been thoroughly debunked, widespread belief in the science of racial difference remains difficult to dislodge as best-selling books such as Charles Murray's and Richard Herrnstein's *The Bell Curve* attest.[5] In many ways, the well-meaning, popular rhetoric of the digital divide inadvertently reaffirms this dangerous but seductive logic. Moreover, I contend that its deployment in high-profile, high-stakes discussions of technology diffusion and state fiscal policies threatens to become a disabling self-fulfilling prophesy of endemic black technological lag. I hasten to add here that in challenging the digital divide's overdetermined signifying power to simultaneously benefit and thwart universal access initiatives, I am in no way denying the distressing fact of unequal technology distribution. My concern is that in the glare of the media spotlight on the digitally disadvantaged, we become blinded to the other fact of significant black technomastery and new media activism despite tremendous odds.

The point is that all too often an essentializing digital divide rhetoric has the effect of reifying dangerous misperceptions about the futility of investing scarce high-tech funding in minority communities, when presumptions are that precious resources might be better allocated elsewhere. This flawed logic of fiscal responsibility is purchased by our collective resignation to the idea that the so-called black permanent underclass naturally translates into the information economy's new class of "information have-nots." Where, after all, is mainstream media's countervailing concern with the fact of the "permanent overclass" and its evolutionary white, male privileged assumption to the top of the information haves heap? Most disturbing in the rhetoric of the digital divide is its overemphasis on the information have-nots, which, in turn, occludes such structural impediments to universal access as biased employment practices in the high-tech industry, deregulation policies that beget corporate megamedia mergers, communications industry consolidation, expensive computer equipment and software (although prices are finally becoming much more affordable), high-cost Internet access fees, difficult computing operations systems, and chronically underfunded public education in minority communities.

Notwithstanding this one-sided discourse, premised upon a putative intellectual lack among underserved groups, the rhetoric becomes untenable upon close inspection because as early as 1995 the U.S. Department of Commerce commissioned a study of disproportionate rates of information technology access and use among the nation's *disadvantaged.* In a federal report entitled "Falling through the Net: A Survey of the 'Have Nots' in Rural and Urban America," studies conducted on the basis of race, class, age, and educational backgrounds made it clear that despite their status at the bottom of the technology adoption curve, Native Americans, Hispanics, and blacks were

> the most enthusiastic users of on-line services that facilitate economic uplift and empowerment. Low-income, minority, young and less educated computer households in rural areas and central cities appear to be likely to engage actively in searching classified ads for employment, taking educational classes, and accessing government reports, on-line via modem [connectivity]. (Irving et al.)

Even as recently as 23 October 2000, the *Los Angeles Times* ran a news item stating "Blacks Find Internet More Useful: Study," which makes the point that "[a]lthough blacks still lag in access to the Internet, a study finds that those who are connected are more likely than whites to use it as an information tool." The article also reported that "blacks were more likely than whites to use the Internet to find information on religion, jobs and housing" ("Blacks Find"). Despite compelling evidence of minority groups' acquisition of high-tech skills and sophisticated computer use, the mainstream media persist in mystifying disproportionate technology access issues, preferring to characterize black computer users overwhelmingly as isolated anomalies and perplexed net novices undertaking a futile Sisyphean effort unequal to their skill levels or intellectual abilities. One black critic of the new information order recently advanced a different rationale for questioning the limitations in the discourse of the digital divide. His observations bear quoting at length. In his article "The Art of Tricknology," entrepreneur Tyrone D. Taborn writes:

> This scam involves the "Digital Divide." For years, we have been saying that African Americans are being left out of the technology revolution, that the tremendous wealth created by the New Economy is bypassing minority communities. Now, after billions of dollars spent in a so-called national effort, we are seeing reports claiming that the Digital Divide is beginning to narrow, that Blacks are gaining in computer ownership, and more of us are getting online than ever before. We have done our job, these reports seem to say: soon every kid will have a computer right next to his or her Playstation. . . . The folks promoting this nonsense—I call them "tricknologists"—are the high-tech equivalent of the three-card Monty dealers you see on street corners. . . . The trick is simple: the first step is narrowing the definition of the Digital Divide, by saying that computer ownership and Internet usage are how we measure minority participation in the new, high-tech economy. In fact, all these statistics prove is that minorities are closing the gap in being consumers of technology, not in being producers or equal partners. . . . [I]f we are not careful, by the time we figure the whole thing out, the only things left for us will be jobs flipping computer-inventoried hamburgers at fast-food restaurants or cleaning out test tubes at high-tech labs. (1–2)

Clearly, Taborn advances a compelling counterview, and many of his concerns are right on the money, so to speak. It is impossible not to appreciate his cogency here: "Saying that the Digital Divide is closing because minorities have greater access to them is like saying minorities have a stake in the automobile industry because they drive cars, or that they are Bill Gates because they own Microsoft Office 2000" (2). For Taborn, the reality is that "the digital divide is widening." He suggests that the effort to put "computers in every classroom" be equally matched by a commitment to "produce just as many [minority] high-tech billionaires as Silicon Valley does." Furthermore, he recommends that we strive to "fill the ranks of the high-tech work force with as great a percentage of [blacks] as you see on the basketball court" (2). While these hyperbolic remarks are not likely to be seriously considered or implemented, his point remains true. For until we systematically redistribute high-tech wealth and economic opportunities along nonracial, nonclass-based lines, the national preoccupation with the digital divide will only continue to benefit the high-tech billionaires that Theodore Roszak calls the new information economy's "data merchants."

Still, my research confirms a crucial aspect of the digital divide debate. Too little attention is focused on the fact that it is not only the highly educated cognoscenti in the African diaspora who continually bound the formidable obstacles to participation in the information revolution, beyond mere consumerism, but so do the grassroots, poorly educated segments of this community,[6] as my Million Woman March chapter demonstrates. Perhaps one reason that black peoples' information technology acumen fails to register on the mainstream media's technology radar screens is black people's imbrication in what Daniel Akst described in 1995 as "The Internet's Dirty, Cheap Little Secret." The secret that Akst uncovered is "that cruising cyberspace takes almost no computing power at all, and the woods are just full of 'obsolete' old PCs that are easily up to the task." Akst's point is that even with "obsolete" technology and inexpensive nonprofit Internet subscription services such as LA Free-Net (fifteen dollars per year at the time), the so-called information have nots could access the Internet's riches, sans the state-of-the-art "graphics capability" and "gigabytes of storage." Akst does note an important consideration here. As he puts it, "for novices who decide to go this route, the help of a computer-savvy friend will make the job vastly easier. In fact, my holiday gift suggestion for all you warm-hearted geeks out there is to haul that ancient PC out of storage and give it to someone who would benefit from a little email" (D4).

Before we turn our attention to the "warm-hearted geeks" in the African diaspora responsible for actually closing some of the technology gap in black communities (that group I am calling "Afrogeeks"), I want to mention another dirty—not so cheap—little secret of the new technocracy. It seems to me that what obviates mainstream media's sustained critical focus on such important structural barricades to technological parity, besides a naturalized new-tech victimization of minority and low-income groups, is the issue of corporate profiteering and late capitalism's sacred cow of "market forces" protectionism. One particularly egregious and unacknowledged consequence of the digital divide's pathologizing gaze trained on economically deprived groups is that it takes corporate, state, and Wall Street financial sectors off the hook by ignoring their complicity in creating the conditions for making the digital divide rhetoric a sort of self-fulfilling prophesy. In effect, by promulgating the view that certain people are incapable of participating in or are outside the new information revolution,[7] the necessary will to invest structurally in overhauling a woefully inadequate educational system charged with leveling the playing field fails to materialize. Consequently, underserved groups cannot participate in new information regimes because they do not have the means to do so. It is a vicious and cynical cycle that authorizes high-tech companies' insistence that they are obliged to import competent and cheaper technology workers from abroad or that they have an understandable need to outsource technology work entirely in foreign countries. This does not even address the emerging structural barriers to higher-ed, high-tech parity, such as for-profit distance learning instruction and hostile online environments (Flaherty "Racist–Email") likely to further exacerbate minority students' diminishing upward mobility options. For example, in her look at the increasing number of state university systems "developing a wide range of courses online," Karen W. Arenson reveals, "Nonprofit universities like N.Y.U. have increasingly turned to profit making ventures to capitalize on their professors' research." Furthermore, she adds, "tapping the capital markets to pay for courses is a new and largely unexplored concept. . . . And educators and education experts say the for-profit approach is likely to become more prevalent" (A20).

After reifying the concept of an inevitable information class structure, this new high-tech division of society and labor becomes desirable because corporations can exploit foreign labor's exemption from health care and other employee benefits legally binding in employment contracts with U.S. nationals. And, as Donna Haraway writes, "The 'New Industrial Revolution' is producing a new world-wide working class . . . neither gender- nor race-neutral." She points out further "that women in Third World countries are the preferred labour force for the science-based multinationals in the export-processing sectors, particularly in electronics" (166). In the main, this amounts to a sort of high-tech slavery or techno-colonialism that injures foreign laborers and completely devastates the high-tech aspirations and employment options of undereducated and undertrained black and other minority laborers in the United States.

In the wake of the horrendous terror attacks on the Pentagon and the World Trade Towers, it is unclear if the new "racial profiling" of Arabs and other foreign nationals implicated in cyberterrorist conspiracies of 11 September 2001 has curtailed the corporate high-tech brain drain from India, Pakistan, the Middle East, and elsewhere. Certainly, the economic benefits of NAFTA (North Atlantic Free Trade Agreement), WTO (World Trade Organization), and other free market programs do not accrue to U.S. black and other minority and low-income groups seeking to stake claims in the still-evolving information economy.[8]

What strikes me as a particularly distressing aspect of highly touted remedies aimed at bridging the digital divide is what I call the cynical "misanthropic philanthropy" of some high-tech companies. Under the guise of assisting the information have-nots to overcome their plight, technology corporations are encouraged and highly compensated to donate their obsolete, no-longer-profitable computers and dated software to economically depressed urban and rural communities with very attractive tax write-off incentives. Despite the fact that possessing old computers is better than having none at all, there is the obvious fact that mastery of old technologies does not assist this sizable segment of the workforce to keep pace with the phenomenal rates of technological change and advancement. Arguably, this approach guarantees the permanence of these groups' technological lag as this one step forward all but assures two steps backward if this model of self-regulated corporate donations is not matched by strategies and policies more systematic and forward thinking.

Regardless of the final dispensations of these recent troubling manifestations of our postmodern and our so-called post–civil rights conditions, black people's struggle for power sharing in the new information economy apparently signifies a new millennial iteration of class conflict along classic Marxist lines; a model of social organization defined by an inevitable capital-versus-labor symbiosis. Fortunately, there are some capable new-tech barbarians pounding at the gate, with demonstrably successful blueprints in hand for assuring black people's homesteading rights on the new information frontier, if only the public and its elected officials would take heed or get out of the way. And since popular press representations of that rarefied group of computer technology elites or experts, better known as geeks and nerds, are overwhelmingly white, middle-class, and male, it is hardly surprising that a cadre of Afrogeeks or technology early adopters became a convenient structured absence in the powerful rhetoric of the digital divide. As exemplary real-life bodies demonstrating the feasibility of universal access and value-neutral, color-blind technology advancement, it is to this invisible group of Afrogeeks and their remarkable achievements as information-age freedom fighters that we now turn.

AFROGEEKS IN THE 'HOOD: BLACK CYBERFLANEURS TAKE IT TO THE STREETS

I got my first computer when I was about 15 years old. . . . Growing up I was not considered a computer nerd because I was athletic.
—Brian Jackson, "AAs in Video Games"

Since 1995, Black Geeks Online has served as a grassroots advocacy network. Many of our "charter members" were technology trailblazers. . . . It has been our goal to connect people of color from around the world—both on and off-line—to share our talents and time to make others aware of the potential and pitfalls of Information Technology.
—Anita Brown, "Welcome, I'm Anita Brown"

In the person of the flaneur, the intelligentsia becomes acquainted with the marketplace. . . . The flaneur plays the role of scout in the marketplace. As such, he is also the explorer of the crowd.
—Walter Benjamin, *The Arcades Project*

Notwithstanding contemporary popular reimaginings of human bodies interacting with machinic technologies, including Madison Avenue's politically correct, multiracial computer advertisements, and Hollywood's casting of black leads in cyber- and tech narratives, for society at large the idea of black or Afrogeeks remains primarily one of cognitive dissonance. If we accept Sandy Stone's view, in a different context, that "[t]he virtual space is most frequently visualized as Cartesian" (104), then perhaps the invisibility of Afrogeeks in our society's high-tech imaginary obtains because the idea of a black "thinking subject" contradicts entrenched assumptions about African diasporic peoples. Since Stone draws upon William Gibson's foundational cybervision, which fictionalizes black characters as *Neuromancer*'s "low-techs," we readily recognize a hypostatization of the problem. It is bad enough that the historical residue of slavery's imprimatur on black peoples' image as beasts of burden has been difficult to eradicate even from modern attitudes, but its recursiveness in the "consensual hallucination" of cyberspace is especially distressing. Apparently this persistent historical construction of blacks as the brawn assisting whites' brains in powering America's new world industrial society helps to authorize the invisibility blues[9] of postindustrial society's ignorance of Afrogeeks' significant participation in the information revolution. In fact, black scientist Philip Emeagwali recounts on his webpage a poignant experience of high-tech racism that eerily recalls the nineteenth-century no-tech racist logic responsible for the reprehensible 1856 Dred Scott Supreme Court ruling that held that black people "had no rights which the white was bound to respect."[10] Apparently, as Emeagwali discovered, a trace of this intended degradation persists since even black scientists possess no intellectual powers that the white man is bound to respect. After discovering that his white peers were disinterested in and disrespectful of his amazing scientific discoveries, for Emeagwali (as with Dred Scott) this was incontrovertible evidence that "whites had the attitude 'there is nothing a black man can teach us [that] we don't already know.'"[11] It is within this ontological binary construction that I propose a new conceptual cyberculture heuristic.

To augment my articulation of the black geek subject, I propose an analogue figuration of the black cyberflaneur in keeping with Walter Benjamin's rich discourse of Baudelaire's nineteenth-century *arcade's flaneur* (man of the crowd—that I revise to *person of the crowd*). In this way, I hope to rethink the Afrogeek idea by marrying the romantic and historical figure of the flaneur to the historic sociocultural uplift agenda and aspirations of black people in so-called developed and *underdeveloped* societies. As I argue elsewhere, in origin narratives of black peoples underacknowledged technolust, modern African diasporic people are among the most ardent early adopters of new media forms[12] and progressive, revolutionary societal transformations. For just as the French Revolution helped to overthrow aristocratic class entitlements and created the preconditions for the upward mobility, self-determination possibilities and influence of nonblue-blood aristocrats to affect large social change, I contend that black people's early adoption of revolutionary digital technologies similarly will help overthrow late twentieth- and early twenty-first-century information regimes and hierarchies. Further informing the online case studies at the center of my Afrocentric digital alchemy matrix is a pass of my Afrogeeks thesis through Mark Reid's formulation of "postnegritude" and Antonio Gramsci's articulation of the organic intellectual.

AFROGEEKS IN THE HOUSE: ONLINE
ORIGIN NARRATIVES OF BLACK TECHNOCULTURE

On November 17, 1994, I logged onto AOL with much trepidation. I quickly started networking and building my address book. On January 26, 1996, 18 men and women from the Mid-Atlantic States gathered in my living room to officially launch "Black Geeks Online."

—Anita Brown, "Update"

Late in 1993, the World Wide Web burst upon the scene and many of us began using it for AFROAM related pages. I ran across Hypermail 1.0, a great little software package that converts a unix mailbox to a page of links to each message. It even cross indexes it by subject, date, thread and author. The idea for a webarchive began to take shape.

—Sandra Hall, "Online Interview"

In 1988, I announced in [a] supercomputer seminar that I had performed the world's fastest computation. Nobody believed me. Then I offered a public demonstration or "demo" of my record-setting calculation. Only one student showed up. He was black. The whites had the attitude "there is nothing a black man can teach us we don't already know."

—Phillip Emeagwali, "It Was the Audacity"

If Afrogeeks remains a novel idea even in 2008, then the fact that the Internet's origins include a black founding father must be unfathomable if not altogether mind-blowing. As a subgroup of a subgroup amid computer technology's guildlike expert culture, Afrogeeks are particularly marginalized when it comes to sharing in the recent cultural capital now enjoyed by the once-maligned, now-celebrated computer geeks and nerds responsible for the late twentieth-century personal computer revolution. Rather than acquiesce to the whiteout of black participation in technology mythologies spread by a white male–dominated popular media and state bureaucracies, enterprising Afrogeeks have righteously hacked some elite centers of computer research and experimentation to insert themselves in the new information order. It is unlikely still that many people are aware that, for example, Afrogeeks John Henry Thompson (chief scientist and software developer at Macromedia) and Mark Dean (IBM fellow and vice president of systems in IBM research) are pioneers of essential computer technology development that have shaped and continue to shape our information technology infrastructures today. Thompson

> developed Lingo, the programming language that drives the interactivity of 90 percent of video games and web sites. The MIT graduate grew up in Harlem where he began playing with computers in high schools. As principal engineer at Macromedia for more than a decade, he used Lingo for programs like Shockwave, Flash and Director. As well, Dean . . . was part of the team that developed the IBM PC in Boca Raton, FL exactly 20 years ago. He continues to develop cutting edge applications for IBM from the Yorktown laboratory. ("Fifty Most Important")

Thriving in spite of their marginalization, black early adopters of digital media and Internet technologies have found other means of gaining entry into high-tech training environments such as the U.S. military, and other science-based governmental institutions. Through some personal acquaintances, and through attentiveness to military recruitment promotions and advertisements, I have learned of the role of the military in providing black people with high-level computer technology skills and training. This underacknowledged source of high-tech training for the African diasporic community is an important corollary to the more traditional route of technology access most commonly available at universities and colleges.

I begin this discussion with a focus on one of the African diaspora's preeminent Afrogeeks recounting his own frustrating experiences with some of the race-based obstacles to universal technology access. As Nigerian computer scientist Philip Emeagwali, whom CNN dubbed "a father of the Internet," tellingly puts it:

FIGURE 5.1. Screen grab of Philip Emeagwali. Nigerian
scientist Philip Emeagwali in traditional African Garb
surrounded by computers is a striking Afrogeek figure.
Circa 1997. © Philip Emeagwali.

I was the first person to invent an international network (in 1975). . . . By
1981, I realized that my HyperBall project is bigger than me [sic]. I realized that I needed interactions with other scientists, institutions and eventually the market. Within walking distance from my home in Silver Spring,
Maryland was a major research laboratory of the United States National
Weather Service. This lab was the ideal place for me to continue my
research, except the tradition is to hire only white scientists for the paid
positions. When I applied and was turned down for a paid position, my
offer to work as an unpaid employee was accepted. In addition to being
unpaid for five years, I was completely ignored by other scientists. I was
ignored because I was black.

It is Emeagwali's revealing and maddening encounters with institutional racism during the early years of the Internet's development that help to concretize my special reinscription of the terms *hack(er)* and *nerd* to signify *Afrogeek* as simultaneously a description and function of black people's guerrilla-style approaches to accessing elite technology centers—in physical space, virtual space, or both. As Emeagwali's experience here points out, Afrogeeks' abilities to insert their often-undesired physical bodies in restricted high-tech environments provokes a more expansive view of hacking beyond trespassing unauthorized "computer code" or "reconfiguring electronic hardware" (Ludlow 125) (figure 5.1). In my view, Emeagwali's "hack" is his decision to trade-off a salary for technology access, which was tantamount to an act of necessary code breaking, only in this case the code in question was not a digital database but an unfair code of biased labor practices and restricted information flows. Indeed, in this instance, Emeagwali used his underestimated black body to submit voluntarily to high-tech slavery in order to hack the white, institutional body of an American information bureaucracy. When that strategy ultimately became unavailing, Emeagwali demonstrated his hacker skills in more traditional and, for the times, more precocious ways. Emeagwali writes:

> In 1987, I changed locations so that I could use a vector supercomputer instead of my HyperBall, to solve the mathematical equations of weather forecasting. First I applied for a supercomputer account and I received an email that I had been granted access to use one. . . . At the appointed time, I showed up to receive my password. The supercomputer manager, a white male, was shocked when he met me. He withdrew my account under the pretext that "supercomputers are for serious researchers." . . . Denied access to supercomputers . . . [m]y only choice was to use the Internet to access thousands of expensive PC processors and then use them to perform supercomputer-level computations.

What recommends Emeagwali as Afrogeek par excellence, especially at this juncture, is that despite his nonpossession of the white skin passkey to supercomputing nirvana, his possession of virtuoso computing and engineering skills enabled him to turn the racist affront into a racial triumph of sorts. Indeed, these maddening experiences among many others led him to become a recipient of the highly coveted Gordon Bell Prize for special achievement in supercomputing in 1989.[13] And while Nigerian scientist Emeagwali represents a special case of black geek inventiveness, there are other black geeks in the house whose interventionist online practices aptly embody the decolonization, liberation ethos at the heart of my early-adopter, cyberflaneur thesis. The other black cyberflaneur (actually a cyberflaneuse—feminine construction) under consideration here is Anita Brown, the founder of Black Geeks Online.

In 1987, a dedicated hacker, writing under the moniker *Mentor*, penned what arguably has become the quintessential hacker manifesto. Mentor's influential essay is entitled "The Conscience of a Hacker" and appeared in the publication *Phrack* (Ludlow 515). Granted, it is in the nature of manifestoes to be polarizing and thought provoking, but this is precisely their allure. Among Mentor's provocative sentiments that resonate powerfully with the imperatives of my cyberflaneur construction are the following:

> I made a discovery today. I found a computer. Wait a second, this is cool. It does what I want it to[. . . .] And then it happened . . . a door opened to a world . . . an electronic pulse is sent out, a refuge from the day-to-day incompetencies is sought . . . a board is found. "This is it . . . this is where I belong. . . . I know everyone here . . . even if I've never met them, never talked to them, may never hear from them again . . . I know you all.

Mentor continues:

> This is our world now . . . the world of the electron and the switch, the beauty of the baud. We make use of a service already existing without paying for what could be dirt-cheap if it wasn't run by profiteering gluttons, and you call us criminals. We explore . . . and you call us criminals. We seek after knowledge . . . and you call us criminals. We exist without skin color, without nationality, without religious bias . . . and you call us criminals[. . . .] Yes, I am a criminal. My crime is that of curiosity. My crime is that of judging people by what they say and think, not what they look like. (132)

It is this final quote that really speaks to the issue at hand: "My crime is that of outsmarting you, something that you will never forgive me for. I am a hacker, and this is my manifesto. You may stop this individual, but you can't stop us all . . . after all, we're all alike" (132). Because of the West's imperialist construction of black people as a monolith, an essential ideological, intellectual, social, and economic bloc, my attraction to Mentor's statement of that powerful utterance might be obvious. For it circulates within a well-known, if clichéd, political economy that authorizes many abuses of black peoples' legal and civil rights—the idea that conflating black criminals and law abiders matters little under a highly politicized, zero-tolerance mandate of strict law and order. However, the larger political economy of this racialized approach is outside the scope of the present work. Be that as it may, the relevance of Mentor's astute articulation of the outsider angst felt by institutionally powerless yet highly competent individuals and groups seeking parity and legitimate participation in the emergent information order is undeniable. It is Mentor's implicit clarion call to well-meaning hackers of the world to unite against a common profiteering opponent that suggests an efficacious return to Nigerian scientist Philip Emeagwali as an anchor study in our quest for online origin narratives of black cyberflanerie (what black cyberflaneurs do) on the electronic frontier.

SAY IT *IS* SO! IS THERE A BLACK FATHER OF THE INTERNET?

As a black scientist whose own work suffered arrested development because of structural racism in the white-dominated scientific community, Philip Emeagwali became painfully aware of the need for black scientists to persevere "under very difficult circumstances." Moreover, he was acutely aware of the need for black scientists not to be doubly victimized through the process of historical erasure. To that end, he set about the task not only of challenging some historical assumptions about the origins of the Internet but also of repositioning himself and his scientific innovations in this important epoch-making phenomenon. When I decided to frame this discussion in terms of origin narratives, I had not yet read Emeagwali's extensive writings on the origins of the Internet published on his personal website. Because I had holes in my Emeagwali file (downloaded from his site's 1997 iteration), I went back to consult his greatly expanded website for more detailed but unexpected updated information. What can you say about serendipity but, thank God for it! In the section of his site entitled "It Was the Audacity of my Thinking: History of the Internet," he counters the view of the Internet's development as originating from a Cold-War government mandate to create an indestructible information-flow system capable of surviving a nuclear attack. It was not the "fourth and investment stages" responsible for the birth of Yahoo or Amazon dot com, nor the development of the World Wide Web or browsers that engendered the Internet according to Emeagwali. "Like email," Emeagwali informs us, "The Web is an application that runs on the Internet." He contends further that, contrary to popular opinion:

> The origin of the Internet is not the creation of the ARPAnet or NSFnet. The NSFnet [was] created on the second or applied research stage. The origin of the Internet was the point at which we understood that many small computers could be harnessed to solve one big problem. The origin is the point where the computer gave birth to the Internet. The point we achieved [was] the technological embodiment of "e pluribus unum," the Latin Phrase "out of many, one."

Lest anyone doubt the veracity of his counterhistory, Emeagwali quotes statements about the Internet's origins from an arguably unimpeachable source "who should know." So, alongside other more technical determinates that he specifies,[14] Emeagwali makes a point of the fact, "While I was working on my proposal for a HyperBall international network, ARPA [was] trying to solve similar computation-intensive problems on a national network." He continues:

> The Advanced Research Projects Agency's (ARPA) approach was to remotely connect computational scientists to remote supercomputers. Contrary to the widely held belief, ARPA's original proposal was not intended to build a national network that will save the United States from nuclear attack. (Was it Mark Twain that said: "A lie will travel half way around the world while the truth is still putting on its shoes?") One person who should know why ARPA built the ARPAnet is Charles M. Herzfeld, the former director of ARPA. Herzfeld explained: ". . . The ARPAnet was not started to create a Command and Control System that would survive a nuclear attack, as many claim . . . in fact, we would have been severely criticized if we tried. Rather, the ARPAnet came out of our frustration that there were only a limited number of large, powerful research computers in the country, and that many research investigators who should have access to them were geographically separated."

Clearly, this explanation does not necessarily preclude the "nuclear attack" theory if one concludes that those "geographically separated" scientists might have been working on a nuclear attack survivability scenario. Still, if the then-director of ARPA admitted that this was not the case, then

Emeagwali's assertions that "ARPAnet was created for computational scientists using supercomputers from remote locations," that supercomputers derived a presumptive collateral benefit of surviving nuclear attack,
and that "secondary applications such as Hypertext, the graphic browsers
and e-commerce were developed later" are tenable. Whatever the actual
facts of the Internet's birth may be, the fact of Emeagwali's scientific
developments and personal historical connection to the developmental
phases and stages of the supercomputing revolution have not been challenged or denied in any way to my knowledge.

Apparently another source of salt put in the wounds excising black
scientists' contributions to the Internet's development was a PBS documentary about this monumental scientific milestone entitled *Nerds 2.0.1.*
According to Emeagwali, "The companion Website for the PBS television
documentary, *Nerds 2.0.1: A Brief History of the Internet,* listed 50 'cast of
characters' who made significant contributions to the Internet." He states,
"I practically rolled on the floor and laughed when I noticed that a whop-
ping forty eight (48) of those 50 pioneers were white males. Not a single
black person is included. . . . For the record, many of the so-called Fathers
of the Internet did not use the Internet until after 1990. The pioneers of
the Internet did their work in the 1970s and 80s." And with his penchant
for peppering his commentary with striking aphorisms, Emeagwali adds
this one to his PBS criticism, "Since white males control the media, 96
percent of the Internet pioneers were white males. The documentary
Nerds 2.0.1 reminded me of the African proverb: 'Only when lions have
historians will hunters cease to be heroes.' As they say, the word 'history'
means HIS-STORY." For Emeawgali, the import of historical accuracy in
determining the Internet's origins is not simply to get his personal props,
but as he puts it, "When we forget why the Internet was invented, we will
end up giving credit to the wrong inventors."

In the subsection of his essay "History of the Internet" that includes
a sub-subsubsection entitled "Three Stages of Invention: Acceptance,"
Emeagwali says:

> The difference between I [sic] and the other "Fathers of the Internet" is
> that they are white Americans and I am a black African. . . . My path was
> strewn with thorns while theirs was strewn with roses. I began my journey
> from an African civil war refugee camp and Bill Gates began his from the
> home of his affluent parents. The destination may be the same but I
> walked the farthest and climbed the highest mountains.

What I found most compelling in mining Emeagwali's provocative revision of "The History of the Internet," among other things, were details of his personal odyssey from Biafrian War refugee to U.S. prizewinning scientist in supercomputing excellence. As he puts it, "The 30 month Nigerian-Biafran civil war ended on January 15, 1970. My family and I walked 60 miles to return to our hometown of Onitsha, which was captured and battered during the war." It is fascinating to discover that someone who had not heard the word *computer* until 1970, and who credits his incredible ascendancy in science to purchasing a slide rule in 1972 that so captivated members of his Nigerian hometown that "curious friends [would] stop by to watch me operate it," could rise to become one of CNN's named "Fathers of the Internet." Quite informative as well is Emeagwali's "Computing Timeline Study Guide," which traces the history of computing from the "469 BC to 1300 AD invention of the Abacus in China, to its global, historical development on through the 1940s invention of the electronic computer, to present times." To his credit, Emeagwali does not slight Persian mathematician Muhammed idn Musa Al-Khwarizmi, English computer visionary Ada Lovelace, and African mathematician Heron in his genealogy. At the same time, one cannot help but be struck by his unabashed self-promotion as he moves through the timeline to the present day. However, given the disinclination of mainstream scientists, historians, and journalists to fairly assess the contributions of women and racial others in their historiographies, Emeagwali's recourse to deserved self-promotion becomes a necessary if immodest corrective. After all, he does not call himself "A Father of the Internet," but who can blame him for foregrounding the fact that CNN does?

Also, it is crucial to bear in mind that an important lure of the pre-commercial Internet for its early adopters and innovators was its counter-public functionality as a digital public arena and parallel universe in opposition to the corporate takeover of modern society's physical public spaces. In talking about the Internet technology's progression to Phase Three—the stage of the SuperBrain—wherein a "a bio-digital brain will be invented and computer hackers will be able to download their minds into the World Wide Brain," Emeagwali discusses his settling on the electronic frontier—the digital public sphere, if you will, is prescient. He adds:

> Also, the successful incorporation of my mind into my Web site means that I will have achieved a non-physical immortality. The content of this website was written over a twenty (20) year period and initially distributed

by e-mail and FTP. . . . As late as 1991, the page had no pictures, no move-ment and no sound. In 1997, we had 100 megabytes of information on our primary server 200 megabytes on our secondary server. . . . With 500,000 visitors a year, www.EMEAGWALI.com is one of the most pop-ular sites on the Internet. Because we have (arguably) the largest personal Web site, our visitors tend to stick around for long periods.

To his rhetorical question, "Am I 'The Father of the Internet?" he writes, "The answer is NO. Since the Internet is a product of overlapping inven-tions, it will be preposterous for one person to claim to be the father of a complex international network." In this section, Emeagwali suggests that his scientific accomplishments demonstrate that he most certainly is *one* of its progenitors. He qualifies his remarks by stating accurately that "the Internet has many fathers, mothers, uncles and aunts."

If Emeagwali is content merely to publicize CNN's induction of himself into the Internet Fathers' pantheon, he is less willing to await mainstream anointing of his status as one of the world's first geeks, Afro or otherwise. Emeagwali claims the moniker in the section of his site called "Down Memory Lane: The '70s [and] Computing in the '80s." In this biographical section chronicling his movement from war refugee to celebrated prize recipient, he foregrounds his protohacking credentials as a student of mathematics, physics, astronomy, and computer science at Oregon State University. Because of the school's deficient computing facilities, Emeagwali began tinkering successfully with the available equipment. These early successes lead him to the conclusion that, "[i]n retrospective [sic], I was among the earliest computer hackers." Where Emeagwali embodies the early-adopter individualist hacker ethos, moti-vated primarily by the desire to learn and explore, other Afrogeeks con-veniently situated at elite U.S. universities, nonprofit organizations, and technology businesses up the ante to advance a group-hack imperative aimed at high-tech information sharing and other modes of community uplift cyberflanerie.

AFROGEEKS AND BLACK CYBERFLANEURS: FORGING AN AFROCENTRIC DIGITAL UNDERGROUND

In some instructive ways Walter Benjamin's articulations of Baudelaire's nineteenth-century flaneur present useful ideas for my construction of a black cyberflaneur subjectivity for the information age. For example, Benjamin writes in his unfinished *Arcades Project*: "The social base of flanerie is journalism" (446). Related to this, Benjamin adds, "The press brings into play an overabundance of information which can be all the more provocative the more it is exempt from any use." (447). I was surprised to learn that Benjamin even uses "information industry" to describe the nineteenth-century press in these discussions (446). As demonstrated in the Emeagwali case, and in what follows, Afrogeeks' understanding of the Internet as an important alternative journalistic sphere for their own counterhegemonic agendas is clear. Benjamin's notions about the power of the flaneur inhering in an ability to be essentially hidden by the law of the incognito—the flaneur as "Man of the Crowd" interpenetrating the urban scene and chronicling the"landscape and the present moment" (419) is equally pertinent to the role of the black cyberflaneur whose intimate knowledge of and affinity with the black masses legitimates his or her particular brand of strategic invisibility amidst the black crowd. It is important here to note my indebtedness to Ralph Ellison's highly influential formulation of the "invisible man" and Sam Greenlee's crafting of the "spook who sat by the door" in my own conceptual imaginings of Afrogeeks' strategic invisibility practices. I want to contextualize these ideas by quoting from the famous opening remarks from Ellison's 1952 masterpiece *Invisible Man*:

> I am an invisible man. . . . I am a man of substance, of flesh and bone, fiber and liquids—and I might even be said to possess a mind. I am invisible, understand, simply because people refuse to see me. . . . It is sometimes advantageous to be unseen, although it is most often rather wearing on the nerves. Then too, you're constantly being bumped against by those of poor vision. . . . [O]ut of resentment, you begin to bump people back. (3–4)

Clearly, these sentiments from Ellison's fictional protagonist resonate with the plight of real-world Afrogeeks such as Emeagwali, discussed above, and many others outlined in this study. It is Ellison's astute characterization of the invisible black man who is "even said to possess a mind" and is willing to "bump back" against this imposed invisibility that is metaphorically rich in my view. As with Benjamin's flaneur, with his ability to disappear within the crowd, Ellison's unnamed hero in the novel recognizes and capitalizes on the strategic advantages in being unseen, especially by hostile agents and forces. This is precisely the case

I am advancing in articulating the subversive strategies of black cyber-flaneurs in the technoir underground. In 1969 Sam Greenlee penned his bestselling novel (adapted to film in 1973) *The Spook Who Sat by the Door*, a text that repurposes Ellison's postwar (World War II) invisibility thesis to meet the revolutionary political demands of the 1970s post–civil-rights-era black nationalism. In this novel-cum-film, Greenlee transposes the powerful trope of black invisibility from Hollywood's stereotypical caricature of blacks being spooked by invisible ghosts of the dark to a dark figure of black revolutionary politics capable of spooking the comfort zone of mainstream America's status quo of white domination. Greenlee's spook is a "mild-mannered social worker . . . [who is] recruited by the CIA as a token black and then proceeds to learn (and later apply) the techniques of urban guerrilla warfare in Chicago"[15] to lead an armed resistance against brutal repression in black ghettoes of that era. In 1973, *Jet* magazine, considering the incendiary nature of the adapted film, wrote: "The movie is 'bad' enough [Ebonics alert—bad is good here] that it won't be surprising if authorities in some cities try to ban it" ("New York Beat"). As a sort of manifestation of *Jet's* prophesy, one online description of the film states: "Possibly the most radical of the 'Blaxploitation' films of the 70s, this movie was an overnight success when it was released in 1973, and then was abruptly taken out of distribution for reasons that are still not entirely clear." What is clear, however, is that black invisibility becomes a dialectic of alarm and power for both the unseen and, as Elision notes, those who refuse to see.[16]

By drawing upon these historical referents, I envision the various stealth practices of community-oriented black cyberflanerie as manifest in Afrogeeks' sophisticated production and maintenance of Afrocentric list-servs, personal and entrepreneurial websites, nonprofit high-tech organizations, and technoliteracy outreach initiatives in black communities. In a reflection on his author function, Ellison makes the point that although he may be "gambling with the reader's capacity for fictional truth" (xxii), his fictional discourse on black people's strategies of converting the liability of invisibility into a tactical strength is grounded in some larger social realities. For Afrogeeks sitting by the doors of entry into technological privilege the burden of invisibility may have yielded less spectacular rewards than found in Greenlee and Ellison's creative imaginings. However, actual Afrogeek invisibility fulfills a needed real world transformation even beyond the most fantastic of literary constructs.

ANITA BROWN'S CYBERFLANEURIE
VIA BLACK GEEKS ONLINE

Another pioneer Afrogeek who early on toiled in the trenches of the technology war between the information-haves and have-nots is the late Anita Brown, founder and chief inspiration officer (CIO) of the now-defunct, but once formidable and well-regarded nonprofit organization Black Geeks Online, based in Washington, D.C. Brown's important history not only gives a material face and body to statistics calculating black women's majority status in the rise of black participation in the information economy,[17] but she also skewed the accepted norm of geekness due to her lack of traditional college education and training, and computer programming expertise. It is precisely Brown's acumen in surmounting such structural barriers to black high-tech literacy and institutional propagation during the height of the Internet's expansion that makes her founding of an innovative and successful community-based, high-tech, nonprofit organization early in the Internet's popularization particularly compelling. Indeed, Brown's pioneering cyberflaneurie enables us to rethink a potent Internet metaphor to help elucidate our particular concerns. While we are most familiar with the Internet's popular electronic frontier metaphor, that "suggests the possibility of a vast, unexplored territory" (Balsamo 116) and unlimited potential, for our rhetorical purposes a reassignment of the metaphor in keeping with the impossible restrictions on urban, ghetto life is more apt. As Guillermo Gomez-Pena writes about the predicament of Mexican artists in "The Virtual Barrio @ the Other Frontier," often the "relationship with digital technology and personal computers is defined by paradoxes and contradictions" (296). The case is likewise with the black diaspora's confrontation with such contradictions as the image of unlimited online opportunities colliding with the reality of the net's virtual redlining and other restrictions to universal access. Unfortunately, this contradiction is played out as a delimited electronic fiefdom that transfers real-world race-based restrictions to the digital realm. In the ghetto streets ("the hood"), substandard housing, lack of access to fair housing and business loans, and other equitable financial, educational, political, and cultural services find their corollary in prohibitive fees to gain basic entry to the infobahn, exacerbating other hidden and obvious costs prohibiting full-fledged participation.

We have already discussed structural barriers to the electronic frontier for blacks such as relatively expensive computers, monthly Internet access fees, steep technology learning curves. However, the far-reaching consequences of monopoly capital, megamedia merger mania, and the new information economy tamp down of minority and non-English-speaking groups remain that crucial reality check on the idealization of the Internet's liberationist digital democracy metaphor. After all, if black professionals and working-class members in the hood cannot secure fair market home and business loans due to racist redlining (read legal exclusionist) practices, how are blacks to compete in an emergent high-stakes information economy dominated by the likes of AOL, TCI, AT&T, Time-Warner, Disney, Microsoft, Newscorp, Verizon, and Bell Atlantic Corp., among others.

Up against this new information disorder, what David Crane has called "a technocapitalist marketing of territory" (88), emblematic in Viacom's takeover of BET (Black Entertainment Television), among other high-profile consolidations that, as early as 1998, could offer merger packages in the $31 billion range,[18] what are blacks in the hood and in the bush to do? Enter, the "ethno-cyborgs" and "artificial savages" (to borrow Guillermo Gomez-Pena's imaginative phrasings). Even though Gomez-Pena's figurations are contextualized within a specific Mexican digital performance art experimentation milieu, with definite creative practices and strategies, the interactive element involving "thousands of anonymous Net-users" can easily be extrapolated to the political empowerment imperative of Afrogeeks in the cyberghettos and the digital bush. What Gomez-Pena and his fellow artists are attempting here is a performative politics of technology to reclaim the realm of bodily otherness and primativeness so that web users end up experiencing their "technodiorama" project as "a sort of visualization of their own postcolonial demons and racist mirages" (306), accessible to those identifying with the oppressed and oppressors alike. Notice the saliency in Gomez-Pena's remarks to our unfolding discussion of cyberflaneurie:

> In other words, the actual Internet responses become the basis for the creation of a series of "ethno-cyborgs," co-created (or rather "co-imagined") collaboratively with thousands of anonymous Net-users. . . . [T]he "ethno-cyborgs" and "artificial savages" incarnate profound fears and desires of contemporary Americans regarding the Latino "other," immigrants, and people of color, and function as mirrors for the (real and virtual) visitors to see the reflections of their own psychological and cultural monsters. (306)

When Anita Brown logged onto AOL in 1994, she subsumed her own fears of a perceived luddite mentality among blacks under a daring personal entrepreneurial maneuver designed to benefit her newly formed t-shirt business. After abandoning her fledgling desktop publishing business, Brown went online to seek "out Baby Boomers who could give her inspiration for her next T-shirt."[19] In an instance where Brown's ethnocyborg collided with AOL's artificial savage, the surprising encounter with this anonymous mass of net users, via computer-mediated communication (CMC) fomented her remarkable Black Geeks Online organization.

Brown's Black Geek cyberflaneurie, then, began with her own perfunctory invisibility as just another newbie subscriber to AOL's cybercommunity in 1994. Describing her experience in an AOL "late night" chatroom where she sought out Baby Boomers for researching a new shirt for her business, Brown brings to light the paradoxical limits and possibilities of anonymity and racial invisibility online. Beyond the Baby Boom nostalgia factor that Brown sought and found in AOL respondents' input contributing to a "shirt titled 'Wayy Back in the Day,'" her disclosures about her AOL online identity in an interview are telling:

> Because I'd chosen a screen name that likely pegged me as African American, several AOL members checked my Member Profile and engaged me via Instant Message. Before long, I was invited to a weekly private chat forum for Black entrepreneurs and professionals. . . . It didn't take long for me to realize the power of email for sharing information and resources. One of the founders of NetNoir dubbed me "The Email Queen" alluding to the quality and quantity of information I forwarded.[20]

What Brown's favorable encounter in that AOL late-night chatroom reveals is that the much-celebrated politics of eschewing identity markers in cyberspace may not be as productive and conducive to certain agendas as the much-touted image of online race, class, and gender neutrality suggests. I am thinking especially of the popular 1996 MCI television commercial that utilizes documentary-style black and white photography in its touting of the Internet's putative ability to nullify these historically divisive social categorizations. The commercial's affective hook inheres in psychosocial appeals claiming that "people can communicate mind to mind," without the barriers of race, gender, class, and physical impairment. The commercial's rhetoric of bodily transcendence ends with this hyberbolic refrain, "Utopia? No. The Internet!" And of course, the long-awaited, posthuman identity neutralizer is the Internet, which significantly, in this instance, is made possible by MCI, an early entrant in the realm of Internet connectivity for the public at large.

Countering the presumed benefits of this posthumanist disembodiment logic is Brown's own poignant example. By refusing a deracinated virtual body and logging onto AOL in 1994 as "MsDCThang," surely an Ebonics-inflected moniker, Brown opts to foreground racial identification in her CMC transactions. This identification strategy secures Brown's admittance to one of AOL's multicultural subcultures culminating in a life-transforming experience for herself and like-minded others in AOL's diverse virtual community. After entering AOL's late-night, black underground chat group, Brown discovered her geek calling. "Subsequently," as she tells it, "I called the first meeting of Black Geeks Online, a virtual organization that would connect and encourage African Americans to get involved in taking IT to the streets. As of June 2000, we have 28,000 registered members" (Ashford). Despite today's more widespread digital sophistication, it is important to bear in mind how radical and forward thinking Brown's pioneering efforts were at that juncture.

That Brown's nontraditional acquisition of technological competency occurs during the era when digital spheres were indifferent, at best, and hostile, at worst, to marginalized groups such as women and racial minorities "that do not possess a historical involvement with advanced technologies" (Silver 138) is significant. If we presume that AOL's gated cybercommunity was insulated from the infamous risk of flaming and explicit racist affronts, then Brown's race and gender identity specification appear less daring. This protectionist expectation seems more reasonable especially in AOL's surveilled social environment than, say, in the more free-wheeling, ribald suceptible e-zones such as MUDs, BBSs, Usenets, and other less panoptic digital environments. Nonetheless, the fact that Brown's raced and gendered virtual body finds expressive freedom and camaraderie in the confines of a late-night chatroom complicates this premise. Still, the fact that Brown's coming-of-age geekness is facilitated in a substratum of a mainstream ISP (Internet Service Provider) underscores my notion of black cyberflanerie and strategic invisibility. Moreover, Brown's AOL experience reverses the appropriate[d] other thesis promulgated by Trinh-T Min ha, whereby the dominated other astutely appropriates the dominator's cultural artifacts and apparatuses in unanticipated self-serving maneuvers. Notably, this is not quite the same thing as postmodern syncretism and cultural hybridity where "minority" contributions often get erased from or flattened out within a universal humanistic (read white, Western) "melting-pot" rubric. The significant inversion here turns on influential "bragging rights" (in Ebonics terms) and the ability to stake a specific participatory claim on a new, revolutionary cultural formation.[21]

Brown's serendipitous appropriation of AOL's ISP cybercasting network apparatus is not the only nodal point of her ascension to the emerging realm of popular geekdom. Indeed, she cites many important influences on her technological awakening, including some politicians with whom she worked. For instance, there were specialists in adult education and her

> brother Maurice Welsh, who was responsible for bringing me that first AOL diskette. He saw the natural match between his sister, the communicator, and the Internet. Maurice worked with the Defense Department in the early years of the Arpanet and retired last year as Director, New Media Development, for Pacific Bell. (Ashford)

Twenty-seven years earlier, "As a single mother in the '60s, she started out as a GS-3 [Government Services-3] clerk-typist at the U.S. Civil Service Commission."

Taking advantage of her invisibility as a low-level clerk-typist, Brown's gender-bending reprisal of Sam Greenlee's spook who sat by the door recodes the potent metaphor to fit the revolutionary demands of the emergent information age. Once she "saw text flow around a graphic on a Mac," Brown appropriated it at an opportune moment, signifying her transformation from mild-mannered, government spook to superwomanist black geek committed to fighting for truth, technojustice and universal access for all. In an interview with *IT Recruiter* Magazine in late 2001, she recalls the transformation or technoconversion experience: "Someday, I'm going to tell Steve Jobs that an Apple changed my life" (Ashford; Durham-Vichr). In founding her nonprofit Black Geeks Online organization, hers was not the only life change in the offing.

BLACK GEEKS ONLINE: AN IT ORGANIZATION OF ONE'S OWN

> At some point, I plan to share more about myself . . . how I launched my first company on an unemployment check, my controversial views on the digital divide "industry," coping with data smog and techno stress.
>
> —AnitaBrown@sistageek.com

From her interpellation in the AOL underground chatroom of black entrepreneurs and professionals and the resources of her one thousand-card
Rolodex collected over a twenty-five-year secretarial career, Brown was
emboldened to launch her Black Geeks Online organization. And true to her
activist roots as a "former 60s warrior" (Ashford), Brown was determined to
take her newly acquired IT skills to the urban streets of Washington, D.C.
Such a radical, midlife shift seems unthinkable given Brown's history of
growing up in Washington, D.C., during the era of segregation and her safe
and stable twenty-five-year career as a secretary in the civil servant corps. She
reflects on her incredible journey in an interview with Peggy Townsend for
TECHDIVAS.com. Through her autobiographical reminiscences Brown's
function as an exemplary organic intellectual becomes evident. Discussing
the sacrifices her parents made to send her away to a Catholic boarding
school in Philadelphia, Brown recalls for Townsend painful lessons that later
she had to unlearn, an unlearning that ultimately set her on the path to
netrepreneurial success. "I learned very early to sit down, shut up and don't
be creative," Brown reveals. Not only did her boarding school fail to suppress
her creative and inquisitive yearnings, but the constraints placed upon her
during her brief college stint were equally unavailing and likely contributed
to her sense of profound restlessness. Brown confesses that she dropped out
of college after six months: "It was read this, take the test and spit it out." At
age forty-five, and clearly fed up with the lack of autonomy, she determined
to wrest control of her life from several disabling external forces, "I was
breaking out of boxes I had been put in my whole life."[22] Apparently, this
life-long frustration with the conformist dictates of institutional power pre-
disposed her to the lure of geek antiestablishmentarianism (figure 5.2).

Despite her bodily nonconformity to the quintessential masculinist
geek/hacker construct, Brown shares some of their key attributes. For
example, in Leslie Haddon's history of videogame development at MIT
and other innovative computer centers we get a strong sense of the
hacker/geek mentality and creative ethos most pertinent here. Haddon
notes these adventurers' nontraditional interests in developing new and
direct forms of computing, experiencing pleasure in and play with the
machines, and exploring interactivity or two-way computer communications' techniques (125–26). When Brown finally took the leap of faith,
quitting her secure twenty-five-year secretarial job to join the insecure
ranks of small business entrepreneurs, she confesses that she was scared to
death. But, compelled by her growing technolust (pleasure and play with
the machines), her newfound experiences with interactive chatrooms, and

FIGURE 5.2. Screen grab of Anita Brown. Grandmother Anita Brown founded the Black Geeks Online organization in Washington, D.C. in the mid-1990s. © Anita Brown.

her demonstrated savvy with desktop publishing's entrepreneurial use of computers, she was unable and unwilling to resist her geek calling. Like the geek personae in Haddon's investigation, Brown's initiation into the technoguild is hardly surprising. As Brown tells it:

> I've always lived and worked in Washington, DC, the capital of information and I learned the power of "contacts" early on. I left the "world of work" on July 1, 1989 to start my own desktop publishing service. I had seen text flow around a graphic on a Macintosh with a 9–inch screen and I was instantly hooked! I bought technical books and software, and studied typesetting, graphic design, and page layout while using my 1,000–card Rolodex to build Desktop Designs. In 1993 I designed a t-shirt (on my Mac) to celebrate my 50th birthday. Little did I know how "IT'S A D.C. THANG" would capture the hearts of native Washingtonians. Eventually I had to close Desktop Designs in order to keep up with the orders for t-shirts. (Townsend)

In the year following her foray into AOL, Brown and others "who were concerned that African Americans would be left behind in the digital revolution" met offline in Washington, D.C., where she convened the "first meeting of Black Geeks Online" (Townsend). From that initial inner circle of eighteen people sharing a vision in the mid-1990s, the organization celebrated a registered membership of 30,000 by 2001.[23] No doubt this phenomenal surge in numbers was augmented by the organization's well-publicized public coming-out event Taking IT to the Streets. This watershed moment in the organization's early years bears witness to Brown's institution-building acumen and speaks volumes about her unique vision of black geekness at a time when the controversial image of the geek in our social imaginary was reified as young, white, male, and often of bourgeois privilege. Sistahgeek Brown, as a grandmother in her fifties, an African American woman, and hailing from the Washington, D.C., enormous working class clearly turns the mythical 1995 geek image on its head.

SISTAHGEEK TAKES IT FROM AOL
TO CHOCOLATE CITY AND BEYOND

What sets Brown's Black Geeks Online organization apart, in terms of institution building, is its real-life community base and outreach efforts. It is the case that Brown's geekness was nurtured in the virtual community of AOL, yet she refused the usual insularity of geek culture and its concomitant guildlike mystification, preferring instead to share "the potential and pitfalls of Information Technology" with everyday community folks in the 'hood. Theodore Roszak's concerns about the "data merchant" class' vested interests in "the extravagant promises that attach to computers" and the "creation of a mystique of information that makes basic intellectual discriminations between data, knowledge, judgment, imagination, insight and wisdom impossible" (xix), are precisely what Brown's measured embrace of technology resists. Like Roszak, Brown too is suspicious of this sort of "strange sect . . . worshipping light bulbs" (xix). Instead, they promulgate the view that "light bulbs are useful devices," not "objects of veneration" dissociated from their useful tool function that works to improve the human condition, not dominate it. Improving the black community's abject condition in the rapidly unfolding information revolution was the motive force behind Black Geeks

Online's 5 July 1997 project of Taking Internet Technology (IT) to the Streets! of urban space in Washington, D.C.

Brown and her cadre of "experienced netizens from around the Washington region [came together] to provide free one-on-one email and web instruction to DC residents, and dispel the myth that this technology is unaffordable and irrelevant to their lives."[24] It is important to note that Black Geeks led the vanguard efforts to close the technology gap before the popular digital divide rhetoric captured the public imagination. To encourage participation in their free event, Black Geeks circulated a flyer, downloadable from their website, that contained this provocative lure to join the ranks of the information haves: "Why should you care? Because if Black folks are not techno-savvy by the year 2000, we'll be left behind! 'Taking IT to the Streets' is our way of bringing the Net to you in a relaxed, informal setting. Join us!."[25] The point that Black Geeks Online strives to make to their unconnected constituency through the rhetorical question "Why should you care?" is well articulated by Howard Rheingold. Rheingold pointed out in 1993 that

> big power and big money always found ways to control new communications media when they emerged in the past. . . . What we know and do now is important because it is still possible for people around the world to make sure this new sphere of vital discourse remains open to the citizens of the planet before the political and economic big boys seize it, censor it, meter it, and sell it back to us. The potential social leverage comes from the power that ordinary citizens gain when they know how to connect two previously independent, mature highly decentralized technologies. (5)

By 1997, Brown's Black Geeks Online organization decided to enter the fray of this high-stakes battle for positioning in the new economy formation. To pull off their interventionist strategy of virtual-to-real-world black cyberflaneurie, Brown and her Black Geeks network garnered support from local and national IT concerns and the stand-up comedian and actor Sinbad.

Taking stock of her organization's status in its impressive sixth year of operation (a important milestone in small business terms and relative to the now infamous volatility of e-commerce), Brown reached some sober conclusions about institutional practices, which she shares on a section of the organizations' website entitled "About Black Geeks Online." Of the organization's status from 1995 through 2001, she states, "Many have asked why, with 30,000 members, we have remained unfunded[?]."[26] Her response to why Black Geeks Online departs from the "frequently-changing web marketing and advertising models that other African American websites employ," bears a lengthy quote:

> I have an issue. I believe "who pays the piper calls the tune." And I've not been willing to solicit money from corporations or the government that consider us to be "hits," "eyeballs," numbers," "a niche market." Say or do something they don't condone—and your funds get snatched. Black Geeks Online is not a "website." We are a network that HAS a website. Our network includes a broad spectrum of African Americans—students, unemployed and underemployed workers, single parents, technology professionals, and entrepreneurs. Our members have come to expect our "read" on IT news. . . . I write a column for Heads^UP [a subsection of the website] called, "A View From the 'Hood," which is, essentially, an op-ed piece. And I call it like I see it. . . . And "the piper" ain't paying for that!

Brown's sense of institutional integrity is particularly resonant and telling in comparison to, say, Black Entertainment Television (BET) as a counterexample. The "Black" in Black Geeks Online does not signify the sort of racial window dressing that has made the "Black" in BET such a magnet for controversy in the black community. By the same token, Brown's integrity and commitment have exacted a high cost in terms of financial solvency over the years. I am reminded here of Actor Debbie Allen's famous opening credit-line statement as the dance instructor character in the short-lived, 1982–83 television show *Fame* (adapted from the feature film of the same name). Allen, as the no-nonsense, tough task master dance teacher named Lydia Grant, who works at an inner-city performing-arts high school, informs her star-struck students of an important trade-off. She tells them: "You want fame? Well, fame costs, and *here* is where you start paying!" Indeed, by the year 2000, Brown was confronted with the impossibility of "payment." Although she refused payment to the piper, apparently, Brown accepted the payment due on her brand of institutional integrity.

As Deborah Durham-Vichr notes in her profile of Brown for *IT Recruiter* Magazine:

> She's a full-time volunteer, making no salary, yet manages to run her organization. . . . Right now, she's grappling with a $10,000 estimate to redesign

her Web site, when her latest fundraiser only brought in $3,000. She's got someone working on it, she says. Brown's a testament to everyone that you can start life over at 45, learn a whole new career, and be successful.

Clearly, Afrogeeks such as Brown and Emeagwali compel us to reconsider ossified and inapplicable capitalist notions of success, especially in the wake of the much-lamented new economy meltdown, or "dot.com bust," incurred by questionable Wall Street speculations in the technology sector of the economy as the new millennium dawned. To help us rethink successful capital, Brown, dubbed the "technorealist," makes the following insightful observations: "There's such a thing as social capital . . . as well as intellectual capital and personal capital. Intellectual capital is what you learn in school, and personal capital is what you own. Social capital is the people you know. That's what I'm rich in" (Durham-Vichr). Indeed, Brown found the elusive gold that many sought prospecting on the electronic frontier. As Durham-Vichr describes her, "She's a social goldmine because—in the Web jargon—she's sticky. Very, very sticky. She's got more links than AltaVista." Put more plainly, Brown and her Black Geeks Online organization have remarkable staying power in the notoriously fickle and ever-changing information economy. When asked in the year 2000, "What is your definition of success?" Brown's response echoes the famous refrain from a Frank Sinatra song; she defines success as the "freedom to live your life in your own way" (Ashford). Although Brown leveraged the high-integrity costs of doing it "my way," she had a lot of help from some very influential friends—those other black technophiles, D.C. politicians, and Internet enthusiasts who were "with Black Geeks Online from its inception" (Ashford).

In the spirit of valorizing the Internet's tool function of enabling free information flows and entrepreneurial networking that typified its virtual community ethos in the early years, Brown readily shares the credit for her organization's success in the section of the Black Geeks Online website "Behind the Scenes."[27] Even as late as February 2002, when I asked Brown to answer my own questions about her experiences, she referred me to a host of Afrogeek individuals and organizations too numerous for inclusion in this study. Brown's readiness to share the many accolades bestowed upon her with her colleagues attests to her understanding of how institutions are built, maintained, and endure beyond the visionary goals of an individual founder. As a counterexample to Roszak's much-lamented class of self-enriching data brokers, Brown has been dubbed "an information broker." Brown describes herself as a "techno realist" (Durham-Vichr). As such, she is not afraid to engage with the vexing contradictions of information age culture. While she was committed to the goal of increasing computer literacy and Internet access among African Americans, as their website states, Brown did not subscribe to the view of computers as the panacea for what ails American civil society. In fact, Brown resented "some of the things technology has done to society. She was deeply suspicious of the way that computer commodification agendas have infiltrated poor peoples' lives, serving primarily as yet a new and improved shopping mall" (Townsend) and not as a resource for job training and other life improvements. Brown, the late-blooming computer geek, "believes it's not good to live only in a virtual community" (Townsend).

While Brown may not have articulated a rejection of cyberculture's posthuman thesis in exact terms recognizable to cultural theorists, such as Kathrine Hayles, Jean Baudrillard, or Jean Franciois Lyotard, it is clear that she shared some of their concerns regarding the problematics of cyborgization. For example, Brown "likes it that people from Southern California to South Africa can now exchange ideas, but she likes the idea of a real community better" (Townsend). In her version of anti-posthumanism and creeping posthuman technologization, Brown writes, "[T]ake care of yourself; your personal, spirtual and family needs. You'll never live to enjoy the fruits of your work if you get caught-up in voice mail, email, Palm Pilots, schedules, cell phones, etc." (Ashford). For Brown, the important thing is for "people to take time off to call their mothers, to run with their dogs or make brunch for their girlfriends" (Townsend). And despite Brown's anti-posthuman leanings, she well understood and shared James Gleick's frustrated acknowledgment of computerization's acceleration of all aspects of everyday life. For Brown, it was necessary to challenge the reality that "[s]earch engines and databases connect us with flat data and resources, and they can do it lightening fast" (Ashford). As she saw it, the fact that "the world we live in doesn't permit contemplation . . . [nor anything] but IPO speed and greed" (Ashford) does not mean that black technology consumers should be caught up in the often-disabling logic of computerized speed and technological greed.

Brown, like Tyrone Taborn, worried about the commodification of technology participation that, as Taborn noticed, threatened to equate minority communities' mere consumption of technology products with a dangerous misperception of their full participation in the new information economy.[28] To Brown's way of thinking, this was the wrong direction. Brown states, "Consumers—name-brand dependent—are always at the mercy of the marketeers. We poke fun at the white man who wears khakis, outdated tennis shoes and drives a pick-up truck. But we also know he's going to the bank!" Furthermore, as Brown comments, "It distresses me that we seem to be united in one thing only: the blind, self-destructive pursuit of stuff. It seems to me that our people bought the hype: portray the ILLUSION of wealth—at all costs." To counter the *stuff-rules* consumerist ideology, including the need to own every latest technology commodity, Brown boasted, "I don't need a new NOTHING as long as the one I have performs. Not a younger partner, not a blender, not a microwave, not shoes, outfits, or furniture. I own no cell phone, no pager, no 'personal digital assistant.' I'm not burdened with credit-card debt" (Ashford).

Brown's cyberflaneurie, then, was about promoting computer use to simplify not exacerbate black people's already complicated lives. As she puts it: "Simplicity is about re-prioritizing, making decisions for ourselves and our families, based on principles. I've used the Power Macintosh computer and printer for the last three years. If my machines are serving me well, I don't need every 'new' upgrade or gadget that engineers design." For sure she offers a viable alternative to the painful and well-known point that "Consumerism [is] built on planned obsolescence" (Ashford), a plan that many black people, positioned as technology outsiders, can ill afford, despite the long-overdue cost decreases in consumer-grade computer technologies.

What makes Brown's mold-breaking geek example so central, in addition to her gender, class, race, and age anomalies, is how she exemplifies an important yet undervalued aspect of black women's disproportionate rates of new technology adoption. In her study of girls and videogame culture, Heather Gilmour happened upon an intriguing factor that helps explain this unexpected female advantage in a male-dominated sphere. To a question posed to high school students regarding which gender "is better at using computers, boys, girls, or neither? What reasons would one give for" such a disparity, if one exists, one female student's response was telling. One girl in Gilmour's survey made the crucial observation that girls were better at using computers "because girls type faster" (283). This is an important revelation to the extent that it echoes the Million Woman March (MWM) webmaster's contention that the phenomenal success of the 1997 MWM was purchased by and large by the efforts of many black women who used their Internet access at work to spread the word and to generate interest in the march for those women who were not online. Brown's own "invisible" woman capitalization on a twenty-five-year career as a secretary for the U.S. government affirms this unanticipated gender advantage in the high-stakes technology war.

However, as with any institution-building enterprise, Brown recognizes the inevitability of handing over the reins of a successful venture to the next generation responsible for ensuring its perpetuation. Brown says as much in late 2000 in her interview with *IT Recruiter* magazine. Talking at that point about what comes next after her amazing successes and numerous accolades for founding and steering Black Geeks Online to its national prominence, Brown states, "It's time the new generation take it to the next level." In an apt summation of her ground-breaking efforts, and with an eye towards distilling her legacy in the world of IT community outreach, Brown conveyed her heartfelt sentiments about the role Black Geeks Online can play in community technology diffusion in the black community: "I want it to be fun, real hands-on, not just leaving people with the Magic Johnson Web site. No, we'll follow up with real info where they can get online for free, buy inexpensive PCs, where their neighborhood programs are" (Ashford). At the time of her untimely death of a heart attack in 2006, sixty-three-year-old Anita Brown could witness the next generation take IT to the next level as underrepresented groups of Latin American and Mexican American youths harnessed social networking sites (MySpace, Facebook), instant messaging, blogs, and other digital media to usher in what *Chicago Tribune* journalist Howard Witt dubbed a "'new' viral civil rights movement" ("Blogs Help Drive"). Emblematic of the viral civil rights movement taking next-gen IT to the streets was the unanticipated but widely covered national protests against the HR 4437 2005 Sensenbrenner Bill (Border Protection, Anti-terrorism, and Illegal Immigration Control Act) led by Latin American youths, Mexican American youths, and others sympathetic to this nationwide opposition to that divisive bill. Afrogeek Brown surely would have been proud.

CONCLUSION

Reflecting on the formidable advances in Internet and other digital media technologies that have ensued since I began this work, I am struck by how *much* and how *little* things have changed where digital technologies and race interface. On the one hand, my snapshot-in-time approach to researching the African and African diasporic presence in cyberspace during the early years of the Internet's formation as a unique if fledgling public mass medium yielded an array of significant studies that portended great strides toward closing the so-called digital divide against tremendous odds. Unquestionably, the research in this volume undermines recalcitrant notions about the position of black peoples across the globe as information technology outsiders and even technophobes. Moreover, the totality of this work confirms that black peoples have not only been enthusiastic early adopters and innovative users of new information technologies, especially of the Internet but that they were also among the key architects in the developmental history of new information technologies, especially in terms of their rapidly evolving social implications.

In fact, during the early days of the IT revolution the sociopolitical climate in America, specifically, fostered a vision of universal access and IT inclusivity that promised nothing short of a radical reinvention of America's fundamental democratic principles. After all, many of us bought into the powerful rhetoric that ultimately the Internet would level the playing field of access to the nation's important public sphere—that idealized Habermassian space venerated for its centrality to the necessary circulation of shared ideas and values at the heart of the nation's democratic functioning. And for a minute—in Internet years—(let us say from 1995 through 1998), that lofty ideal seemed easily achievable even to the nation's disadvantaged groups and to an extent was achieved, as the Million Woman March chapter illustrates.

On the other hand, it is apparent that most of this progressive activity was coterminous with that far-reaching period of media deregulation and its baleful consequences brought on by the Federal Communications Commission's (FCC) passage of the 1996 Communications Act that ultimately changed the media landscape drastically. Media consolidation eroded much of the diverse, independently owned media outlets, especially radio. Not only did this act open the floodgates to an unprecedented number of corporate media mergers and their resultant proprietary monopolies and oligopolies, but it also created the precondition for big media companies' near-total usurpation of the public broadcast spectrum (arguably our society's most influential public sphere). In effect, the 1996 Communications Act rescinded all prior claims to and expectations for universal access to the public marketplace of ideas for many of the newly empowered, computer savvy, nontraditional players who helped to make the Internet the global force for change that it became precisely because it was outside the panoptic gaze and radar screens of the traditional media powers.

Exacerbating this troubling development on America's national legislative front, the newly evolving media wars, impelled by the emergence of new digital technologies and the phenomenal "old" and "new" media competition, and the government's response to the tragic events of 11 September 2001, all but assured that the experiment with universal access to the new information technologies and the reinvention of democracy would be dead on arrival as the Internet came under increasing suspicion in America's newly christened twenty-first-century war on terrorism. And although I fear that the phenomenal strides made by Afrogeeks chronicled in this volume and those outside of its purview are jeopardized by such developments, I also recognize the looming possibilities for even greater progress and participation in the maturing global IT economy for African peoples on the continent and throughout the diaspora. In recent years, however, my deep ambivalence has given way to a more enthusiastic optimism as a result of my face-to-face contact with several key players who comprise my case studies in this book and numerous others not directly affiliated with this volume. This optimism is heightened further by what I learned from many Africans, African Americans, Afro Britons, and numerous others doing cutting-edge work on blackness and technology who all contributed to a series of race and technology conferences that I helped to organize and participated in from 2001 through 2005.[1]

FROM MOTHERBOARDS TO THE MOTHERLAND: MORE AFROGEEKS ARE IN THE HOUSE

During the final phases of this research project, I was appointed director of the University of California, Santa Barbara (UCSB), Center for Black Studies Research, which enabled me to convene two conferences on blackness and new ITs. As a result of the wealth of research contained in this volume and in my position as center director, I was empowered to make personal conference invitations to a wide range of IT workers in the realms of new media arts, community activism, scholarship and research, e-business, and other progressive IT practices. The response to our calls for participation over two years was overwhelmingly positive as the two IT conferences on blackness and technology that I organized successfully brought together an unprecedented variety of IT specialists from across the globe, including those from the United States, Africa (Sao Tome, Uganda, Ghana, and South Africa), Australia, Britain, Canada, and Hawaii. In 2004 we launched our first Afrogeeks conference, Afrogeeks: From Technophobia to Technophilia. One year later, we convened a follow-up conference, Afrogeeks: Global Blackness and the Digital Public Sphere.

These conferences were a revelation. It was clear to me that in the years that passed since I began this important research, much had changed for the better, despite the facts of big media mergers and industry consolidation, the horrific terror attacks in the United States on 11 September 2001, and the subsequent 2003 Operation Iraqi Freedom war. In effect, the shifting demands of geopolitics and changed international relations that reflected what media pundits after 11 September term our "new normal" condition had a direct impact on the Afrogeeks conference as many of the international participants encountered more cumbersome travel demands directly related to newly defined (real and imaginary) Homeland Security concerns. Still, the resolve of most international participants to attend the conferences was evident and impressive as all but two speakers from Africa were able to join the proceedings. Moreover, those who attended the conferences conveyed firsthand knowledge and experiences that support my contentions that the global focus on the racial digital divide in the burgeoning IT economy obscured from view the important progress and innovations in IT taking place in black communities across the globe. The consequence, I fear, is that indeed we remain in danger of this thinking becoming a self-fulfilling prophesy as necessary funding sources for successful models of global IT inclusion get redirected to fund the expensive and seemingly perpetual war on terrorism.

Still, the two Afrogeeks conferences revealed many powerful examples of actually existing programs that are, at once, effective and easily replicable cases of innovative IT adoption and sustainable infrastructure development in Africa and throughout the diaspora that cry out for support and recognition. Clearly, it is beyond the scope of this work to enumerate here all the important technology work on display at the two conferences. Nonetheless, I want to conclude this volume with references to several significant projects from our second race and technology conference in 2005 and then expound a bit more on several exemplary cases that I discovered at the conclusion of my years of research for this volume. In fact, it was the impressive information gleaned from the websites of several special projects that led me to feature them in the conferences. For example, the compelling work being conducted by the project leaders of the Ugandan women's technology collective prompted us to include this surprising project among our keynote presenters at the Afrogeeks: Global Blackness and the Digital Public Sphere conference. The unexpected strength and power of the Ugandan women's multimedia presentation of their NGO's technology work set them apart as an overwhelming crowd pleaser at the second conference in 2005 and what I believe is a telling example for the conclusion of this present work.

At the first conference in 2004, Afrogeek technology researcher and computer programmer Jorge Coelho presented findings from his field research on the growth of Internet cafes and computer learning centers on the small island nation of São Tomé e Principe (STP), a former Portuguese colony in central Africa, noted for recent discoveries of vast oil deposits of interest to America and other Western powers.[2] Coelho, a native of STP, was a visiting researcher at the UCSB Center for Black Studies charged with conducting onsite research concerning the impact and value of technology adoption in his homeland, as part of his postgraduate studies. Another key component of Coelho's 2003–04 research trip was to conduct computer literacy workshops for STP's high school youths as a result of his own specialized computer science training at both Russian and U.S. universities. In addition to acquainting the Afrogeeks conference attendees with historical and contemporary data on STP, Coelho incorporated photos of his teaching experience with the students and their engagements with computers in his conference presentation. Pertinent for our consideration of Africa's and African diasporic peoples' often unacknowledged or dismissed participation in the ascendant global IT economy are several of Coelho's telling findings.

First, Coelho's experiences disclose a particular hollowness to claims of universal technology access (that in a world after 11 September are characterized as less desirable) and the forging of new digital democracies through the Internet when the language gateways to the web and other digital technologies are not available in dominant African languages or even in Portuguese (the dominant language of STP), in some instances. Second, he calls attention to the lack of a modern IT infrastructure capable of ensuring reliable, affordable, and pervasive computer connectivity on the small, impoverished island nation. Third, Coelho reminds us that despite the citizenry's (especially the youth's) interest in and yearning for securing their participation in the information society, that nation's complex postcolonial realities and contemporary geopolitics often conspire to frustrate STP's modernizing ambitions in the realm of IT. Still, computer education and training continues, IT infrastructure and literacy development advances, Internet cafés exist, recent discoveries of oil in the region beckon, and the exertion of new external pressures on the powerful European nations (that from the G-8 organization) for African "debt relief," all leave me reasonably optimistic that tiny STP, among other African countries, will emerge as an increasingly relevant if unlikely global player on the international scene as this millennium progresses (figure C.1).[3]

ON DIGITIZING THE MOTHERLAND WITH WOMEN TECHNOLOGY WORKERS IN UGANDA

Among the more surprising and impressive models of socially conscious technology work occurring in Africa are WOUGHNET, Isis-WICCE, and IWTC, three separate but related rural and semiurban community-based IT networking centers organized for and managed primarily by African women in Uganda. The Women of Uganda Network (WOUGNET) is an NGO established in May 2000 by several affiliated women's groups united to promote and support the development of a

FIGURE C.1. Photo of STP students in computer lab, and satellite in rural and urban spaces. IT education is a priority for these select students, and the nation of STP. The juxtaposition of these satellites and the local STP landscape is striking in its representation of technology development and the country's global IT aspirations.

viable information communication technology (ICT) network devoted to Ugandan women's goals of information sharing and political empowerment. As articulated on their website, WOUGNET recognized,

> The new ICTs, in particular, [and how] email and the Internet facilitate communication with each other and the international community. Indeed, access to information about best practices, appropriate technologies, ideas and problems of other groups working on similar concerns have been identified as critical information and communication needs of women's organisations in Africa.[4]

WOUGNET is essentially an online information clearinghouse specializing in a wide range of IT-related news and services of particular interest to African women in general, and women in Uganda in particular.

Among its plethora of offerings are links to organizational websites, a newsletter, and tech support services, including virus prevention, data back-up tips, software tutorials, managing email and instant messaging, and step-by-step guides to setting up firewalls and blogs. Assistance with website design and development and access to satellite radio services are also available to WOUGNET's listserv members. The award-winning WOUGNET website also provides its mailing list of subscribers with the latest ICT policy news bearing on Uganda and other African nations. Presenting the case for WOUGNET at the second Afrogeeks conference was Milton Aineruhanga (a last minute replacement for his boss, Director Dorothy Okello).

Founded in 1974, Isis-Women's International Cross-Cultural Exchange (Isis-WICCE) obviously predates the contemporary IT revolution. Nonetheless, its mission "to promote justice, and empowerment of women globally through documenting violations of women's rights and facilitating the exchange of information and skills, to strengthen women's capacities, potential, and visibility,"[5] remains as pertinent today (if not more so) as when the organization began. Additionally, when Isis-WICCE moved administrative operations to Kampala, Uganda, in 1993, it not only maintained a fealty to the visions of its progressive white feminist founders (Jane Cottingham and Marilee Karl of Geneva, Switzerland), which included "communicating ideas, creating solidarity networks and sharing information to overcome gender inequalities," promoting women's self-determination and "building a culture of peace" (Isis-WICCE). In Kampala Isis-WICCE set forth a bold, new agenda designed specifically to better incorporate African women's unique needs, perspectives, and ideas for fundamental change in the status of women at an international level. A key component of this move was the organization's effort to develop national and regional programs capable of facilitating the flow of utilitarian technology information from Uganda to other parts of Africa and the rest of the world and strengthening Uganda's and other African nations' incipient women's movement (Isis-WICCE).

Whereas the new digital media technologies that enabled WOUGNET's very existence justify the location of its information resources and operational activities primarily in cyberspace, Isis-WICCE's founding and successful operations prior to the IT revolution explain its base of operations in the real world now augmented by the expanded global reach of the Internet. Among Isis-WICCE's programs that call attention to and seek redress for the human rights violations against

African women in conflict and war zones are international, national, and regional exchange programs, research, and documentation of wartime abuses of women in print, video, online, and DVD formats, information dissemination and advocacy projects by any media possible, among other self-help and self-determination strategies.

In addition to several published research reports produced in print by Isis-WICCE (such as "Women's Experiences of Armed Conflict Situations in Uganda: The Case of Gulu District 1986–1999," "Medical Interventional Study of War Affected Gulu District, Uganda," and "Women's Experiences in Situations of Armed Conflict, 1987–2001: The Teso Experience"), Isis-WICCE produced two video documentaries of armed conflict and war's atrocities against Ugandan women as told through testimonials from women victims, health care providers, and educators in 2000 and 2002. The documentaries also released on DVD are titled *Women, War, Trauma* (2000) and *A Lingering Pain: Her Experience* (2002). The women's stories are heartbreaking, poignant and, in a remarkable way, inspiring in their testaments to these women's humanity, dignity, perseverance, and the Isis-WICCE organization's involvement in and contribution to these affected communities beyond the importance of telling these horrific stories. Not only did Isis-WICCE provide visual evidence of the often ignored but particularly harrowing crimes against women in Africa's too numerous armed conflicts, but the NGO (with the assistance of trained medical professionals) also intervened in these struggles through their procurement of essential medical care and treatment for some of Uganda's most severely traumatized women.

What makes Isis-WICCE's case so compelling is its focused work on and publicity about the unique predicament of African women and girls' suffering that frequently gets elided in Western media's myopic coverage of African as a continent always in some form of postindependence degenerate, man-made crisis. Conspicuously absent in these international reports (in both print and video) from Western media conglomerates are detailed background narratives about women's victimization. Thus Isis-WICCE provides a much-needed corrective by drawing attention (online and in print) to such women's issues as rape as a war crime, the powerful social stigmas of unwanted pregnancies from rape, the fundamental unfairness to victims of government amnesty programs for perpetrators of violence against the women, matters concerning the rehabilitation for amputee victims of land mines and psychological trauma, and the state of medical and psychological treatment for women and girls of sexually transmitted diseases through rapes—including AIDS. When Isis-WICCE's current director, Ruth Ojimbo Ochieng, addressed the Afro-geeks conference in 2005, her passionate presentation to this international gathering about the work of this organization was met with rapt attention and frequent applause as she outlined the formidable challenges and remarkable successes of the group's experiences. Based on the conference audience's response to Ojimbo Ochieng's revelation, it is clear that the sophisticated levels of IT engagement and the rates of technology diffusion among rural and other women and girls in Uganda came as a great and welcome conference surprise.

Finally, our third and last group is the International Women's Tribune Center (IWTC). Founded in 1976 after the United Nations' International Women's Year World Conference in Mexico City, this long-standing global network of women activists tackles African women's issues from several strategic trajectories of need. On their website, IWTC relays their mission as a nongovernmental agency dedicated to the special needs of impoverished women in developing nations, including Africa. According to their website's mission statement: "IWTC provides communication, information, education, and organizing support services to women's organizations and community groups working to improve the lives of women, particularly low-income women, in Africa, Asia and the Pacific, Latin America and the Caribbean, Eastern Europe and Western Asia."[6] What struck me most about IWTC's work as I encountered it during the final phases of this current research project was the organizations' emphasis on "the use of the new information communication technologies (ICTs) for poverty alleviation and empowerment" (IWTC).

I became acquainted with the IWTC's work in 2002 when a conference colleague directed me to the organization's website featuring, at that time, the Nakaseke Telecenter Project in Uganda. The Telecenter, in conjunction with the IWTC, was spearheading the pioneering work of integrating ICTs into the everyday lives and "day to day income generating activities"[7] of rural women agricultural workers in Uganda. Among the more compelling items on the website was a story about the local women's enthusiastic participation in the computer literacy program replete with a striking entry on and photograph of the Nakaseke Telecenter's most famous student, project spokesperson, and techevangelist, the seventy-year-old Anastasia Namisango, sitting in front of a computer (figure C.2). The important story behind the Nakeseke Telecenter and IWTC partnership (along with several others including Isis-WICCE and

FIGURE C.2. Cover image of DVD for Ugandan women's microbusiness venture, and photo of seventy-year-old Technophile Anastasia, at computer.

WOUGNET) was its development of a unique CD-ROM designed as an introductory tool of ICT training for "first time users of computers" with the innovation of adapting the program in the language of the Nakaseke women users (online only) "to ensure widespread replicability and viability."[8]

It is hardly surprising that the IWTC and the Nakaseke Telecenter recognized the promotional value and recruitment potential of its elder spokeswoman, Anastasia Namisango, to spread the word that new information technologies could become an important tool of modernization and income generation for poor, rural farm women in Uganda. Then seventy-year-old Namisango's enthusiastic embrace of the IWTC's pioneering CD-ROM, entitled *Rural Women in Africa: Ideas for Earning Money*, became a cause-celebre for numerous organizations and groups involved with matters of gender equity and ICTs, including UNESCO and the BBC. One such organization involved with the global computer literacy movement is the International Information Center and Archives for the Women's Movement (IIAV), whose program director, Lin McDevitt-Pugh, conveys Namisango's global appeal. In a 2004 online query about the feasibility of ICTs among "rural women in developing countries," McDevitt-Pugh states:

> Anastasia Namisango was one of the first women trained by the Nakeseke Telecentre to use the CD Rom. Ms Namisango felt the informa-

tion in the CD Rom was so important that she had a printout made and traveled with the printout to speak with women in nearby villages, inviting them to come to the Telecenter to use the product. This was so effective that it was decided that Ms Namisango should have a laptop to take with her on these visits. So her having a laptop became a way for her to teach women, in the village setting, how to use a computer, and to invite them to come to the Telecenter to use computers to find information that will benefit their lives. Unfortunately, there is still very little content available in languages these women speak, and this is a need that must be addressed. Regarding the ability to learn new skills, one of the women from the Telecenter we interviewed on being asked how difficult it was to learn to use the computer replied "It was a little bit easy. I only needed two lessons." Women who can wield complex farming equipment can wield a mouse.[9]

What makes wrapping up this study with these more inspiring contemporary examples of successful integration of new media technologies in the lives of poorly educated, rural women agricultural workers in Uganda and other underserved African communities so important is their visible, enthusiastic, and unexpected black bodies as exemplars of what I term "not the usual cyborg subjects" of technoculture. During this final phase of the study that included the two Afrogeeks conferences, I was further assisted by Anne S. Walker, then director of the IWTC and force behind the *Rural Women in Africa: Ideas for Earning Money* CD-ROM. Despite Walker's initial hesitation to participate in the conference because, as she expressed to me, she was a white, Australian woman, fortunately she was persuaded to participate by our logic of considering as an Afrogeek anyone committed to the work of advancing the cause of bridging the "digital divide" for African peoples across the globe. After all, it was Walker who had introduced me to the other Ugandan women and male technology workers behind the Isis-WICCE and WOUGNET organizations who also helped make Afrogeeks: Global Blackness and the Digital Public Sphere conference an unqualified success; and they ultimately bore out many of the early empowerment theses supporting viable strategies and tactics for achieving universal access to technology outlined in the early pages of this work.

At the conference, Walker demonstrated the *Rural Women in Arica* CD-ROM product, which illustrated an important and visionary element of the IWTC team's inclusive approach to promoting computer literacy training for the Telecenter's participating rural and semiurban Ugandan women agricultural workers. A simple yet profound strategy of the CD-ROM was the formulation of a "computer book" interface that incorporated an African woman avatar/narrator figure who spoke all the computer directives and narrated, word for word, the entire contents of the on-screen texts. In this way, the target audience was provided an immediate and user-friendly computer tool for all the women despite literacy or computer compentency levels. Additionally, the pragmatics of presenting an oral narration component and African-inspired illustrations and iconographies in the CD-ROM meant that long-standing literacy obstacles were eliminated as the women learned sound business practices for their microbusiness endeavors shown to be adaptable and pertinent to familiar cultural frameworks.

Significantly, there is a shared organizational and networking logic informing each of these sister organizations rooted in their emphasis on adopting information technologies, especially computers and the Internet, as advocacy tools for African women's issues, which is precisely what led me to feature them at the second Afrogeeks conference. In an unexpected turn, an African American woman in the conference audience asked the Ugandan women representatives for strategies and tips that African American women, who, despite popular assumptions of technological advantage by virtue of being in America, might use to replicate the Ugandan women's apparent successes at recruiting uneducated, rural women to the benefits and opportunities of embracing new information technologies.

HIGHWAY AFRICA 2005 CONFERENCE

From 12 through 14 September 2005, I had the opportunity to participate in what I learned was the Ninth Annual Highway Africa Conference, sponsored by the journalism department of the University of Rhodes in Grahamstown, South Africa. The significance of the Highway Africa Conference to this study is its role in advancing ICT development and infrastructures across the African continent over a period of years that happens to coincide with my research arc. The unofficial tally of attendees at the 2005 conference was approximately five hundred from among the ranks of journalists, scholars, researchers, media company executives, and other technology workers from Africa and the West. We eagerly welcomed our roles as contributors to this dialogic encounter with the Highway Africa Conference theme of reinforcing journalism in the information society. In his address to the gathering, Highway Africa director Chris Kabwato gives us a sense of the organization's relevance to this present research project and my excitement about participating in it. Kabwato writes in the conference program:

> The Highway Africa Conference 2005 is the ninth edition of an event that had rather humble origins but has now become the largest annual gathering of African journalists in the world. In 2004 we had 430 delegates from 28 African countries and a few from outside our beloved continent. . . . This year's conference interrogates something that touches on the core of our profession—the underpinnings of African journalism. . . . [S]hould Africa have its own form of journalism? We are also doing a bit of navel-gazing—looking at journalism and ethics in the advent of new media (mostly web-based) and attendant new forms of "journalism" such as blogging. The conference takes place just two months before the final phase of the World Summit on the Information Society (WSIS) in Tunisia (16–18 November). We shall discuss how the media will be involved in this most important event that will determine the direction of contentious issues such as the management of the Internet and the funding of ICT infrastructure in Africa.[10]

This lengthy quote points to a number of compelling aspects that drew this year's constellation of conference participants from such diverse nations as South Africa, Zimbabwe, Uganda, Senegal, Ghana, Kenya, Mozambique, Ethiopia, Sweden, Norway, the Netherlands, the Czech Republic, and the United States. For example, the question of whether or not Africa should have its own form of journalism resonated throughout several conference panels as the introductory plenary session, Towards a Philosophy of "African Journalism": Africa and the Politics of Identity in a Globalized World, Journalism in Africa, Africa in Journalism, generated lively discussion and debate and became a persistent frame of reference as Western journalistic conventions and traditions came under scrutiny in the face of African inroads with new ICTs. One participant's statement that "ICTs can be used to beat back poverty and hunger"[11] in Africa articulates well a number of points that I have consistently tried to make concerning the necessity of IT investment in Africa during the course of this research. Of major consequence also was the conference organizers' and participants' efforts to have an impact on the second World Summit on the Information Society (WSIS) in Tunisia in November 2005, as many

Highway Africa Conference (and the UCSB Afrogeeks conference) participants would be attending the WSIS summit as well.

I was very pleased to be a member of the drafting committee charged with the Highway Africa Conference statement to the second WSIS convention, a statement designed to prevent the marginalization of Africa's particular IT issues, and to promote the continent's say and involvement in the larger deliberative body's agenda of this influential United Nations–led initiative. In 2003, the first phase of the WSIS meeting was held in Geneva, Switzerland, where ideas and recommendations were solicited in the global effort to bridge the "digital divide." According to the WSIS website:

> The objective of the first phase was to develop and foster a clear statement of political will and take concrete steps to establish the foundations for an Information Society for all, reflecting all the different interests at stake. At the Geneva Phase of WSIS nearly 50 Heads of state/government and Vice-Presidents, 82 Ministers, and 26 Vice-Ministers and Heads of delegations from 175 countries as well as high-level representatives from international organizations, private sector, and civil society provided political support to the WSIS Declaration of Principles and Plan of Action that were adopted on 12 December 2003. More than 11,000 participants from 175 countries attended the Summit and related events. The scope and nature of this ambitious project requires new public-private partnerships, many of which were formalized during the Geneva Summit. Some of them were specifically targeted at bridging the digital divide.[12]

Not only were WSIS and its United Nations–backed mission of establishing foundations for a progressive and inclusive information society welcome discoveries for me, but being privy to and included in the Highway Africa delegates' committed efforts to make a strong showing at WSIS particularly on behalf of the African continent somehow seemed an uncanny set of fortunate confluences and validation at this concluding stage of my current research project. I initiated this research into the African diasporic presence online and other issues of blackness and new information technologies in the mid to late 1990s when the Internet was becoming a mass medium, and as expected there was virtually no work on this topic. Finally, momentum on blackness and technology has been gathering in the last few years. Be that as it may, my participation in the

Highway Africa Conference and as a Fulbright Fellow in Tunisia, both in 2005 and 2007, have enabled me to see aspects of my African-inflected research from the unique contours both of cyberspace and in real or material African spaces. In Tunisia I visited and made use of a popular Internet café and indeed relied on it for my own transnational communication needs during my stay. In South Africa, at the Highway Africa Conference in Grahamstown, I met an impressive array of African media executives, journalists, and scholars who were engaged with and doing leading-edge work on achieving universal technology access to global media audiences and consumers.

At the Highway Africa Conference, I was struck particularly by the fact that Highway Africa and the South Africa Broadcasting Corporation (SABC) sponsor an annual live, prime-time television broadcast of New Media Innovation Awards that celebrate the accomplishments of those African nations using ICTs in journalistic practices to progressive and modernizing ends. Of particular interest for me was Highway Africa's 2005 awards show that featured a very futuristic interactive segment in which the show host interviewed a speaker from a remote location via a wrist phone. While videoconferencing is not new, it certainly was new and a revelation to see such a dramatic demonstration of this Dick Tracyesque technology on display in Africa!

It is difficult to conclude this research project after so many productive and generative years of immersion into this growing field of race and technology studies. I am, however, heartened by the prospect that the ever-expanding nature of cyberculture and cybertextuality continues to engender an endless horizon of new research possibilities centering around blackness and the new global information order. Conceived from the outset as a revisionist history of Africa's and the African diaspora's engagement with the Internet during the early years, this volume consists of important moment-in-time case studies that, although not comprehensive, do set forth a useful historical framework and foundational basis for further work that I know others are currently pursuing. I end with this cautiously hopeful quote from new media educator and entrepreneur Patrick Awauh, the founder and president of Ashesi University in Ghana. Addressing the Afrogeeks conference in 2005, Awauh remarked:

> More important than what we teach is how we teach. . . . It is important that we teach our leaders how Ghana is effectively exploring technology.

Our government clearly recognizes the importance of technology in our world . . . but recognition is not enough. . . . [W]e are not moving as quickly as we wish or should. . . . [E]veryone is radiating up in the skies . . . rationing bandwith in a way that I do not understand. . . . [W]orse yet is that our government taxes us for this technology . . . Ghana is connected— it deployed v-sat when other African countries did not . . . mobile phones and fm technologies . . . [and] there are internet cafes everywhere, so Ghana is not doing so bad. ("Ashesi University")

As a project designed to reframe and recontextualize the digital divide rhetoric, this book concurs with Awauh's observations and goes further to add that in terms of ICTs the African digital diaspora is not doing so bad either (figure C.3).

FIGURE C.3. Photo montage of images from both the Afrogeeks and Highway Africa conferences that convened May 2005 in the United States of America, and later in October 2005 in South Africa, respectively. Pictured clockwise at Afro-geeks conference: Alondra Nelson, Mendi and Keith Obedike, Floyd Webb and Mark Dery, and Guy Berger. At Highway Africa conference: Jimi Adesina and audience of South African journalists.

UPDATE! AFROGEEK ELECTED PRESIDENT OF THE U.S.

As this book goes to press, a significant development of unprecedented dimensions has transpired for the United States, in general, and for the African digital diaspora, in particular—the successful presidential campaign and subsequent election of President-elect Barack Obama as the 44th President of the United States of America and first African American elected to the office. It has been widely acclaimed that Obama's historical campaign was masterful in harnessing the exponential growth, influence and pervasiveness of the Internet and other digital media technologies in his phenomenal 2008 Presidential primary and general campaigns. This was a significant factor in Obama's successful bid to become the nation's first black president, with the added distinction of garnering a decisive portion of the popular and electoral college votes. In many ways, the transformative election of President-elect Obama represents a fulfillment of the promise of black disaporic empowerment through the Internet and other digital technologies outlined in the foregoing chapters. With his coterie of tech savvy youths who have never known a world without the Internet, and those others who have learned to master its language and protocols, groups who Marc Prensky has termed "digital natives and digital immigrants," Obama and his political campaign upped the ante of effective online grass roots activism instantiated by such early exemplars as the Million Woman March, the Black Geeks Online, and the "'viral' civil rights movement" of black and Latino/Latina youths (Howard Witt "Jena Protests"), among many others.

Significantly, President-elect Obama's campaign journey signifies a level of next-generation online activism that advances beyond the abovementioned, and the technologically sophisticated case of Dr. Howard Dean's 2004 Internet-driven presidential primary campaign. And for our purposes, Obama's ability to tap into what Pierre Levy terms our "new knowledge space" and "cosmopedia" as concepts to help leverage "the potentials of the new media environment . . . for transforming existing structures of knowledge and power" (quoted in Jenkins, *Fans, Bloggers and Gamers* 136) is nothing short of astounding. It seems that having an African American President as the Afrogeek in-Chief, or the HAIC (Head Afrogeek in Charge) would go a long way toward prompting us to rethink, redefine, and move beyond certain debilitating aspects of the digital divide discourse as proffered throughout this book, particularly for black communities in Africa and throughout the African diaspora.

At the same time, it has been interesting to watch the media's fascination with Obama's technophilia and his penchant for the Blackberry as his PDA of choice. In fact, a few stories centering on Obama's future as a president deeply engaged with ubiquitous computing, high-tech gadgets, and the question of how online community organizing will be reconciled or negotiated with the sensitive demands of his public office bears some consideration here. On November 16, 2008, for example, MSNBC Political Correspondent David Shuster guest-hosted the popular MSNBC news magazine show *Countdown*, and broached the subject in a humorous but serious manner. In the show segment titled "Countdown to January 20th," Shuster interviewed political columnist Ana Marie Cox on the necessity for stripping Obama of his beloved Blackberry. Shuster, for his part recognized the irony in the apparent rules that U.S. presidents must give up personal email, cell phone numbers, etc. in their official capacities and for national security reasons especially, as Shuster noted: "It is a little shocking that Obama will be the first sitting President to use a laptop, so he's really dragging the Oval Office into the late twentieth century." For Cox, the real question, jokingly, was: "Will Obama choose a Mac or PC?" She made the point that Obama is closely identified with the Mac brand. It is significant that many mainstream media pundits have been taken with and have remarked on the fact that Obama's successful campaign was defined and largely determined by the Internet, the blogosphere, and other digital cultures and technologies.

Moreover, the phenomenal success of the Obama campaign's deployment of the Internet and other digital technologies (cell phones, PDAs, and digital games, etc.) has led some, including Arianna Huffington, founder of the wildly successful online news outlet *The Huffington Post*, to proclaim, if tentatively, that Barack Obama's Administration will usher in "the first Internet Presidency." Sitting in as guest host on MSNBC's *Rachel Maddow Show*, Huffington also reminded us that: "FDR had his radio fireside chats," but that "Obama's first weekly address was posted on YouTube." When she asks, "Is the medium the message," we understand that this is an important question particularly as it redounds to our overall discussion in this historical study. Eric Schmidt, Chairman and CEO of Google joined Huffington in this discussion about Obama's as the first Internet presidency. What Huffington revealed that is also pertinent to our discussion is the fact that Obama is on record to "appoint the nation's first Chief Technology Officer (CTO)" which then will function "to bring government into the twenty-first century" (Huffington).

Eric Schmidt, also a member of the Obama Transition Economic Advisory Board, addressed Huffington's view that without the Internet Obama likely would not have been elected. She queried him about what role the Internet would assume in an Obama Administration. After agreeing that Obama would not have been elected without the Internet, Schmidt added that: "One of the great winners of the election that just happened was the Internet itself." Schmidt made the point that no politician returning to government in 2009 can ignore the Internet "to communicate directly with its citizens." What he emphasized was the two-way flow of information that characterized and energized Obama's transformative online presence in the age of the Internet and YouTube. Remarking

FIGURE C.4. Scanned image of 2008 campaign button for now-President-Elect Barack Obama.

upon Obama's brilliant use of YouTube to disseminate his first weekly address, Schmidt stressed the point that unlike the FDR fireside radio chats, Obama's YouTube Chats feature user commentary and involvement, where "they could say I agree or disagree." He noted further that such a platform or new media structure "drives more engagement . . . which is a cornerstone of democracy." The interview segment revealed that "Obama's first weekly YouTube Address rack[ed] up more than 700,000 views." For anyone failing to recognize the political paradigm shift, the new normal condition occurring, or the powerful digital writing on the screens all across America today, take heed. To quote journalist Alison Stewart on the 19 November 2008 *Rachel Maddow Show*, such a failure to see "is *so* November 3rd" (figure C.4).

NOTES

INTRODUCTION

1. I began writing this manuscript on a late 1990s-era PC coded with a DOS-based string of boot-up commands. However, I have since upgraded to a 2005 Dell Inspiron model PC and a number of Macintosh PCs, including the Powerbook and the 2008 MacBook Air. I have always been bi-platform, though I began my PC experience with a Mac. In completing this work, I alternate between all machines. My newer computers do not reveal the textual language of its boot-up string of commands and codes as a new graphical interface has replaced the older format, and users are instantly transported and given access to the desktop environment, sans the "master" and "slave" coding references. Nonetheless, I did photograph and still recall the image of this relic or artefact of computing's earlier discursive modes of conveying certain operational protocols.

CHAPTER ONE. TOWARD A THEORY
OF THE EGALITARIAN TECHNOSPHERE

1. The Bakke decision became the legal watershed event that set the stage for the successful passage of Proposition 209 and the rest. The U.S. Supreme Court ruled on 3 November 1997 that 209 would stand and that appeals against the measure would not be heard. The *New York Times* reported on 2 November 1997 that "the number of minorities entering U.S. Medical schools dropped 11% this year, most drastically in states affected by affirmative action roll-backs. . . . Some educators," the story continues, "fear the figures show that actions of a federal court in Texas and the voters of California to end educational preferences for minorities are echoing through the nation." The report cites med-

ical schools in California, Texas, Mississippi, and Louisiana as particular cases in point (A23).

2. See Theodore Roszak, *The Cult of Information,* for an insightful discussion of the symbiosis obtaining between the 1948 discovery of cybernetic information theories and microbiological research into cracking the "genetic code" of DNA. According to Roszak, Norbert Weiner's "too esoteric" work on cybernetics "found its most dramatic support from another, unexpected quarter: Biology—or rather, the *new* biology, where the most highly publicized scientific revolution since Darwin was taking place. In 1952, microbiologists James Watson and Francis Crick announced that they had solved the master problem of modern biology. They had broken the 'genetic code' hidden deep within the molecular structure of DNA. The very use of the word 'code' in this context is significant. . . . It immediately seemed to link the discoveries of the biologists to those of the new information theorists, whose work had much to do with the 'encoding' of information. . . . Since its inception, the new biology has been so tightly entwined with the language and imagery of information science that it is almost impossible to imagine the field developing at all without the aid of the computer paradigm" (16–17).

3. These ideas are found throughout Jacques Derrida's writings, including his books *Of Grammatology* and *Writing and Difference.*

4. For a thorough treatment of the confluence of African and European musical traditions, see *Blues People,* by LeRoi Jones.

5. See *Sisterhood Is Powerful,* ed. Robin Morgan, for a rare acknowledgment of the civil rights movement's direct influence on 1970s feminism in America.

6. See for example J. Fred MacDonald, *One Nation under Television;* Douglas Kellner, *Television and the Crisis of Democracy;* and Todd Gitlin, *Channels of Discourse,* for varying perspectives on television's "turn to relevance," as MacDonald terms it, during the 1960s upheavals in American civil society.

7. The effects on society due to media reporting on violence have been the subject of several studies, including two independent 1997 studies conducted by the University of Miami's communications school and by the Rocky Mountain Media Watch. Citing these studies in his article for the Associated Press, David Bauder quotes researchers' observations: "Crime coverage has remained steady over the past few years even though the crime rate has dropped, Klite said. 'You get this body-bag journalism over and over again,' said Joseph Angotti, who directed the Miami study. 'I think it has a numbing effect on the public. People withdraw from activities because of fear.'" Bauder's report was reprinted in the 12 May 1997 issue of the *Denver Post*: 6A.

8. Derrick Bell argues from the outset of his book *Faces at the Bottom of the Well: The Permanence of Racism,* that "racism is an integral, permanent and indestructible component of this [American] society" (ix).

9. See also George Lipsitz's important study of television's role in popularizing the homogenizing concept of 'whiteness' while undermining the heterogeneity of white ethnic identity in America during the postwar years, in *Logics of TV.*

10. There are numerous online exegeses of Marinetti and his celebration of the mechanical age. Among the sites conveying information on Marinetti are "Marinetti: 'Joy' and 'Manifesto,'" http//www.english.upenn.edu/~jenglish/English104/marinetti.html, and "Marinetti, Filippo Tommaso, The Columbia Encyclopeida: Sixth Edition. 2000, http://www.bartleby.com/65/ma/marinetti.html.

11. Author Chansanchai's article conclusion includes the following quote from a 131st Street Block Association administrator, "The idea behind Jerra's self-esteem is that she knows she is somebody, that she is a leader in her own right and not a struggling kid. On 110th and Lexington, when she walks out, the whole path from here to the school is negative. The whole environment is negative."

12. See Randal C. Archibold's technology feature story "The Virtual Pie Shop and Other Cyber Dreams," *Los Angeles Times*: E1–2.

13. For the entire contents of this provocative consideration of black science fiction literature, see Mark Dery's important anthology on the evolving cyberculture discourse featuring this interview with Delany, Tate, and Rose in *Flame Wars: The Discourse of Cyberculture*, 179–222.

14. For a recent discussion of the two-way influence of black hip-hop music's "backbeat" and "scratch" styles on both American and German techno-music electronic aesthetics, see Tom Terrell's account in "The Second Wave: 1980–1983," in *The Vibe History of Hip Hop*, edited by Alan Light.

15. Despite Marinetti's technological progressivity, his passionate future vision is forever tained by his fascism and antifeminism.

16. For several full translations of Marinetti's futurist manifesto, see <http://www.english.upenn.edu/~jenglish/English104/marinetti.html> and <http://www.unknown.nu/futurism/manifesto.html>.

17. On 10 August 1995, the *Los Angeles Times* featured a story on Netscape's founder Marc Andreessen and the Internet browser innovation in its business section, D1.

18. For a photo essay of the 1997 "Taking IT to the Streets" event, see their webpage: <http://www.blackgeeks.com/2takinit.html>.

19. My own searches on 6 February 2001 *African American* yielded these results from the following search engines: Excite—120,065; HotBot—907,600; Look Smart—2000; Lycos—1,651,895.

20. In 1987, Ben Bagdikian commented on the role of big media corporations in narrowing the information spectrum of American citizens. In his perennially in-press book *The Media Monopoly*, Bagdikian writes: "Each year it is more likely that the American citizen who turns to any medium—newspapers, magazines, radio or television, books, movies, cable, recordings, video cassettes—will receive information, ideas, or entertainment controlled by the same handful of corporations, whether it is daily news, a cable entertainment program, or a textbook. Any surprise of a few years ago is replaced by the demonstration that media giants have become so powerful that government no longer has the will to restrain them. Corporate news media and business oriented governments have made common cause. The public, dependent on the media giants for its basic information, is not told of the dangers" (ix). Prefiguring this cross-media consolidation or corporate cartelism, the film industry, led by Thomas Edison, effected its own brand of media monopoly. For a cinema history discussion of the Edison trust, see for example, "Edison's Trust and How It Got Busted," in Robert Sklar, *Movie Made America.*

21. See Misty L. Bastian's excellent history of "Immigrant Nigerians on the Internet" at <http: www.westafricareview.com/war/vol1.1/bastian.html>.

22. I discuss this usage of "recolonize" in more detail in my article, "Recolonizing Africa for the 21st Century," *UFAHAMU: Journal of African Activist Association.* (21:1–2): 26–38.

23. I borrow this phrasing from Saskia Sassen, which is the title of this author's recent book, *Globalization and Its Discontents*, published in 1998 by the New Press.

24. When my research lurking led me to ANA in 1997, I had no prior knowledge of its splintering from Niajanet and thus its informative prehistory. As a nonparticipant observer of these first steps in the development of an emergent black digital diaspora, coming of age with the mass-culture oriented World Wide Web portion of the Internet, I opted for as much critical distance as possible, given my obvious enthusiasm for this phenomenon. Also, in grappling with privacy issues and the spirit of "freedom to lurk" around Internet Relay Chat (IRC) groups and communities at the beginning of my research, I discovered that there were a few instances where identification requests were made part of the virtual interaction. In that case, I opted for the familiar and accepted practice of using avatars or pseudonyms to gain entry to some virtual communities. To honor the privilege of access on condition of identity concealment, I determined to reciprocate in kind by extending the same privacy by creating avatars for those under my observation and discussed in this project. In the concluding phase of my research, and to answer some important questions, I made contact with some members of a few digital domains, who were often quite forthcoming and pleased to learn about my ongoing research and focus on their particular communities or websites. It is from

this experience later in my own research agenda that I can appreciate Bastian's more intimate, participant-observer knowledge of Niajanet members's origin stories, as my case study of one Naijanetter's two-year-long archival documentation of his Naijanet correspondences will no doubt convey. It is my hope that in the following chapter my discussion of this specific instance of Naijanet's "database as discourse" (to Mark Poster's phrasing) provides an interesting micronarrative and corollary to Bastain's more macrohistorical overview. See Poster 175–92.

25. See for example the text of the ANA press release, which is interesting because of its international list of members and the particular demands it outlines for progressive netusers. The information is available at ANA online-1995: "The Association of Nigerians Abroad (ANA)," <http://www.prairienet.org/acas/ana. html.

26. ANA online 2004, Scholarship http://www.ananet.org/.

27. In mid-1997 I accessed ANA's website to discover a "Welcome Letter" from the organization's president. It is here that site visitors are informed of ANA's "window on the world" and told about some of the goals of its diverse and far-flung membership base. See Usman G. Akano's "Welcome Letter" page of the ANA site.

28. Akano's ANA "Welcome Letter."

29. See ANA at http://www.ananet.org/.

30. For the full text of the letter to President Obasanjo, visit the site at http://www.ananet.org/Sharia.html.

31. See the new ANA website at <http://www.ananet.org/>.

32. Duncan Harford graciously consented to an online interview with me via email in December 2000. All quotes and specified information regarding the ANC's website are attributed to those email communiques and the ANC website itself.

33. The current Unwembi Communications website is located at <http://www.unwembi.co.za/>.

34. The ANC's revamped website is available at <http://www.anc.org.az>.

35. You will find this description in the Random House *Webster's Collegiate Dictionary* 773.

CHAPTER TWO. DIGITAL WOMEN

1. See for example, Micheal Janofsky's report on the Million Woman March in his article "At Million Woman March, Focus Is on Family," *New York Times* 26 October 1997: A1+.

2. For a thorough discussion of this and other ongoing concerns, see for example, "Million Man March: Almost a Blackout," *Los Angeles Sentinel,* 26 October 1995, A6.

3. On the one year anniversary of the Million Woman March, Karen E. Quinones Miller's article that mentions the march organizers' backgrounds appears on the *Philadelphia Inquirer* website: http://www.philly.com/package/wmill/Inq/MILL102598.asp.

4. See the *Final Call* interview with Phile Chionesu and Asia Coney, 1997 at http:www.netset.com/~Kandi/index8.html/guests.html/intrvw1.htm.

5. The significance of the Internet in the Million Woman March's (MWM) success was relayed to me via an email communication with MWM website manager Ken Anderson, 30 October 1997.

6. A similar charge of whiting out matters of concern within the black community by television broadcasters was reported with respect to the noncoverage of the Million Man March two years earlier, in "Million Man March: Almost a Blackout," *Los Angeles Sentinel,* 26 October 1995, A6. Despite the avoidance of this story by the national TV media, some mainstream print media outlets, CSPAN, and Philadelphia's local stations were compelled to cover the MWM as it unfolded because the unprecedented numbers made the event unquestionably newsworthy.

7. For a creatively insightful look at women's underacknowledged participation in computer science, see Sadie Plant's *Zeroes + Ones.*

8. In "Chatter in the Age of Electronic Reproduction: Talk Television and the 'Public Mind,'" Paolo Carpignano and colleagues discuss the shifting construction of the mass media as today's problematic public sphere.

9. See Houston A. Baker Jr.

10. I borrow this terminology from Sohnya Sayres in her article"Accepted Bounds."

11. See my essay "Civil Rights Movement and Television."

12. For a complete discussion of Fannie Lou Hamer's pivotal role in the civil rights movement, see Kay Mills' biography, *This Little Light of Mine* 45.

13. A fuller account of the contested history of Truth's legendary utterance can be found at <www.britannica.com/women/pri/Q00160.html>.

14. <www.britannica.com/women/pri/Q00160.html>.

15. I must confess that the text is mediated from my own painstaking transcription from videotape of the event sent to me by march webmaster Ken Anderson. I hasten to add that I did not alter the words. I did add punctuation that is virtually absent in orature (oral + literature).

16. Ken Anderson, MWM email to me, 30 October 1997.

17. The issue of the digital divide has captured the public imagination and has been, and continues to be, debated at length. See for example, the PBS documentary *The Digital Divide*, January 2000, and Jube Shiver Jr., "Racial Divide Is Growing in Internet Use," and "More Blacks Are Using Internet, Survey Finds."

18. See Michel de Certeau's dedication page in *The Practice of Everyday Life*, and Eric Auchard, "World Leaders Take Fresh Look at Digital Divide."

19. Anderson, MWM email.

20. I borrow this term from Chela Sandoval (375).

21. Marchers were instructed to mail their material to the Philadelphia headquarters; see <"Video, Photos, Experiences at the Million Woman March," at <http://timesx2.com/mem/page39.html>.

22. Cf. Hakim Bey, "The Temporary Autonomous Zone," <http://www.t0.or.at/hakimbey/taz/taz3a.htm.>.

23. Anderson, MWM email.

24. I take this quote from Patricia Mellencamp's article "Video and the Counterculture" 213.

25. See the 3 June 1998 article, "Successful Million Woman March Generates $21.7 Million," <http:www.afamnet.com/NationalPage/frontpage/110597_million.htm.

26. This quote is from the original 1997 Million Woman March website (now defunct) that outlined the march's twelve articulated "Platform Issues."

27. Print journalists' coverage of the Million Man March includes Mark Cooper, "Missing the Message: How the Media Managed to Ignore One Million Black Men" 4, and "Million Man March: Almost a Blackout" A6.

28. "For more detailed information on the Million Man March, see the page 1, contemporaneous coverage of the monumental event in a weekend edition of the *Chicago Defender* newspaper, "Two Million March on D.C.: Event Made History."

29. See Nancy Fraser, "Rethinking the Public Sphere: A Contribution to the Critique of Actually Existing Democracy."

30. More information on the premarch convention held in Philadelphia from 16 to 19 1997 can be found on http://www.netset.com/~khandi/index8.html/guests.html/milsis.htm.

31. See "Million Woman March: International Scam Alert."

32. See the full text of Hull's article at <http://www.aynrand.org/medialink/tribalism.html>.

33. The complete editorials from these readers can be found at "Missteps on Women's March," Letters to the Editor, *Daily News* 31 October 1997, <http://www.philly.com/packages/wmill/Opin/DN/LMAR31.asp>.

34. See "The Million Woman March," Letters to the Editor, *Philadelphia Inquirer* 2 November 1997, <http://www.philly.com/packages/wmill/Opin/Inq/CORN02.asp>.

35. Ifama's Buttnaked Truth about the Million Woman March. <http://home.earthlink.net/~ifama4maat/mwmthoughts.htm>.

36. For explanations and extensive examples of emoticons, go to the following websites: <http://www.chirpingbird.com/netpets/html/computer/emoticon.html> and <http://www.pb.org/emoticon.html>.

37. Mama Khandi, "Million Woman March Online Commentary before—during—the *Aftermath.*" <http:www.netset.com/~khandi/indexx8.html/guests.html/comment.htm>.

38. I borrow this term from Chris Hables Gray's book, *Cyborg Citizen*, which concerns the impact of the cybernetic systems revolution on our changing ideas and practices of participatory democracy.

39. This is Stuart Hall's terminology in his article "Black and White in Television," in the anthology *Remote Control*, ed. June Givanni, 17.

40. See Jacqueline Bobo's important book on black women's media activism and production, *Black Women as Cultural Readers* 36–43.

41. At one point Khandi begins calling CNN's reporter Cynthia Tornquist "Rinquist," perhaps a Freudian slip associated with high-profile antiaffirmative action proponent Supreme Court Judge Rhenquist, in Mama Khandi, "Million Woman March Online Commentary."

42. Here Jacquie Jones is writing about narrow representational options for the image of black women in dominant media culture. In her commentary on the cinematic reduction of the black woman's image to either the "bitch" or "ho" archetype, Jones notes, "I now realize that this positioning is "not ironic at all. It's functional. It assigns the accusatory space from which representation in the media, and more generally in society, can continually be reprogrammed along gender lines. . . . The news became the factory for Black mass media imagery in cautious, conservative times. The boys, of course, were in the forefront, but always behind them, just inside the frame, was the corps of silent girls, standing on the curb or sitting on a couch. Somehow these girls seemed to me to exist in the space of the accused. After all, according to the news of the early eighties, it was those teenage, female-headed households that produced these boys," in "Accusatory Space" (69).

43. See Donna Haraway, "A Cyborg Manifesto: Science, Technology, and Socialist-Feminism in the Late Twentieth Century" 151, where she writes,

"Cyborgs are not reverent . . . they seem to have a natural feel for united front politics, but without the vanguard party. The main trouble with cyborgs, of course, is that they are the illegitimate offspring of militarism and patriarchal capitalism, not to mention state socialism. But illegitimate offspring are often exceedingly unfaithful to their origins. Their fathers, after all, are inessential." This seems quite applicable to Mama Khandi's cybernetically facilitated street-wise analysis of mainstream media coverage of the Million Woman March.

44. Miller, "Million Woman March Split Group"; see also her article, "A Year Later, Marching Apart."

45. The April 2001 Race in Digital Space conference is one that I helped to organize. Chionesu and Coney's gracious acceptance to participate was particularly reassuring considering their public parting of the ways. It was apparent that the larger goal of advancing black women's collective empowerment efforts trumped any personal differences that developed as these women set about the difficult course of orchestrating a historic event of this magnitude.

46. In his discussion of the concept of the TAZ as a more viable approach to world change, Hakim Bey writes, "I distrust the word revolution. . . . [E]ven if we replace the revolutionary approach with a concept of insurrection blossoming spontaneously into anarchist culture, our own particular historical situation is not propitious for such a vast undertaking. Absolutely nothing but a futile martyrdom could possibly result now from a head-on collision with the terminal State, the megacorporate information State, the empire of Spectacle and Simulation." Hakim Bey, "The Temporary Autonomous Zone."

CHAPTER THREE. NEW BLACK PUBLIC SPHERES

1. Armistead S. Pride and Clint C. Wilson II make the important distinction between "a strictly a Negro newspaper," which *Freedom's Journal* initiated, and an "abolitionist newspaper run by whites with Black assistance" (9). See their book *A History of the Black Press*. Apparently, the distinction turns on the fact of black fiscal and editorial control over all aspects of the newspaper in question. In this case, of course, the model is Cornish and Russwurm's weekly newspaper, *Freedom's Journal*.

2. It is true that without black press venues the literary careers of Langston Hughes, Zora Neale Hurston, and George Schuyler among many, many others would likely have been impossible given the racial chauvinism of the white literary establishment. In fact, the remarkable science fiction texts *Black Empire* and *Black Internationale*, written as novellas by Schuyler and appearing in the *Pittsburgh Courier* during the mid-1930s were nearly lost to us until their recent republication by the Northeastern University Press. According to the editors of

the recent edition of *Black Empire*, Schuyler wrote more than four hundred pieces of fiction for the *Pittsburgh Courier* during the thirties alone. See Hill and Rassmussen 259–60.

3. Michel Foucault, and other poststructuralist theorists, posit the notion of writing's metamorhposis from the idea of narrative or writing as means of warding off death because of its historical role in perpetuating the immortality of the hero to a new emphasis on "the work" that "now possesses the right to kill, to be its author's murderer. . . . [T]his relationship between writing and death is also manifested in the effacement of the writing subject's individual characteristics. . . . [T]he writing subject cancels out the signs of his particular individuality" (102). Modernity's emphasis on the work as opposed to the author shifts the task of the critic or reader so as to privilege "the work through its structure, its architecture, its intrinsic form, and the play of internal [textual] relationships" (103). See Foucault, "What Is an Author," in *The Foucault Reader* 101–20.

4. In my essay "Digitextuality and Click Theory: Theses on Convergence Media in the Digital Age," I discuss this new media technology formation in *New Media: Theories and Practices of Digitextuality* 3–28.

5. Pride and Wilson, in *A History of the Black Press*, have observed of the nineteenth-century black presses, "There was no prospect of making money out of the papers . . . as the circulation could not be expected to be large among recently freed slaves." It was to the children of freedmen that black press editors looked for their future viability and support (170). Writing of black press fiscal conditions a century later in his autobiography entitled *A Man Called White*, Walter White states, "The Negro press has been is today the only large segment of American journalism whose major support comes from its readers rather than its advertisers. It has therefore of necessity remained more responsive to its readers' wishes than has any other" (209). And though White mistakenly believed that the disproportionate lack of advertising revenues finding its way to the black press likely would "not last much longer," Robin Pogrebin's 25 October 1997 *New York Times* article reported a big story about black magazines today in which he found that "advertising still eludes publishers" even as black readers and the country, in general, prosper (B1).

6. *The Conduit* has since been dissolved. It is uncertain if the enterprise will resume operations either online or in print.

7. James R. Grossman writes of the influence of earlier southern "migrants who returned home to visit, looking prosperous and urbane and bursting with wondrous tales of their exploits . . . 'just to tell how well they had done in the North'" 93.

8. Named for Charles Mason and Jeremiah Dixon, this is the boundary line between the northern and southern states.

9. See for example, Rymer, Russ 48–50; Reed 24–29.

10. Another black press entity online, *The Network Journal*, boasted of its early adopter status on its website in July of 1997. In the article "*The Network Journal* Celebrates a Successful First Year on the Internet," the editors announce: "*The Network Journal* was one of the first African American publications to have an online edition and still one of the few where you can read the entire stories that are in the print edition. *The Network Journal's* website is a pioneer that blazed the Internet trail before *Black Enterprise, Essence, Emerge,* and *YSB,* among others and had established an Internet presence before the *New York Times,* the *Daily News* or the *New York Post.*" <http://www.tmj.com/birthday/htm>.

11. For example, the *New York Age* newspaper had its own weekly radio show on the WOV. The *Age's* "radio:-: drama" columnist Vere E. Johns was the host of the radio program as well, see front page advertisement for the show, *New York Age,* 14 May 1932. In "Negro History Week Radio Shows; Other Coming Events," *New York Amsterdam News,* 12 February 1949, 24, there is a catalog of black programs to air over various radio stations, national and local. The *New York Amsterdam News'* special "Television Section" contained this optimistic view of TV: "Most of our readers probably want to know—how do Negroes fit into this TV picture. They have a fair start, and should go much further—especially so, if the public demands such. At present the following Negroes have their own TV shows. Bob Howard is heard daily over CBS-TV. . . . The Three Flames, instrumental group, is heard and seen four times each [sic] over WNBT. Amanda Randolph has her own unusual show over WABD each week day. She plays piano, talks chatter and interview[s] guests—not the big names but little people"; in "TV High Spots for your Daily Entertainment," *New York Amsterdam News,* 26 February 1949, 19. What is interesting about the *Amsterdam News'* supplemental section on television is the half-page-sized advertisements for the General Electric television sets. It seems that there is no concern about the competition this new, rival medium posed at that time.

12. Bagdikian first considered this issue in 1983. However, once the Sherman antitrust act was undermined with the advent of the multinational or global media oligopolies of the Reagan-Bush years, Bagdikian updated his influential book to encompass these significant changes. See Ben Bagdikian, *The Media Monopoloy.*

13. See any number of alarmist discourses lamenting the Internet's complicity if not downright causality in promoting pornography, bomb making, and dysfunctional domesticity in broadcast and cableTV, newspapers, magazines, civic organizations, churches, and political organizations (bear in mind that all these social forces, or what Louis Althusser terms "ideological state apparatuses" are rivals of the new Internet technology).

14. To date, I have found no independent corroboration tracing this independent North Carolina newspaper's existence back to the nineteenth century in the literature on the black press.

15. See Flanders and Willis 25.

16. For a complete history of the black press in the Midwest, see Henry Lewis Suggs, ed., *The Black Press in the Middle West: 1865–1985* (Westport, CT, London: Greenwood, 1996), 2.

17. See their 2004 online publications at <http://www. indianapolis-recorder.com/news/default.asp>.

18. In her article "Passing for White, Passing for Black," that discusses a 1980s legal case about a white woman who challenges the racial identity on her birth certificate, Adrian Piper explains the legal ramifications of the nation's long-standing "'one-drop' rule that uniquely characterizes the classification of blacks in the United States even where no longer in law." She adds, "So according to this long-standing convention of racial classification, a white who acknowledges any African ancestry implicitly acknowledges being black—a social condition, more than an identity, that no white person would voluntarily assume, even in imagination." See Piper 427.

19. I am thinking here of the senseless race-based murder of Ennis Cosby, the son of famed entertainer Bill Cosby, in 1997.

20. I borrow this concept from George Lipsitz, *The Possessive Investment in Whiteness: How White People Profit from Identity Politics.*

21. I borrow this descriptor from Laura Mulvey's highly influential discourse on masculine privilege in objectifying female bodies. See her paradigm-setting essay "Visual Pleasure and Narrative Cinema."

22. See "*Jet* Cover Story: R. Kelly," *Jet*, 1998. <http://www.ebony-magazine.com/jet/jetcover.html>.

CHAPTER FOUR. SERIOUS PLAY

1. For almost everything you ever wanted to know about the *Super Mario Brothers* games, go to the online *Super Mario Brothers* Headquarters at <http://www.smbhq.com\who.htm>.

2. I follow Marsha Kinder's usage of this term in her important book *Playing with Power in Movies, Television and Video Games* 3.

3. Henry Jenkins treats the subject of immersive play and interactivity in computer games more thoroughly in "'Complete Freedom of Movement': Video Games as Gendered Play Spaces."

4. Hayden White has been very influential in advancing the critical project of writing revisionist historiographies. See his essay "The Burden of History" 43.

5. See for example, Carey Goldberg's article "Children and Violent Video Games: A Warning" A14, which begins, "It's almost Christmas. Do you know what your children are playing? Might they perhaps be ripping out the spines of their enemies, perpetrating massacres of marching bands and splatting their screens with sprays and spurts of pixelated blood?"; see also John M. Glionna, "Computer Culture Breeds Ambivalence" A30; a Routers wire story on video game violence picked up by the *Philadelphia Enquirer* newspaper. The story was entitled "Study Questions Video-Game Ratings," *Philadelphia Enquirer* 1 August 2001, A3; and for a less condemnatory perspective see, Steve Lohr, "The Virtues of Addictive Games: Computer Pastimes No Longer Viewed as Brain Poison" C1+; Austin Bunn, "Video Games Are Good for You: Blood, Guts, and Leadership Skills?" 31; and Ted C. Fishman, "The Play's the Thing: The Video-Game Industry, Already a Juggernaut, Plans to Swallow Even More of Children's Time. So Who's Complaining" 27.

6. For important scholarly discussions of gender bias in videogaming that address the subject of girls' problematic positionings within gaming culture, see Marsha Kinder, Yasmin B. Kafai, and in the same anthology, Heather Gilmour.

7. For an important analysis of contemporary race relations see George Lipsitz 1.

8. I rephrase and repurpose Justine Cassell and Henry Jenkins's statement that "the theory of gender differences constructs gender practices," in "Part One: The Girls' Games Movement" 2–45.

9. For historical perspective on the issue of media effects, especially on children, see for example, Shearon A Lowery and Melvin L. DeFleur's excellent study, especially the chapters "Personal Influence: The Two-Step Flow of Communication," and "Communication and Persuasion: The Search for Magic Keys," in *Milestones in Mass Communication Research*. For a more recent view of communication theories regarding issues of behaviorism, magic bullet theories, the two-step flow of information and influence, see Stanley J. Baran, and Dennis K. Davis.

10. To access the study's Children and the Media Home Page, see "Fair Play? Violence, Gender and Race in Video Games," <http://www.childrenand-media.org>.

11. Hanley's other remarks appear at the section head in the series of epigraphs, in Marriott D7.

12. In one of the first journalistic investigations of race matters in gaming culture, Chansanchai's article makes us privy to how some of the gaming industry's creative minds were thinking about race and their place in games' increasingly sophisticated character developments. See Chansanchai, "Yellow Perils" 25.

13. For a discussion of social science media effects researchers' responses to the cultural studies challenge, see Baran and Davis 16.

14. See the Children Now study for the specifics of which game titles and platforms comprised the analytical universe of study.

15. For details, see <www.childrenand media.org>.

16. Specifics of the Children Now focus on black female criminal victimization are outlined in their 14 December 2001 press release. See <www.childrennow.org/media/video-games/2001/>.

17. See the March 2000 cover of *Incite* magazine's video gaming. *Incite* also published a PC gaming magazine version.

18. *Prima's Official Strategy Guide* made this boast on the cover of its special 2000 *Tekken Tag Tournament* issue.

19. The game developer for *Urban Chaos* is the United Kingdom–based company Mucky Foot. I point this out to highlight the international discourse of racial difference and otherness in gaming design.

20. See *International Hobo's* very smart discussion of computer game genres and the usefulness and limitations of generic categorizations on the "Forum" section of their website at <http://www.ihobo.co.uk/forum/articles/genres.html>.

21. I borrow this phrasing from JanMohamed 18.

22. See a game description and several reviews of *Civilization* at the website called FunagainGames, at <www.funagain.com>.

23. I conducted this interview on gaming culture with a former lawyer, now a PhD candidate, Rebecca Hall on 5 May 2002 in Santa Barbara, California.

24. The game *Ethnic Cleansing* could be found during the first months of 2002 at <http://www.resistance.com/ethniccleansing/catalog.htm>.

25. The NPD Group, who conducted the study, noted that video game accessories also posted record-breaking sales. The top-selling PC games were the Sims by Electronic Arts. See the full online report, "NPD Reports Annual 2001 U.S. Interactive Entertainment Sales Shatter Industry Record," 7 February 2002, <http://www.npd.com/corp/content/news/releases/press_020207.htm>.

26. Norris and Koppel. This show explores the popularity of the first-person sim game *Grand Theft Auto 3*.

CHAPTER FIVE. THE REVOLUTION WILL BE DIGITIZED

1. When Howard Rheingold wrote the *Virtual Community: Homesteading on the Electronic Frontier* in 1993, he gave us an insiders' look at one of the first

online communities, called the "Whole Earth 'Lectronic Link" (the WELL). Rheingold describes it as a "full-scale subculture . . . growing on the other side of [his] telephone jack" (2). Since the Internet gained widespread recognition during the early 1990s in the wake of the Internet's graphical interface innovation, Rheingold's discussion of his membership in the WELL dating back to 1983 (1) clearly provides an introduction to the World Wide Web's text-dominant prehistory of thriving virtual communities.

2. Among the more distressing aspects of Netmyths that Thompson identifies is a sea change in the speed of dissemination of these unverified stories, because "Netmyths explode instantly around the globe, duplicated word-for-word with the click of computer mouse" (E1).

3. See, for example, the 1998 anthology *Race in Cyberspace*, edited by Beth E. Kolko, et. al, published in 2000, and other critical essays on race in volumes, such as *High Noon on the Electronic Frontier*, edited by Peter Ludlow (1996), and *The Cybercultures Reader*, edited by David Bell and Barbara M. Kennedy (2000). In earlier chapters of this work, I have already discussed some of mainstream media's print and electronic treatments of this subject matter.

4. See, for example, *Cyberspace: First Steps*, ed. Michael Benedikt; Rheingold, *The Virtual Community: Homesteading on the Electronic Frontier*; Taylor and Saarinen, *Imagologies: Media Philosophy*; Negroponte, *Being Digital*.

5. For a thorough treatment of how specious research on scientific racism is advanced in the U.S. particularly, see William H. Tucker's excellent study in *The Funding of Scientific Racism: Wickliffe Draper and the Pioneer Fund*.

6. In addition to the case studies in the earlier chapters of this book, see for example such journalistic reports as "Blacks Find Internet More Useful: Study" A-16; Alex Klein's "Closing the Digital Divide"; and Douglas Century's "A World Divided into Two-Way Pager Camps: The Hip-Hop Elite Loves Motorola, While Gore and Blue Chippers Favor Blackberry" B14.

7. In some influential early discussions of the Internet haves and have nots, there is a troubling reification of substandard education and high poverty levels in urban and rural communities to explain the "Falling through the Net" phenomenon as the information economy develops. See for example Jube Shiver Jr.'s 9 July 1999 *Los Angeles Times* article entitled "Racial Divide Is Growing in Internet Use." This article notes the "Commerce Department's third annual examination of the Internet across the nation found big increases of Americans going online. But the gap between minority and white households using the Internet nearly doubled. . . . Officials said differences in the income and education and geographical distances hindered minorities who want to use a global network that is fast becoming an essential communication and research tool. . . . Commerce Department officials said that poor blacks and Latinos who live in rural areas and

have little education are the least likely to be wired and benefit from the Internet's information resources."

8. In fact, it is not only minority women and Third-World inhabitants that need to be concerned about the development of what Richard Gordon has called the new "homework economy," that increasingly determines the contours of the new information revolution. Citing Gordon's formulation of the homework economy concept, Donna Haraway writes, "Gordon intends 'homework economy' to name a restructuring of work that broadly has the characteristics formerly ascribed to female jobs, jobs literally done only by women. Work is being redefined as both literally female and feminized, whether performed by men or women." For Haraway, it is important to consider additionally the repercussions of the conflicts involving the fact that "men in advanced industrial societies have become newly vulnerable to permanent job loss, and women are not disappearing from the job rolls at the same rates as men" (166).

9. I borrow this term from Michele Wallace, and her 1990 book entitled *Invisibility Blues: From Pop to Theory.*

10. For the full text of this egregious legal ruling, see the U.S. Supreme Court case law concerning *Dred Scott v. Sandford,* 60 U.S. 393 (1856), 60 U.S. 393 (How.), *Dred Scott, Plaintiff in Error v. John F. A. Sandford,* December Term, 1859, <http://caselaw.lp.findlaw.com/scripts/getcase.pl?court=US&vol=60&invol=393>.

11. In the section of his quite extensive website entitled "It was the Audacity of My Thinking: History of the Internet," African scientist Phillip Emeagwali details the struggles he encountered as a black, independent scientist working on computer technologies during the early years of the Internet and the reinvention of the supercomputer. See his site at <http://emeagwali.com/history/internet/index.html>.

12. In my book *Returning the Gaze: A Genealogy of Black Film Criticism: 1909–1949,* I discuss how black people seized upon the then-new technology of film to affect a transformation of themselves as New Negroes as opposed to their reification as and relegation to slavery's Southern antebellum plantation darkies—passim.

13. "While working for Digital Equipment Corporation (DEC) in the 1960s, Gordon Bell helped build the PDP series of minicomputers, the first minicomputers introduced to the commercial data processing market. He also oversaw the development of the industry's most successful computer lines, DEC's VAX series. He is currently one of several experts employed by Microsoft to direct that company's future path." This background information on C. Gordon Bell can be found at the Jones Telecommunications & Multimedia Encyclopedia website: <http://www.digitalcentury.com/encyclo/update/bell.html>.

14. For Emeagwali, then, the problem of determining the Internet's true origin is the problem of the wrong question being asked. Rather than ask, "At what point did the computer give birth to the Internet?" for him the better question is, "What is the difference between the Intranet and the Internet?" a question for which, of course, he provides an answer. "The answer: a computer utilizes one microprocessor, while the Internet is a network of millions of computers. The latter answer is obsolete. The reason is the computer has been reinvented from one that is one-processor based to one that is multiple-processor based. The 21st century definition is that the computer is a network of [multiple-processors], while the Internet is a network of computers. However, by the 22nd century, the computer and the Internet will be a network of processors. In other words, the computer and the Internet will become one and the same. Therefore, the Internet originated in the minds of computer scientists whose inventions enabled us to reinvent the computer as a 'network of processors' and the development of the Internet as a 'network of computers.'"

15. This description of the film can be found, in full, at Political Film Series, <http:www.illegalvoices.org/films/archive.html>.

16. I love the Web. Even in 2002 and with the corporate takeover, it was awesome! When I entered the key words "Sam Greenlee" into my Google search, it returned fifty-two matches. I was expecting none.

17. In an article entitled "Digital Divide Revisited: Study: Blacks Online More Likely to Appreciate Net's Value," appearing on ABCNews.Com in 2000, it is reported that a PEW study found that "Black women make up 56 percent of the black online population, while white users are equally split between men and women." <http://myabcbews,gi,cin/PRINTERFRIENDL...tech/dailyNews/digitaldivide001023.html>.

18. On 25 June 1998, the front page of the *New York Times* carried three stories relevant to our discussion. The lead story, "With Cable Deal, AT&T Makes Move to Regain Empire: $31 Billion TCI Purchase," appearing in column one, was accompanied by a three-column-width photo of two AT&T and TCI executives lol (laughing out loud—in internetspeak), at a press conference announcing the deal. The third, above the fold—as they say—on that day were two other stories of interest. Column two contained a story entitled "Hooking Up the Nation: Internet Is the Future, and Faster Is Better." But, most notably, in columns three and four was the story "White House Revises Policy on Contracts for Minorities." What makes this story notable is that it juxtaposed details of the grudging concessions to regulations permitting modest gains to black and other minority "small businesses" to the striking photo of the jubilant white CEOs of "big businesses" basking in the fruits of 1996 degregulation policies responsible for this megamerger. See Seth Schiesel, "With Cable Deal, AT&T Makes Move to Regain Empire" A1. See also Saul Hansell, "Hooking Up the

NOTES TO CONCLUSION

Nation" A1, David E. Rosenbaum, "White House Revises Policy on Contracts for Minorities" A1.

19. In a February 2002 email, Anita Brown forwarded to me an informative interview conducted with Peggy Townsend of TECHDIVAS.com. The interview itself was a journalistic document sent with no URL information. It was titled "Profile: Anita Brown," which contained information about Brown's t-shirt business and much more.

20. This information is from a February 2002 personal email communication between Brown and myself. Brown sent me an email attachment of an interview that she granted with Terry Dway Ashford of *US Black Engineer* Magazine, dated 23 August 2000.

21. I am thinking here of the early systematic erasure of "primitive" African art and its aesthetic influences on such formalist, high-brow Western modernist traditions as cubism, most popularized by the "experimental" creative "genius" of Pablo Picasso.

22. This information is contained in a February 2002 email forwarded to me by Brown, there are no specific URLs. The interview was conducted with Peggy Townsend of TECHDIVAS.com.

23. See Brown's update of the organization which is posted on the Black Geeks Online website: "Update: Black Geeks Online, 1995–2001," http://black-geeks.net/2about.html>.

24. This is how Venard R. Gray, a Black Geeks associate and webmaster, described the "Taking IT to the Streets!" program in an email to invitees of the event. This information is contained in a personal email communiqué to the author months after the event transpired.

25. Black Geeks Online flyer, available in 1997 at <http://www.black-geeks.net/TakingIT5.html>.

26. See Brown's reflections on the organization's persistence since its inception, on the website's "About Black Geeks Online" page, which is entitled "Update: Black Geeks Online, 1995–2001," <http://black geeks.net/2about.html>.

27. For a listing of Brown's geek friends, such as "All Net Electronic Media Co, AutoNetwork, MelaNet, NetNoir, Inc., InterCHANGE, and the individuals behind these companies, see "Behind the Scenes," 1997, <http:www.blackgeeks.net/>.

28. See Tayborn, "The Art of Tricknololgy."

CONCLUSION

1. Beginning in 2001, Tara McPherson, Henry Jenkins, Erika Muhammad, and I organized the first Race in Digital Space (RDS) conference that took

place on the campus of the Massachussetts Institute of Technology (For a full list of participants and topics, see the RDS conference website at <http://cms.mit. edu/race>). Following in 2002, Tara McPherson, Henry Jenkins, and I organized the second Race in Digital Space conference (RDS 2.0) on the University of Southern California campus in Los Angeles. (That conference website can be accessed at <http://www.annenberg. edu/race>).

In 2004, I organized the first international conference specifically designed to draw from the research contained in this volume and thereby focus the discussion about the racial digital divide on blackness and IT issues. That conference was entitled Afrogeeks: From Technophobia to Technophilia, and it was held on the University of California, Santa Barbara (UCSB), campus. The tremendous success of the first Afrogeeks conference spurred us to organize a second conference in May 2005. This second conference was entitled Afrogeeks: Global Blackness and the Digital Public Sphere, and it too was convened on the UCSB campus. In September 2005, I had the pleasure of participating in the Ninth Annual Highway Africa Conference in Grahamstown, South Africa, as a plenary speaker. The South African Highway Africa Conference is the largest annual gathering of African journalists and other IT workers devoted to ensuring the African continent's full participation in the new global information economy.

Most exciting for me about the Race in Digital Space and the Afrogeeks conferences was the fact they provided a forum for bringing together many of the key individuals and organizations who are profiled and analyzed in this volume. For example, we brought Nigerian scientist Philip Emeagwali, grassroots organizers of the Million Woman March (march organizers Asia Coney and Phile Chionesu, and their Webmaster Ken Anderson), Afrofuturist theorizers Mark Dery and Alondra Nelson, and Afrogeek pioneer and founder of Black Geeks Online Anita Brown. Of course, the conferences featured many others who are currently engaged in making real and realizable the incredible promise of creating a new vision of the Habermassian public sphere accessible to all thanks to the wonders of digital technologies.

2. For more information on São Tome é Principe's oil discoveries and its value to Western nations, see, for example, Jon Lee Anderson's *New Yorker* magazine article of "Our New Best Friend: Who Needs Saudia Arabia When You've Got Sao Tome?"

3. President Bill Clinton's visit to Africa in late March 1998 signaled not only a major shift in U.S. international policy, as he was the first American president in twenty years to do so, but it also began the dialogue about the moral responsibilities of powerful Western nations to reduce substantially, if not cancel altogether, Africa's massive debt. For more details on Clinton's landmark 1998 visit and subsequent visits to Africa by the president and other high-level officials, see the Stanford University Library's "Africa: South of the Sahara" website at

<http://www-sul.stanford.edu/depts/ssrg/africa/clinton.html>. More recently, 2 July 2005, musician and political activist Bob Geldof organized an international music conference, billed as "Live 8," to exert pressure on the powerful G8 nations to end poverty in Africa in our lifetime. Geldof is quoted as saying, "By doubling aid, fully cancelling debt, and delivering trade justice for Africa, the G8 could change the future for millions of men, women and children." See the website devoted to Live 8, at <http://www.live8live.com/whatsitabout/index.shtml>. This website ends with this statement: "NOW IS THE TIME, THIS IS THE YEAR—OUR LEADERS HAVE THE POWER TO END POVERTY—BUT WE HAVE THE POWER TO MAKE THEM USE IT."

4. See the WOUGNET website for more information, at http://www.wougnet.org/, particularly the sections entitled "About WOUGNET," "Tech Tips," "ICT Policy Issues in Uganda," and "Links and Resources."

5. For a thorough introduction to Isis-WICCE and its programs, see the "About US" page on the group's website.

6. See the International Women's Tribune Centre website, particularly their Mission Statement.

7. The IWTC is a member of the WOUGNET collective, and thus archival information on IWTC's activities dating back to 2002 is available at WOUGNET and no longer on IWTC's revamped website. For information on the IWTC's involvement with the Nakaseke Telecenter, see WOUGNET's site, an entry entitled "A CD-ROM for Rural Women in Africa: Development of a New Information Tool," at <http://www.wougnet.org/News/cdupdate.html>.

8. See "Information and Communication Technologies (ICTs) and Gender Equality," on the World Bank Group, DevForum: E-Discussions & Communities page at <http://www.dgroups.org/groups/worldbank/Gender-ICT/index.cfm?op=dsp_showmsg&listname=Gender-ICT&msgid=132496&cat_id=6188>.

9. For a more complete description of this 2005 conference and the Highway Africa Conference Vision and Mission Statements, see the website at <http://www.highwayafrica.ru.ac.za/mission.cfm>.

10. Chairman of the South African Broadcasting Corporation (SABC), Eddie Sonwabo Funde, made this comment during his plenary talk at the Highway Africa Conference on 12 September 2005.

11. See the World Summit on the Information Society (WSIS) website for detailed information about goals, expectations, and results deriving from both the Geneva and Tunis gatherings at <http://www.itu.int/wsis/basic/about.html>.

WORKS CITED

A., H. "Ethnic Cleansing: The Game!" *Afrofuturism* list, 20 Feb. 2002. <http://www.afrofuturism.net>.

———. "Racist Video Games Target Youth." *Afrofuturism* list, 25 Feb. 2002. <http://www.afrofuturism.net>.

"About Us." *Charlotte Post.* <http://www.thepost.mindspring.com/about%20info/ABHME.html.1998>.

AFROAM-L. <http://list.bowdoin.edu/mailman/listinfo/afroam>.

Akano, Usman G. "Welcome Letter." <http:www.rain-org/-ananet-welcome.html>.

Akst, Daniel. "The Internet's Dirty, Cheap Little Secret." *Los Angeles Times* 26 Nov. 1995: D4.

Allen, H. "Ethnic Cleansing: The Game!" *Afrofuturism,* 20 Feb. 2002.

Anderson, Christopher. "The Internet: The Accidental Superhighway." *The Economist* July 1995: 3–18.

Anderson, Jon Lee. "Our New Best Friend: Who Needs Saudia Arabia When You've Got Sau Tome?" *New Yorker* 7 Oct. 2002: A.

Anderson, Ken. "The Internet and the March." Email to Anna Everett. 30 Oct. 1997.

"Anonymizer FAQ, The." 1995 http://www.anonymizer.com.

Archibold, Randal C. "The Virtual Pie Shop and Other Cyber Dreams." *Los Angeles Times:* E1–2.

Arenson, Karen W. "N.Y.U. Sees Profits in Virtual Classes." *New York Times* 7 October, 1998: A20.

Arthur, Paul. "Jargons of Authenticity: Three American Moments." *Theorizing Documentary*. Ed. Michael Renov. New York and London: Routledge, 1993. 108–134.

Ashcroft, Bill, Gareth Griffiths, and Helen Tiffin, eds. "Feminism and Post-colonialism: Introduction." *The Post-Colonial Studies Reader*. London and New York: Routledge, 1995. 247–250.

Ashford, Terry Dway. Anita Brown Interview. *U.S. Black Engineer* Magazine 23 Aug. 2000.

Awauh, Patrick. "Ashesi University: Moving the Information Economy Forward in Ghana, Opportunities and Challenges." Keynote Speech. AfroGeeks Conference, University of California, Santa Barbara, 20 May 2005.

B., Mr. "Re: Racist Video Games Target Youth." *Afrofuturism* list, 26 Feb. 2002. <http://www.afrofuturism.net>.

Bagdikian, Ben. *The Media Monopoloy*. Boston: Beacon, 1983, 1987,1990.

Baker, Houston, A. "Critical Memory and the Black Public Sphere." *The Black Public Sphere*. Ed. the Black Public Sphere Collective. Chicago and London: University of Chicago Press, 1995. 5–38.

Balsamo, Anne. Technologies of the Gendered Body: Reading Cyborg Women. Durham and London: Duke University Press, 1996.

Baraka, Amiri. "Technology & Ethos: Vol. 2 Book of Life." *Raise Race Rays Raze: Essays since 1965*. New York: Random House, 1971. 155–157.

Baran, Stanley J., and Dennis K. Davis. *Mass Communication Theory: Foundations, Ferment, and Future*. Belmont, CA: Wadsworth, 1995.

Barthes, Roland. *S/Z: An Essay*. Trans. Richard Miller. New York: Hill and Wang, 1974.

Barwell, Graham, and Kate Bowles. "Border Crossings: The Internet and the Dislocation of Citizenship." *The Cybercultures Reader*. Ed. David Bell and Barbara M. Kennedy. London and New York: Routledge, 2000. 702–711.

Bastian, Misty L. "Immigrant Nigerians on the Internet." *West Africa Review*. <http: www.westafricareview.com/war/vol1.1/bastian.html>.

Bell, David and Barbara M. Kennedy, Ed. *The Cybercultures Reader*. London and New York: Routledge, 2000.

Bell, Derrick. *Faces at the Bottom of the Well: The Permanence of Racism*. New York: Basic Books, 1992.

Benedikt, Micheal, ed. *Cyberspace: First Steps*. Cambridge, MA, and London, England: MIT P, 1991.

Benjamin, Walter. *The Arcades Project.* Trans. Howard Eiland and Kevin McLaughlin. Cambridge, MA, and London, England: Belknap of Harvard UP, 1999.

Bey, Hakim. *The Temporary Autonomous Zone.* Brooklyn: Autonomedia, 1985, 1991.

Bigham, Darrel E. "The Black Press in Indiana." *The Black Press in the Middle West, 1865–1985.* Westport, CT: Greenwood, 1996.

"Blacks Find Internet More Useful: Study." *Los Angeles Times* 23 Oct. 2000. A16.

Bobo, Jacqueline. *Black Women as Cultural Readers.* New York: Columbia UP, 1995.

Bolter, Jay David, and Richard Grusin. *Remediation: Understanding New Media.* Cambridge, MA, and London, England: MIT P, 1991, 2000. 2001.

Braxton, Joanne M. *Black Women Writing Autobiography: A Tradition within a Tradition.* Philadephia: Temple UP, 1989.

Brooks, Peter. *Reading for the Plot: Design and Intention in Narrative.* Cambridge, MA, and London, England: Harvard UP, 1984.

Brown, Amos. "'Just Tellin': A Last Look Back at 1998." *The Indianapolis Recorder.* 1998. <http://www.indianapolisrecorde.com/current/justtellinit_122498.htmlr>.

Brown, Anita. "Welcome, I'm Anita Brown aka Miss DC Sistahgeek." <http://www.sistahgeek.com/welcome>.

Brown, Elsa Barkley. "Negotiating and Transforming the Public Sphere: African American Political Life in the Transition from Slavery to Freedom." *The Black Public Sphere.* Ed. the Black Public Sphere Collective. Chicago and London: U of Chicago P, 1995.

Bunn, Austin. "Video Games Are Good For You: Blood, Guts, and Leadership Skills?" *Village Voice* 21 Sept. 1999: 31.

"Bust-A-Move." TV Commercial. Priceline.com. 2000.

Cadet, Ron. "Net Emerges as Delivery Tool for Black News and Views." *The Conduit,* Fall 1995 (defunct). <http://matrix.the conduit.com>.

Carpignano, Paolo, et al. "Chatter in the Age of Electronic Reproduction." *Social Text* 25/26 (1990): 33–55.

Cassell, Justine, and Henry Jenkins. "Chess for Girls? Feminism and Computer Games." *From Barbie to Mortal Kombat: Gender and Computer Games.* Ed. Justine Cassell and Henry Jenkins. Cambridge, MA, and London, England: MIT P, 1999.

Century, Douglas. "A World Divided into Two-Way Pager Camps: The Hip-Hop Elite Loves Motorola, While Gore and Blu7e Chippers Favor Blackberry." *New York Times* 15 Jan. 2001: B14.

Chansanchai, Athima. " Tech Tyke: A Six-Year-Old Brings Computer Education to the Projects." *Village Voice* 29 July 1997: 31.

———. "Yellow Perils: Online 'Coolies" Rile Asian Americans." *Village Voice,* 7 Oct. 1997: 120.

Children Now Study. <http://www.childrenandmedia.org>.

Chionesu, Phile. <http://www.netset.com/khandi/index8.html/intrv1.htm.>.

City, The. Dir. Ralph Steiner and Willard Van Dyke. American Institute of Planners. 1939.

Clark, Archie T., II. "Dolls Reflect, Shape Cultural Identity." Charlotte Post, 1998. http://the post.mindspring.com/news/com/news2%20Page.html.

Cornish, Samuel and John S. Russwurm. "To Our Patrons." *Freedom's Journal* 1:1: 16 March 1827.

Crane, David. *"In Medias* Race: Filmic Representation, Networked Communication, and Racial Intermediation." *Race in Cyberspace.* Ed. Beth E. Kolko, et al. New York and London: Routledge, 2000. 87–116.

Crowley, David, and Paul Heyer. "New Media and Old in the Information Age." *Communication in History: Technology, Culture, Society* 2nd edition. Ed. David Crowley and Paul Heyer. White Plains, NY: Longman, 1991, 1995. 307–310.

Crummell, Alexander. "Hope for Africa." *Call and Response: The Riverside Anthology of the African American Literary Tradition.* Ed. Patricia Liggins Hill, et al. Boston and New York: Houghton Mifflin, 1998. 335–370.

C_Splash. "Re:—Racist videogames target youth—." *Afrofuturism* 26 Feb. 2002.

Davis, Richard Pierre. Interview by author. Tape recording, London, England, 9 July 2001.

de Certeau, Michel. *The Practice of Everyday Life.* Berkeley and Los Angeles: California UP, 1984.

Derrida, Jacques. *Of Grammatology.* Baltimore and London: Johns Hopkins UP, 1976.

———. *Writing and Difference.* London: Routledge & Kegan Paul, 1978.

Dery, Mark. "Black to the Future:" Interviews with Samuel R. Delany, Greg Tate, and Tricia Rose." *Flame Wars: The Discouse of Cyberculture.* Ed. Mark Dery. Durham and London: Duke UP. 179–222.

"Digital Divide Revisited: Study: Blacks Online More Likely to Appreciate Net's Value." *ABC News.com.* <http://my.abcnews.go.com/ PRINTERFRIENDI …tech/DailyNews/digitaldivide001023.html>.

"Digital Racism Is Already Here." Email Post. AFROAM-L Archives. 26 Feb. 1995. <http://www.afrinet.net/~hallh/afrotalk/afrofeb95/0894.html>.

Dixon, Wheeler Winston. *It Looks at You: The Returned Gaze of Cinema.* Albany: State U of New York P, 1995.

Downey, John. "Black Weeklies to Merge." *Charlotte Post,* 1997. <http://www. triadbusiness.com/chronicle4197.html>.

Durham-Vichr, Deborah. "Techie to Watch: Grandmother vs. the Digital Divide." *IT Recruiter* Magazine, Sept.–Oct. 2000.

Eagleton, Terry. *Literary Theory: An Introduction.* 2nd edition. Minneapolis: U of Minnesota P, 1996.

Ellison, Ralph. *Invisible Man.* New York: Vintage International, 1947, 1948, 1952, 1980.

Emeagwali, Philip. "It Was the Audacity of My Thinking: History of the Internet." undated. <http:emeagwali.com/history/internet/index.html>.

Enzensberger, Hans Magnus. "Constituents of a Theory of the Media." *Video Culture: A Critical Investigation.* Ed. John G. Hangardt. Layton, UT: Peregrine Smith Books, 1990. 96–123.

Ethnic Cleansing Game. 2002. <http://www.resistance.com.>.

Everett, Anna. "The Black Press in the Age of Digital Reproduction." *The Black Press: Literary and Historical Essays on the 'Other Front Page.'* Ed. Todd Vogel. Rutgers UP. New Brunswick, NJ, and London: Rutgers University Press, 2001. 244–257.

———. "Digitextuality and Click Theory: Theses on Convergence Media in the Digital Age." *New Media: Theories and Practices of Digitextuality.* Ed. Anna Everett and John T. Caldwell. New York: Routledge, 2003. 3–28.

———. "P.C. Youth Violence: 'What's the Internet or Video Gaming Got to Do With It?" *Denver University Law Review* 77:4 (2000): 689–698.

———. Recolonizing Africa for the Twenty-First Century." *UFAHAMU: Journal of African Activist Association* 21:1–2: 26–38.

———. *The Revolution Will Be Digitized: Afrocentricity and the Digital Public Sphere. Uitgave Faculteit der Lettern: Universiteit Utrecht, 2001.*

"Fair Play: Violence, Gender and Race in Video Games." Children Now report. 2001.<http://publications.childrennow.org/publications/media/fairplay_2001.cfm>.

Farnsworth, Robert M. *Melvin B. Tolson 1898–1966: Plain Talk and Poetic Prophecy.* Columbia: U of Missouri P, 1984.

Fishman, Ted C. "The Play's the Thing: The Video Game Industry, Already a Juggernaut, Plans to Swallow Even More of Children's Time. So Who's Complaining?" *New York Times* Magazine 10 June 2001:27.

Flaherty, Julie. "Racist E-Mail Is Sent to 13 at Boston College." *New York Times* 7 October, 1998: A20.

Flanders, Vincent, and Mike Willis. *Webpages That Suck: Lear Good Design by Looking at Bad Design.* San Francisco: Sybex, 1996.

Foucault, Michel. "What is an Author?" *The Foucault Reader.* Ed. Paul Rabinow. New York: Pantheon Books, 1984.

Fraser, Nancy. "Rethinking the Public Sphere: A Contribution to the Critique of Actually Existing Democracy." *Social Text* 25/26 (1990): 56–80.

Funagain Games. "Sid Meier's Civilization: The Boardgame." <http://www.funagain.com/control/product/~product_id=013615/~reviewsShowAll=true#reviews>.

Gilmour, Heather. "What Girls Want: The Intersections of Leisure and Power in Female Computer Game Play." *Kids' Media Culture.* Ed. Marsha Kinder. Durham and London: Duke UP, 1999. 263–292.

Gilroy, Paul. *The Black Atlantic: Modernity and Double Consciousness.* Cambridge: Harvard UP, 1993.

Gleick, James: *Faster: The Acceleration of Just About Everything.* New York: Pantheon, 1999.

Glionna, John M. "Computer Culture Breeds Ambivalence." *Los Angeles Times* 19 Nov. 2000: A30.

Goldberg, Gary. "Children and Violent Video Games: A Warning." *New York Times* 15 Dec. 1998:A14.

Gomez-Pena, Guillermo. "The Virtual Barrio @ the Other Frontier." *Race in Cyberspace.* New York and London: Routledge, 2000. 295–308.

Gray, Herman. *Watching Race: Television and the Struggle for "Blackness."* Minneapolis and London: Minnesota UP, 1995.

Grossman, James R. *Land of Hope: Chicago, Black Southerners, and the Great Migration.* Chicago: U of Chicago P, 1989.

g-Tech. "Re:—Racist video games target youth—." Afrofuturism 26 Feb. 2002.

Gutierrez-Jones, Carl. *Critical Race Narratives: A Study of Race, Rhetoric and Injury.* New York and London: New York UP, 2001.

Haddon, Leslie. "Interactive Games." *Future Visions: New Technologies of the Screen.* Ed. Philip Hayward and Tana Wollen. London: British Film Institute, 1993. 123–147.

Halberstam, Judith, and Ira Livingston, eds. *Posthuman Bodies.* Bloomington and Indianapolis: Indiana UP, 1995.

Hall, Sandra. Online Interview. <http://www.list.bowdoin.edu/mailman/listinfo/afroam>.

Hall, Stuart. "Black and White in Television." *Remote Controle: Dilemmas of Black Intervention.* Ed. June Givanni. London: British Film Institute, 1995. 13–28.

———. "Encoding/decoding." *Culture, Media, Language: Working Papers in Cultural Studies, 1972–79.* London, Melbourne, Sydney, Auckland, Johannesburg: Hutchinson, 1980, 1981, 1984, 1986.

Hamamoto, Darrell. *Monitored Peril: Asian Americans and the Politics of TV Representation.* Minneapolis and London: U of Minnesota P, 1994.

Hanley, Orpheus. Quoted in Michael Marriott, "Blood, Gore, Sex and Now: Race: Are Game Makers Creating Convincing New Characters or 'High-Tech Blackface'?" *New York Times* 21 Oct. 1999, D7.

Hansell, Saul. "Hooking Up the Nation." *New York Times* 25 Feb. 1998: A1.

Haraway, Donna J. *Simians, Cyborgs, and Women: The Reinvention of Nature.* New York: Routledge, 1991.

Hill, Robert A., and Kent Rassmussen, eds. *Black Empire.* Boston: Northeastern UP, 1994.

Holt, Thomas C. "Afterword: Mapping the Black Public Sphere." *The Black Public Sphere.* Chicago and London: U of Chicago P, 1995. 325–328.

Huffington, Arianna. *The Rachel Maddow Show.* MSNBC. 18 Nov. 2008.

Hull, Gary. "Pied Pipers of Tribalism: The 'Million Woman March' Should Have Promoted Individualism Not Tribalism." <http://www.aynrand.org/medialink/tribalism.html>.

International Hobo. "Forum—A Guide to Computer Game Genres." <http://www.ihobo.co.uk/forum/articles/genres.html>2003 (now defunct). Now at <http://www.ihobo.com>.

International Women's Tribute Centre. Mission Statement. <http://www.iwtc.org>.

Irving, Larry, et al. "Falling through the Net: A Survey of the 'Have Nots' in Rural and Urban America." Report of National Telecommuncations and Information Administration. 1995. <http://www.nita.doc.gov/nitahome/fallingthru.html>.

Iser, Wolfgang. *The Implied Reader: Patterns of Communication in Prose Fiction from Bunyan to Beckett.* Baltimore and London: Johns Hopkins UP, 1974.

Isis-WICCE. "About Us." <http://www.isis.or.ug/about.htm>.

Jackson, Brian. "AA's in video Games." Email conversation with author, 7 Dec. 1997.

James, C. L. R. " *The C. L. R. James Reader.* Ed. Anna Grimshaw. Oxford: Blackwell, 1992.

JanMohamed, Abdul R. "The Economy of the Manichean Allegory." *The Post-Colonial Studies Reader.* Ed. Bill Ashcroft, Gareth Griffiths, and Helen Tiffin. London and New York: Routledge, 1995. 18–23.

Jenkins, Henry. "Complete Freedom of Movement: Video Games as Gendered Play Spaces." *From Barbie to Mortal Combat: Gender and Computer Games.* Ed. Justine Cassell and Henry Jenkins. Cambridge, MA, and London: MIT P, 1998, 1999. 262–297.

———. *Fans, Bloggers and Gamers: Exploring Participatory Culture.* New York and London; NYU Press, 2006.

Johnson, L. D. "Racist Video Games Target Youth." *Afrofuturism* list, 25 Feb. 2002. <http://www.afrofuturism.net>.

Jones, Jacquie. "The Accusatory Space." *Black Popular Culture: A Project by Michele Wallace.* Ed. Gina Dent. Seattle: Bay, 1992. 95–98.

Jones, LeRoi. *Blues People: The Negro Experience in White America and the Music That Developed From It.* New York: Morrow, 1963.

Kafai, Yasmine B. "Video Game Designs by Girls and Boys." *Kids' Media Culture.* Ed. Marsha Kinder. Durham and London: Duke UP, 1999. 293–316.

Kellner, Douglas. *Television and the Crisis of Democracy.* Boulder, San Francisco, Oxford: Westview,1990.

Khandi, Mama. "Million Woman March Online Commentary: Before-during-the Aftermath." <http://www.netset.com/~Khandi/index.html/guests. comment.html>.

Kinder, Marsha. *Playing with Power in Movies, Television and Video Games.* Berkeley and Los Angeles: U of California P, 1991.

Klein, Alex. "Closing the Digital Divide." *Washington Post Online* 16 Aug. 2000. <http://www.washingtonpost.com/wp-dyn/articles/A32559–2000Aug15 html>.

Kolmos, Keith. *Ready 2 Rumble Boxing, Round 2: Prima's Official Strategy Guide.* Roseville, CA: Prima Communications, 2000.

Kolko, Beth E., Lisa Nakamura, and Gilbert B. Rodman, eds. *Race in Cyberspace.* New York and London: Rougledge, 2000.

Kroker, Arthur and Marilouise, eds. *Digital Delirium*. New York: St. Martin's, 1997.

Lamming, George. "The Occasion for Speaking." *The Post-Colonial Studies Reader*. Ed. Bill Ashcroft, Gareth Griffiths, and Helen Tiffin. London and New York: Routledge, 1995. 12–17.

Landow, George P. *Hypertext: The Convergence of Contemporary Critical Theory and Technology*. Baltimore and London: Johns Hopkins UP, 1992.

———. "What's a Critic to Do?" *Hypertext Theory*. Ed. George P. Landow. Baltimore and London: Johns Hopkins UP, 1994. 1–48.

Laudon, Kenneth C. "Promise versus Performance of Cable." *Wired Cities: Shaping the Future of Communication*. Boston: Hall, 1987. 27–40.

Levy, Steven. "Crypto Rebels." *High Noon on the Electronic Frontier: Conceptual Issues in Cyberspace*. Cambridge, MA, London, England: MIT, 1996. 185–205.

Liggins Hill, Patricia, et al. *Call and Response: The Riverside Anthology of the African American Literary Tradition*. Boston and New York: Houghton Mifflin, 1998.

Light, Alan, ed. *The Vibe History of Hip Hop*. New York: Three Rivers, 1999.

Lipsitz, George. *The Possessive Investment in Whiteness: How White People Profit from Identity Politics*. Philadelphia: Temple UP, 1998.

Lohr, Steve. "The Virtues of Addictive Games: Computer Pastimes No Longer Veiwed as Brain Poison." *New York Times* 22 Dec. 1997: C1+.

Lowery, Shearon A., and Melvin L. DeFleur. *Milestones in Mass Communication Research*. New York: Longman, 1983, 1988.

Ludlow, Peter. "How Should We Respond to Exploratory Hacking/Cracking/Phreaking." *High Noon on the Electronic Frontier: Conceptual Issues in Cyberspace*. Cambridge, MA, London, England: MIT, 1996. 124–129.

Lyotard, Jean-Francois. *The Inhuman: Reflections on Time*. Stanford, CA: Stanford UP, 1991.

Marinetti, Filippo Tomasso. "The Joy of Mechanical Force." Trans. Eugen Weber. <http://www.english.upenn.edu/~jenglish/English104/marinetti.html>.

Marriott, Michael. "Blood, Gore Sex, and Now: Race," *New York Times* 21 Oct. 1999, D7.

McConnaughey, James W., et al. "Falling through the Net II: New Data on the Digital Divide." Report of National Telecommunications and Information Administration, 1998. <http://www.nita.doc.gov/nitahome/net2/falling.html>.

McDonald, J. Fred. *One Nation under Television: The Rise and Decline of Network TV.* New York: Pantheon Books, 1990.

McLuhan, Marshall, and Bruce R. Powers. *The Global Village: Transformations in World Life and Media in the Twenty-first Century.* New York and Oxford: Oxford UP, 1989.

McPherson, Tara. "I'll Take My Stand in Dixie-Net: White Guys, the South, and Cyberspace." *Race in Cyberspace.* Ed. Beth Kolko, et al. New York and London: Routledge, 2000. 117–132.

Meehan, Eileen R. "Why We Don't Count: The Commodity Audience." *The Logics of Television: Essays in Cultural Criticism.* Ed. Patricia Mellencamp. Bloomington and Indianapolis: Indiana UP, 1990. 117–137.

Mellencamp, Patricia. "Video and the Counterculture." *Global Television.* Ed. Cynthia Schneider and Brian Wallis. New York: Wedge, 1988. 198–223.

Meston, Zack. "Conquest of the New World: Strategy Guide." *Computer Player* Oct. 1996.

Miller, Karen E. Quinones. "Million Woman March Split Group." *Philadelphia Inquirer* 12 Oct. 1998. <http://www.philly.com/packages/wmill/Inq/MRCH12.asp>.

———. "A Year Later, Marching Apart." *Philadelphia Inquirer* 25 Oct. 1998. <http://www.philly.com/packages/wmill/nq/MILL102598.asp>.

Miller, Laura. "Women and Children First: Gender and Settling of the Electronic Frontier." *Resisting the Virtual Life: The Culture and Politics of Information.* Ed. James Brook and Ian A. Boal. San Francisco: City Lights, 1995. 49–57.

"Million Man March: Almost a Blackout." *Los Angeles Sentinel* 26 Oct. 1995: A6.

"Million Woman March: International Scam Alert." <http://www.timesx2.com/mwm/page42.html>.

Mills, Kay. *This Little Light of Mine: The Life Story of Fannie Lou Hamer.* New York: Plume, 1993.

Minh-ha, Trinh T. *Woman, Native, Other: Writing, Postcoloniality and Feminism.* Bloomington: Indiana UP, 1989. Rpt. in *The Post-Colonial Studies Reader.* Ed. Bill Ashcroft, Gareth Griffiths, and Helen Tiffin. London: Routledge, 1995. 264–268.

"Money Makes the Games Go Round." *Next Generation* Oct. 2000: 58–63.

Morgan, Robin, ed. *Sisterhood Is Powerful: An Anthology of Writings from the Women's Liberation Movement.* New York: Vintage Books, 1970.

Mulvey, Laura. "Visual Pleasure and Narrative Cinema." *Movies and Methods.* Ed. Bill Nichols. Berkeley, Los Angeles, London: U of California P, 1985. 303–314.

Narayan, Uma, and Sandra Harding. *Decentering the Center: Philosophy for a Multicultural, Postcolonial, and Feminist World.* Bloomington and Indianapolis: Indiana UP, 2000.

Nakamura, Lisa. "Where Do You Want to Go Today? Cybernetic Tourism, the Internet, and Transnationality." *Race in Cyberspace.* Ed. Beth Kolko, et. al. New York and London: Routledge, 2000. 15–28.

Negroponte, Nicholas. *Being Digital.* New York: Vintage Books, 1995.

Newcomb, Horace, ed. *Television: The Critical View.* 4th edition. New York and Oxford: Oxford UP, 1987.

"New York Beat." *Jet.* 13 Nov. 1973: 62.

Nielsen, Aldon L. *CLR James: A Critical Introduction.* Jackson: UP of Mississippi, 1997.

———. *Reading Race: White American Poets and the Racial Discourse in the Twentieth Century.* Athens and London: U of Georgia P, 1988.

Norris, Michele, and Ted Koppel. "Just a Game." ABC TV's *Nightline* 10 June 2002.

Okoli, Emeka, J. "Ethnicity, the Press and Integration in Nigeria." *The International Journal of Africana Studies* 5 (1999): 32–48.

Ow, Jeffrey, A. "The Revenge of the Yellowfaced Cyborg: The Rape of Digital Geishas and the Colonization of Cyber-Coolies in 3–D Realms' Shadow Warrior." *Race in Cyberspace.* Ed. Beth Kolko, et. al. New York and London: Routledge, 2000. 51–68.

Penn, I. Garland. *The Afro-American Press and Its Editors.* New York: Arno, 1969.

Petersen, Kirsten Holst. "First Things First: Problems of a Feminist Approach to African Literature." *The Post-Colonial Studies Reader.* London and New York: Routledge, 1995. 251–254.

Pham, Tri, Jeff Barton, and Michael Littlefield. *Prima's Official Strategy Guide: Tekken Tag Tournament.* Roseville, CA: Prima Communications, 2000.

Pierre-Davis, Richard. Mongrel.org. Interview by author, tape recording, London, England, 9 July 2001.

Piper, Adrian. "Passing for White, Passing for Black." Critical White Studies: Looking Behind the Mirror. Ed. Richard Delgado and Jean Stefanicic. Philadelphia: Temple UP, 1997.

Plant, Sadie. *Zeroes + Ones: Digital Women + the New Technoculture.* London: Fourth Estate, 1997.

Poster, Mark. "Databases as Discourse; or, Electronic Interpellations." *Computers, Surveillance, and Privacy.* Ed. David Lyon and Elia Zureik. Minneapolis and London: U of Minnesota P, 1996. 175–192.

Prensky, Marc. "Computer Games and Learning: Digital Game-Based Learning." *Handbook of Computer Game Studies*. Eds. Joost Raessens and Jeffrey Goldstein. Cambridge, Massachusetts and London, England; MIT Press, 2005. 97–124.

Pride, Armistead S., and Clint C. Wilson II. *A History of the Black Press*. Washington, D.C.: Howard UP, 1997.

Reed, Adolph, Jr. "Dangerous Dreams: Black Boomers Wax Nostalgic for the Days of Jim Crow." *Village Voice* 16 April 1996: 24–29.

Reid, Mark A. *PostNegritude:Visual and Literary Culture*. Albany: State U of New York P, 1997.

Rheingold, Howard. *The Virtual Community: Homesteading on the Electronic Frontier*. New York: HarperPerennial, 1993.

Rhymer, Russ. "Integration's Casualties: Segregation Helped Black Business. Civil Rights Helped Destroy It." *New York Times* Magazine 1 Nov. 1949: 48–50.

Roszak, Theodore. *The Cult of Information: The Folklore of Computers and the True Art of Thinking*. New York: Pantheon, 1986.

Ross, Andrew. "Techno-Ethics and Tele-Ethnics: Three Lives in the Day of Max Headroom." *The Logics of Television:Essays in Cultural Criticism*. Ed. Patricia Mellencamp. Bloomington and Indianapolis: Indiana UP, 1990. 138–155.

Russwurm, John, and Samuel Cornish. "To Our Patrons." *Freedom's Journal* (vol. 1, no. 1) 16 March 1827.

Said, Edward. *Orientalism*. New York: Vintage Books, 1979.

Sandoval, Chela. "New Sciences: Cyborg Feminism and the Methodology of the Oppressed." *The Cybercultures Reader*. Ed. David Bell and Barbara Kennedy. London and New York: Routledge, 2000. 374–387.

Santisteban, Ray. "A Program for Change: Latino Media into the Next Millennium." *The Future of Latino Independent Media: A NALIP Sourcebook*. Ed. Chon Noriega. Los Angeles, CA: UCLA Chicano Studies Research Center, 2000. 107–115.

Sayres, Sohnya. "Accepted Bounds." *Social Text* 25/26 (1990): 119–128.

Schiesel, Seth. "With Cable Deal, AT&T Makes Move to Regain Empire." *New York Times* 25 Feb. 1998: A1.

Seiter, Ellen. "Television and the Internet." *Electronic Media and Technoculture*. Ed. John Thornton Caldwell. New Brunswick, NJ: Rutgers UP, 2000. 227–243.

Senghor, Léopold Sédar. "Negritude: A Humanism of the Twentieth Century." *Colonial Discourse and Post-Colonial Theory: A Reader*. Ed. Patrick Williams and Laura Chrisman. New York: Columbia UP, 1994. 27–35.

Shiver, Jr., Jube. "Racial Divide Is Growing in Internet Use." *Los Angeles Times* 9 July 1999: A10.

Shklovsky, Victor. "Art as Technique." *Russian Formalist Criticism: Four Essays*. Trans. and intro Lee T. Lemon and Marion J. Reis. Lincoln and London: U of Nebraska P, 1965. 3–23.

Silver, David. "Margins in the Wires." *Race in Cyberspace*. New York and London: Routledge, 2000. 133–150.

Singleton, Solveig. "Encryption Policy for the Twenty-first Century: A Future Without Government-Prescribed Key Recovery." *Cato Policy Analysis No. 325*. <http://www.cato.org/pubs/pas/pa-325es.html>.

Sis, Mickey. "Congratulations Sistahs." Email Communication with author. 29 Oct. 1997.

Sklar, Robert. "Edison's Trust and How IT Got Busted." *Movie Made America: A Cultural History of American Movies*. New York: Vintage Books, 1975.

Spivak, Gayatri Chakravorty. "Three Women's Texts and a Critique of Imperialism." *The Post Colonial Studies Reader*. Ed. Bill Ashcroft, et al. London and New York: Routledge, 1995. 269–272.

Spook Who Sat by the Door, The. Dir. Ivan Dixon. United Artists. 1973.

Stewart, Alison. *The Rachel Maddow Show*. MSNBC. 19 Nov. 2008.

Stone, Allucquere Rosanne [Sandy]. "Will the Real Body Please Stand Up? Boundary Stories about Virtual Cultures." *Cyberspace: First Steps*. Ed. Michael Benedikt. Cambridge, MA, London, England: MIT P, 1991. 81–118.

"Study Questions Video-Game Ratings." *Philadelphia Enquirer* 1 Aug. 2001: A3

Sudan, Rajani. "Sexy SIMs, Racy SIMMS." *Race in Cyberspace*. New York and London: Routledge, 2000. 69–86.

Suggs, Henry Lewis, ed. *The Black Press in the Middle West: 1865–1985*. Westport, CT and London: Greenwood, 1996.

Sundaram, Ravi. "Beyond the Nationalist Panopticon: The Experience of Cyberpublics in India." *Electronic Media and Technoculture*. Ed. John Thornton Caldwell. New Brunswick, NJ: Rutgers UP, 2000. 270–294.

Taborn, Tyrone D. "The Art of Tricknology." June 2000. http://www.blackengineer.com/articles/june00/tricknology.htm.

Tate, Greg. "15 Arguments in Favor of the Future of Hip Hop." *The Vibe History of Hip Hop*. Ed. Alan Light. New York: Three Rivers, 1999. 385–393.

———. Quoted in Dery, Mark. "Black to the Future: Interviews with Samuel A. Delany, Greg Tate, and Tricia Rose." *Flame Wars: The Discourse of Cyberculture.* Mark Dery. Durham and London: Duke UP, 1995. 179–222.

Taylor, Lane. "Not a War Game?" *Funagain Games* <http://www.kumquat/ funagain/04253>.

Taylor, Mark C., and Esa Saarinen. *Imogologies: Media Philosophy.* New York: Rougledge, 1994.

Terrell, Tom. "The Second Wave: 1980–1983." *The Vibe History of Hip Hop.* Ed. Alan Light. New York: Three Rivers, 1999. 43–51.

Thompson, Tracy. "Net Fiction." *Los Angles Times* 27 Feb. 1996: E1.

Townsend, Peggy. "Profile: Anita Brown." TECHDIVAS.com final draft 21 March 2001.

Tucker, William H. The Funding of Scientific Racism: Wickliffe Draper and the Pioneer Fund. Chicago: U of Chicago P, 2002.

Walker, David. "Major Abolitionist Voices." *Call and Response: The Riverside Anthology of the African American Literary Tradition.* Ed. Patricia Liggins Hill, et al. Boston and New York: Houghton Mifflin, 1998. 245–370.

Wallace, Michele. *Invisibility Blues: From Pop to Theory.* New York: Verso, 1990.

Walton, Lester A. "The Degeneracy of the Moving Picture." *New York Age* 5 Aug. 1909.

White, Hayden. *Tropics of Discourse: Essays in Cultural Criticism.* Baltimore: Johns Hopkins UP, 1978.

White, Walter. *A Man Called White.* New York: Viking, 1948.

Witt, Howard. "Blogs Help Drive Jena Protest." *Chicago Tribune*.com <http://www.chicagotribune.com/news/nationworld/chicago_blog>.

———. "Blogs Help Drive Jena Protests." Online posting. 18 Sept. 2007. *Chicago Tribune* <http://www.chicagotribune.com/services/newspaper/printedition/wednesday/chi-jena_blog_web19,0,4298165.story>.

Wolseley, Roland E. *The Black Press USA.* 2nd ed. Ames: Iowa State UP, 1971, 1990.

Wright, James. "Congressional Roundup." *Afro-Americ@.* National News, Washington, DC 21 Dec. 1998. http://www.afro-com/iinformation/news/current/ capitoltext.html.

Yette, Samuel F. "Clinton Attack on Iraq Shows He Is Out of Control." *Philadelphia Tribune,* 1998. <http://www.chicagotribune.com/news/nationworld/chi-jena_blog.>.

INDEX

Italicized page entries/folios refer to illustrations.